A PROGRESSIVE VOICE
IN THE CATHOLIC CHURCH
IN THE UNITED STATES

A PROGRESSIVE VOICE
IN THE CATHOLIC CHURCH
IN THE UNITED STATES

Association of Pittsburgh Priests, 1966–2019

Arthur J. McDonald

Foreword by Thomas J. Gumbleton

WIPF & STOCK · Eugene, Oregon

A PROGRESSIVE VOICE IN THE CATHOLIC CHURCH IN THE UNITED
STATES
Association of Pittsburgh Priests, 1966–2019

Wipf & Stock
An Imprint of Wipf and Stock Publishers
199 W. 8th Ave., Suite 3
Eugene, OR 97401

www.wipfandstock.com

PAPERBACK ISBN: 978-1-5326-9147-8
HARDCOVER ISBN: 978-1-5326-9148-5
EBOOK ISBN: 978-1-5326-9149-2

Manufactured in the U.S.A.   09/27/19

We dedicate this book to our founders and to all our Association of Pittsburgh Priests' brothers and sisters, who have gone before us, whose faith and courage inspire us, and whose humor encourages us. We humbly stand in their company and on their shoulders as we look to the future.

Contents

Foreword

OCTOBER OF 1962 WAS an exciting time to live in Rome. I was there at the graduate house of the North American College, the major seminary for priesthood students from the United States.

It is easy for me to remember the morning of October 11. I was at St. Peter's Square watching 2,500 bishops from around the world process into St. Peter's for the start of Vatican Council II.

The decision to summon an Ecumenical Council had been announced by Pope John XXIII in January of 1959. It had been envisioned by Pope John as an opportunity to "open windows" and "let in fresh air" for the Church. More precisely he described his hope for the Council as an *aggiornamento,* a chance to update the Church in line with developments in the world since the abrupt ending of Vatican Council I in 1870 when revolutionary troops entered Rome and Pope Pius IX fled Vatican City.

After Pope John's announcement in 1959, the Roman Curia with assistance from bishops around the world, began the task of preparing the initial agenda documents on a wide range of topics. These would serve as the basis for the discussions at the Council. After the solemn opening of the Council on the 11th with Mass and opening statements regarding arrangements and procedures that would be followed, the bishops dispersed for the day.

The Council was underway, or so everyone thought. Two days later, shortly after the opening prayer, word began to circulate around Rome and quickly arrived at our house. Bishops were streaming out of St. Peter's. There would be a delay. The meeting of the first General Congregation, intended for electing the 160 members of the ten Commissions ended within a few minutes. Cardinal Lienart, from France, supported by Cardinal Frings from Germany, proposed deferring the first rounds of voting to Tuesday, October 16, so that the Council Fathers could get to know each other, and consult among themselves about the candidates, a proposition accepted by acclamation.

This dramatic change made it clear that the Assembly of Bishops was moving to take leadership of the Council rather than simply following the direction of the Bishops from the Curia who had hoped for a quickly concluded Council with only superficial changes in the understanding of the Church and its role in the world. No windows would be opened. No fresh air would enliven the Church.

However the world's Bishops took charge and made it clear they wanted dramatic changes in the Church—changes that would fulfill the hopes of Pope John for an understanding of the Church as the "people of God," a community of believers in which everyone is "equal in freedom and dignity" with a call "to transform the world into as close an image of the reign of God as possible."

Over the years from 1962 to 1965 the Council developed sixteen documents that make up the teachings of Vatican Council II. These were officially promulgated by Pope Paul VI on December 8, 1965.

The Council had completed its work. Now the bishops were to return to their dioceses to implement the teachings.

However, the divisions that were present in the Council were reflected in the bishops of the United States. Just as at the Council, where most were enthusiastic for the changes proclaimed in the Council documents, there was a minority who were opposed to any significant changes.

That held true when the bishops returned home. For some there was a willingness to change but hesitation in how to make it happen. And there were some who adamantly rejected change.

In Detroit we were very blessed. Archbishop John Dearden had been on the Preparatory Commission. Then throughout the Council he was on the Doctrinal Commission which was responsible for developing the two most important documents, the document on the Church and the one on the Church in the modern world. These were fundamental in bringing about the new understanding of the Church as the people of God and the Church's call to be immersed in the world.

Very soon in Detroit we had discussion groups in all the parishes for the purpose of learning about the Council and finding ways to reflect the Council in the life of our parishes and in the Archdiocesan structure itself. First was the need to begin to understand the Church as the people of God with co-responsibility among bishops, priests, and people. After that it was necessary to discuss and implement changes in the liturgy, in parish and diocesan governance, adult religious education, the role of women in church ministry and leadership. Lay leadership would be implemented through parish councils and a diocesan pastoral council. Lay Catholics really began to experience "fresh air" blowing through the "open windows."

This was a monumental change from the top down leadership that characterized the Church previously. How did this work out in practice? It was best described by Archbishop Dearden himself not long after his retirement when he was asked what his style of leadership was. He thought for a moment and said, "Well, I tried never to get in the way of the Holy Spirit."

As a leader he allowed the gifts of the Spirit to burst forth from the people. This style of leadership was difficult for everyone to respond to. Priests who were used to always making decisions for their people found it difficult at times to realize they were there to serve the people, not dominate them. And people who had been taught their role was "to pray and obey" sometimes found it difficult to step forward and take leadership and share in decision making for their parish.

But gradually a flourishing of parish life was being realized. And at the diocesan level a very vital diocesan council began to experience the responsibility of shared decision making.

This way of being Church was challenging certainly. But gradually the majority of Catholics realized in a new way the call to live out their baptismal anointing to be "priest, prophet and king" and to be "doers of the word" as the apostle James had exhorted the Church of Jerusalem.

For a variety of reasons this way of being a Vatican II expression of the Church did not happen everywhere in the U.S.

Sometimes bishops did not have a deep understanding of the Council or the fundamental skill to be a leader who could draw forth and support priests and lay leaders who would share co-responsibility for the life and work of the Church.

Such was the case to a greater or less degree at various times in the Church of Pittsburgh. As this book makes clear it took courageous priests and lay people to struggle for a church which would develop a style of co-responsible leadership and a Church which would live out the call, later articulated in The Synod of 1971, that "action for justice and participation in the transformation of the world are constitutive dimensions in preaching the Gospel."

This book is a compelling history of the priests, and later the lay people, who were committed to make the Church of Pittsburgh an inspiring example of helping to fulfill the dream and challenge of St. John XXIII to bring about a conversion of the Church to enable it to proclaim and live the gospel message in the modern age. The task goes on in Pittsburgh and throughout the Church in the U.S. Inspired by this account of the Association of Pittsburgh Priests, all of us are invited to continue this work.

Bishop Thomas J. Gumbleton, Detroit, Michigan

Preface

MY FIRST ENCOUNTER WITH the Association of Pittsburgh Priests occurred in the summer of 1982. After having spent ten years as a Dominican Friar, six in theological and pastoral training, and four as an ordained priest serving in a team ministry with two Dominican sisters, Mary Moynihan and Ann Lovett, in a parish in the Highbridge section of the South Bronx, I took a leave of absence. A job possibility drew me to Pittsburgh. When I arrived at the Thomas Merton Center, a hotbed of peace and justice activities in the city of Pittsburgh, where I was to interview for an organizer's job, I was told by a staff person that he was headed to an anti-nuclear rally downtown and I was welcome to come along. So I and my traveling companion from the Bronx, Melanie Hodorowski, a recently resigned Sister of Mercy, later to become my spouse, accompanied him to the federal building. As we approached the demonstration, we heard a strong, clear voice through a bullhorn decrying the use of taxpayer dollars to fund nuclear weapons. The speaker was wearing a Roman collar. We were told he was an activist priest, part of an organization called the Association of Pittsburgh Priests (APP), a group that helped initiate the Thomas Merton Center back in 1972. His name was Fr. Jack O'Malley. We noticed other Roman collars in the crowd and felt a certain comfort in knowing that the Catholic Church in Pittsburgh seemed well represented in activist circles.

After spending the remainder of the summer of 1982 traveling to various cities in the South and Midwest in pursuit of other job leads, we returned to Pittsburgh and I accepted employment at the Merton Center as a meagerly paid community organizer. At that point we met another APP member Fr. Don Fisher, who offered to put us up in his rectory, while we sought more permanent housing. He was happy to accommodate us as long as it didn't last too long! He was joking, we thought at the time. Nevertheless, we were out in a week after finding our own apartment. But our deep friendship with Fisher lasted for thirty-six years until his untimely death in 2018.

As a staff person at the Thomas Merton Center, I had frequent contact with APP activists, and Melanie and I became active members of Fisher's East End parish. Then, in the spring of 1983, another APP member Neil Mc-Caulley asked me to give a talk on the topic of the U.S. Catholic bishops and foreign policy in history at the annual meeting of the National Federation of Priests' Council to be held in Pittsburgh. APP served as host.[1]

Over the next twenty years, while living in Pittsburgh, I participated, along with APP members, in any number of marches and demonstrations, including a number of arrests due to acts of civil disobedience. Whenever there was a call for advocacy and protest on important issues of social justice, APP almost always had representation. I collaborated with the group frequently.

Although Melanie and I moved back to my home state of Massachusetts in 2003, we often returned to Pittsburgh for major events, but also just to visit good friends. We kept in touch regularly. When APP decided to celebrate its fiftieth year of existence in 2016, the group asked me to give a keynote address on its stellar history. Since I could think of no group of religious activists I'd rather talk about, I agreed to the request. Along with the request to deliver the keynote, I was also asked if I would consider writing APP's history. What a privilege, I thought. I never hesitated, despite my intimidation at the task. Though trained theologically and social-scientifically, I'm not an historian. But I did have a very helpful starting point: a priest friend of APP, Fr. Frank Brown of the diocese of Steubenville, Ohio, had written a fifteen-page brochure on APP in 1987. It was entitled: "The Association of Pittsburgh Priests: A Brief History." So, along with my many years of experience with APP, I had a decent starting point for the project with Brown's brochure, which highlighted key events from the group's first twenty years. Unlike me, Brown was a trained historian. Previously, Brown had written a history of the Steubenville diocese, as well as a history of the National Federation of Priests' Council, a national independent Catholic clergy group founded in 1968, of which APP was a member.[2]

Actually, another trained historian, Timothy Kelly from Saint Vincent College in Latrobe, PA, who had already published a book on the Catholic laity in Pittsburgh, was approached in 2010 about writing APP's history.[3] Though he had expressed serious interest at the time, full-time teaching and

1. McDonald, "The U.S. Catholic Church and Foreign Policy."
2. Brown, "The Association of Pittsburgh Priests"; Brown, *Priests in Council.*
3. Kelly, *The Transformation of American Catholicism.*

other writing projects got in the way of his availability for the APP history project. Since Frank Brown was deceased, and Kelly unavailable, I was next in line. Thus, given the opportunity to undertake this exciting project, I seized the moment. And I am thrilled I did, as this has been an exhilarating experience of tracing the history of a group of prophetic and future-oriented priests, whose vision is as clear today as it was nearly fifty-three years ago. Nevertheless, although most APP members have enthusiastically embraced this project, a few current and past APP members had doubts that it was worth undertaking. Fortunately, I didn't share their misgivings. And, along the way, I've received tremendous encouragement, even from some of those who had initial doubts. For me it has been a true labor of love, even though it involved tediously poring through seven boxes of materials, filled to the brim with documents, press releases, op-ed pieces, and endless minutes of meetings from 1966 until the present, and conducting numerous interviews and e-mail correspondences with any number of APP members and friends, involving frequent visits to Pittsburgh. I now understand better, and have great respect for, the challenges that real historians face.

Regarding the writing genre of this book, what might be considered a straight-forward institutional history of APP, I would like to say something about methodology. A good friend, Jack Rossi, whom I was ordained with back in 1978, and who also left the Dominican Order and wound up teaching high school English and literature for approximately thirty years, graciously and generously agreed to edit this book. During the editing process, at several points, he warned me about my decision to occasionally insert myself into the narrative. As an historical study, he felt it might be deemed inappropriate and, possibly, would compromise the book's worth as less than accurate or objective. In some cases I agreed and removed personal references. But in other cases, I left personal commentary in the story. I, alone, of course, am responsible for such decisions and greatly appreciated Jack's concern that the narrative maintained some academic character.

I also received very helpful and affirming feedback from the aforementioned Dr. Tim Kelly, professor of history at St. Vincent's College in Latrobe, PA. Tim has expressed great interest in this project and has been exceedingly generous with his time and commentary. After having read one chapter, Tim expressed his professional viewpoint to me in an e-mail that, "Your narrative falls somewhat between a personal account and an academic monograph. It's not quite a memoir, because you convey not your own experiences but rather the stories of participants. But your inclusion throughout the text of your own reactions and responses to the information that you discovered in your research puts it outside the standard academic genre as well . . . the result is a narrative that falls in between familiar genres."

Tim refers to this as my "personal approach" and my "own encounter with the APP history" as central to the study. He went on to suggest ways I could make the study better and more effective if I chose to stay with such an approach. This was enormously helpful to me and I am grateful to Tim. And after careful consideration, I made the decision to basically stay with this more personal approach, despite its possible downsides, mostly because of my close relationship to APP and many of its key members, but also because of my participation over the years with many APP actions.

In writing my doctoral dissertation on liberation theology in Peru,[4] I took an approach that sociologists and anthropologists refer to as "participant-observer" or "participant-insider," that is, I wrote about liberation theology from the perspective of one who was both an advocate of the theology, and also an activist and practitioner of the theology in my own ministry. I argued then that academic objectivity, the usual approach of researchers who are merely trying to understand the reality they are investigating by maintaining a distance from the subject matter, while a very valid and understandable approach to social-scientific research, is not the only one. Another approach, my own in this study, involving direct participation, thus somewhat more subjective, is also a legitimate methodology and, in some cases, may actually unearth a more accurate analysis of what is actually happening. As a sympathetic insider, if you will, there is also the possibility, at times, of actually better understanding and interpreting what might be going on with any particular group and its mission or activity. As an insider, one also has the trust of those who are the subjects of the study, which offers unusual access to what the group really thinks, thus gaining access to information such participants might not be willing to share with a total outsider, a merely interested investigator with no particular attachment to the group or its mission.

Nevertheless, still harboring some doubts about the wisdom of my approach, I was curious how two other studies of progressive priest organizations, written by priests who were also members of the groups they wrote about, handled the issue of their own participation. In one of the books, Frank Brown's aforementioned study of the National Federation of Priests Council, Brown acknowledges that he was "one of the 284 priests who attended the first national planning meeting" of the group in 1968 and "had an intense interest in the possibilities offered by such an organization." He went on to write that he eventually participated in the organization "at its

4. McDonald, "The Practice and Theory," 3–7.

top level" and expressed the concern that he "hoped that the occasional use of the first person throughout this volume is acceptable to the reader."[5]

In the other study I consulted written by Dominican priest Charles Dahm about Cardinal Cody and the Association of Chicago Priests, of which he was an active member, Dahm writes the following: "To understand what this book is not may enhance appreciation of its strengths. It is not clinically objective, for it includes very little of the evidence that the major figure—Cardinal Cody of Chicago—might have offered in explanation or defense." Dahm explains that Cody declined his request to comment on the study or offer his own perspective. Dahm then admits that the book offers a "sharp critique of the Catholic Church," but suggests that this represents "not just the author's personal opinions about one particular bishop," but rather reflects an institutional problem of the entire Catholic Church, citing another study of "eighty-five dioceses" across the country, about to be released. Dahm also acknowledges that as a priest-participant in the Chicago association, "he favors the efforts of Chicago's priest-reformers."[6]

Unlike Dahm, who gave Cardinal Cody an opportunity to offer his perspective, which he declined, I did not make an attempt to contact either Bishops Wuerl or Zubik in Pittsburgh, or any other diocesan officials. Nevertheless, I would argue that my deep connections with key APP actors and my participation in their actions and overall mission has actually given me profound insider information, insight and perspective that might not necessarily be available to a stranger, an outside, primarily academic investigator. In the process, of course, I hope that my reporting has not been compromised by my admiration or sympathies for APP and its mission, that is, I am hoping that my account of the history of APP is still accurate and appropriately critical. I'll let the reader judge all of that.

5. Brown, *Priests in Council*, xi-xii.
6. Dahm, *Power and Authority*, xvi-xvii.

Acknowledgments

FIRST AND FOREMOST, I want to thank Marcia Snowden, without whom this book would never have been undertaken. As APP was planning to celebrate its fiftieth anniversary in October of 2016, with Marcia as its point person, I was asked to offer the keynote address. Previous to that celebration, Marcia had approached me about taking on this project. For years she has been advocating for this history to be written. In preparation for the 2016 speech, I had to quickly pore over materials from the early years of APP, of which I knew little. Once I did that, I was determined to see this through. Marcia has been the guiding light throughout. Some had doubts; what would it cost? Was it really worth telling? We'll find the money, she said. The next generation needs to know there was such a group as APP, she argued. I am so grateful to Marcia.

Part of the joy in doing this study has been interviewing key participants. I interviewed over forty people, some multiple times. Though all interviews were valuable and insightful, a number were especially helpful. Though some had doubts as to the worth of telling this story, they still wanted to talk about APP. Jim Hohman, Joe DiCarlo, Phil Gallagher, Tom Harvey and John Groutt, early APP members who left ministry, were very helpful, especially for the early years. Groutt sent me articles he had written, both in the 1960s, as well as a wonderful memoir he wrote in 2014. Other resigned priests, Pat Fenton and Denny Kirk, were also of enormous help as very active members during their time with APP, especially Fenton who read two draft chapters and offered critique. Of all my interviewees, Fenton had the best memory for details and actions.

Long-term APP activists Gary Dorsey, Regis Ryan, John Oesterle read individual chapters and offered critique, insight and encouragement. I had many follow-up phone calls with these three. Mark Glasgow, a civil rights activist even before the formation of APP, had great memories of marches

in Selma and Jackson in the mid-1960s. Revs. Bernie Survil and Greg Swiderski also provided helpful insights.

Several key APP clerics have died before the completion of this book:
three before I even undertook the project, and two during the writing. Don
McIlvane, Neil McCaulley and Warren Metzler were already deceased by
the fiftieth anniversary in 2016, so I was never able to interview them, despite their major roles in moving APP's agenda forward. Given his wealth
of first-hand knowledge about APP, as well as his prolific writing skills, I've
often thought that Neil McCaulley should have written this. Don Fisher and
Eugene Lauer have died more recently, and I had the privilege of interviewing them both for the book. Fisher, especially, would have loved to have
witnessed the study's completion.

Although he died many years before I undertook this endeavor, I am
grateful for the work Fr. Francis Brown did in writing a short pamphlet on
the first twenty years of APP. Unlike myself, Brown was serious historian
and I learned a lot about APP's early history from reading his pamphlet.
Earlier, Brown had written about the national priests' group, the National
Federation of Priests Council, and that, too, was helpful to this study.

Many thanks as well to non-clerical APP activists, Sr. Barbara Finch,
Joyce Rothermel and Michael Drohan, Molly Rush, Jim McCarville, John
Pillar, David Aleva and Kevin Hayes, all of whom provided insights and
encouragement as the project moved along.

I especially enjoyed conversations with two Pittsburgh diocesan priests,
Lou Vallone and Michael Stumpf, who while never having been members of
APP, expressed great admiration for the group and its members, even while
offering friendly criticism.

I also want to thank a great friend from seminary days, Jack Rossi, who
agreed to edit this manuscript. I'm not a great writer and Jack helped clean
up my mess as best he could. Also, Dr. Tim Kelly, a history professor from
St. Vincent's College, Latrobe, PA., has been extraordinarily helpful to me in
offering insights and ideas, both for the content of the work but also for the
methodology. Tim read one of the chapters and made suggestions as to how
I might improve it. He also opened doors to potential publishers.

As mentioned above, one early concern about this project was the
potential expense involved. That was solved early on by a number of generous donors: Jim Browne, Bonnie and Joe DiCarlo, Eileen Colianni and Phil
Joyce, Fr. Don Fisher, Philip Gallagher, The Hayes Design Group of Archi-
tects, Jim Hohman, Robert Jedrzejewski, Fr. Eugene Lauer, Fr. Jack O'Malley
and John and Jane Pillar. Thanks to all of them for such generosity.

Professor Thomas Groome from Boston College deserves a special
note of gratitude for suggesting I send this manuscript to my publishers,

Wipf and Stock. Somehow Tom sensed that this type of study would interest Wipf and Stock. I was overjoyed upon receiving this acceptance.

A number of close friends helped encourage me to both undertake and complete this project. I want to thank them. Their encouragement helped keep me on course when the research dragged on. When I mentioned to my friend Jules Lobel, professor of Constitutional Law at the University of Pittsburgh, that I was considering undertaking this project, he immediately thought it a great idea. I was more than mildly surprised. Though very spiritually centered and religiously curious, Jules, a Jew, is not a practitioner of the Jewish faith or any other religious tradition. However, he knows well a number of APP clerics and has always been in admiration of their work and dedication. He always thought this story should be told. He was so supportive from the very beginning that he was asked to introduce me at APP's fiftieth-anniversary celebration.

I also want to acknowledge my very good friends and now, fellow authors, Donna and Ed Brett. Ed and Donna have recently published a wonderful book about Catholic martyrs in Central America and they have been an inspiration to me for years. When I just couldn't burden Ed and Donna one more time for computer and formatting tips, I asked for help from two special women in the congregation I now worship in. Thanks to Mary Carlin and Tori Rosati for their gentle, loving and patient ways with me when I hit a wall. I called them on a number of occasions when I needed tips on how to make the world of computers more user-friendly to a hopelessly computer-phobic writer and friend. They were very patient with my most basic of questions.

A shout out, also, to Chuck Dahm, OP, an old friend from my days in the Dominican Order, who not only encouraged me in this endeavor and tried to open a publishing door to me, but his excellent study of Chicago priests and Cardinal Cody has been very helpful in my writing this this current work.

Finally, a most special thanks to Fr. Jack O'Malley, a wonderful friend and a key APP activist from its initial days right up to the present. I have had endless conversations about APP with Jack over these many years of friendship. I have also spent a few nights with him and others in jail after acts of civil disobedience. He embodies the very best that APP has offered through all of these years. Even better, he's a brother who has offered me and my wife, Melanie, hospitality, ever since we moved from Pittsburgh in 2003. As our Latin sisters and brothers often say, with their endless offers of hospitality, *mi casa es tu casa*. My home is your home. With Jack, that's always been the case. Need a book, need a ride, need a bed, need a car, need a hug, need a buck, Jack is always there. What a gift to us all. If only church leaders had followed his and APP's lead over the years, we would have a renewed church, in line with the vision of Vatican II.

And to my partner in connubial bliss, my spouse, Melanie, I offer my most heartfelt gratitude. She has loved me so deeply through all our experiences together, starting in the South Bronx in the late 1970s, to Pittsburgh to Boston to Peru—where she nearly lost her life—back to Pittsburgh and, finally, to Salem, MA. When I decided to undertake this project, she offered only loving support and encouragement, even though she knew it would affect our daily rhythms greatly, as I kept returning to the office to write just one more page before quitting for the day. Her love has been a healing force in my life and she shares in my joy at completing this project.

Introduction

THE ROOTS OF THE Association of Pittsburgh Priests (APP) are primarily twofold: the civil rights' movement of the 1950s and 60s and the international Catholic Church's Second Vatican Council, which ended in 1965. As part of the civil rights' movement, a number of future APP members helped form the Catholic Interracial Council of Pittsburgh in the early 1960s, most notably Fr. Don McIlvane. In 1965 and 1966 Frs. McIlvane, Don Fisher and Mark Glasgow, all initial APP members, traveled to Selma, Alabama and Jackson, Mississippi, to participate in the great civil rights' marches with Dr. King and so many others. Glasgow recalls an inspirational all night meeting with actor and activist Dick Gregory in Jackson. At the same time, priests throughout the diocese were beginning to read some of the key documents promulgated at the Second Vatican Council, and they were anxious to meet and discuss the contents of these pronouncements. It was an exciting time in which the international Catholic Church was finally engaging with the modern world. Young clergy were anxious to consider what this might mean for their ministries. But they were fearful of the bishop's reaction if they gathered independently, so in the summer of 1966 nineteen priests met clandestinely at 9 p.m. in the parish hall of a suburban Pittsburgh church at the initiation of Fr. John Groutt. The meeting went until almost 1 a.m.

Although Vatican II produced sixteen documents, dealing with issues regarding divine revelation, liturgy, priestly life and training, the role of bishops, the place of laity, ecumenism, non-Christian religions and religious liberty, what most interested the early APP clergy was the document "*Gaudium et Spes*: The Pastoral Constitution on the Church and the Modern World." Just what is the role of the priest in the modern world, they wondered? Furthermore, what is the nature of the relationship between the priest and the laity? Does the reclaiming by the bishops at Vatican II of the notion of common priesthood, shared by all the baptized, mean we are all equal in the church? And what is the significance of Vatican II's new image of the church as "the people of God," as articulated in the document *Lumen Gentium*, Dogmatic Constitution on the Church?

At a time in priestly ministry when morale was low, as many young clerics were assigned to dysfunctional living situations in rectories with difficult older pastors, whom they often couldn't relate to, coming together as priest brothers in solidarity and excitement over new ideas, it was an exhilarating moment. Vatican II was encouraging the opening of windows to the world and dialogue about worldly concerns. After a second summer meeting that went late into the night, the nineteen decided to form an independent group of clergy with their own voice. APP was born.

Among other things, APP members desired a positive and mature relationship of equality with their local bishop, so they sent a letter to the entire Pittsburgh clergy, as well as a separate letter to Bishop John Wright, announcing their formation and inviting participation of all. Their initial thrust was to simply study Vatican II documents and consider how such documents might be implemented to renew the church. They received a cordial response from Bishop Wright, who somewhat surprisingly, expressed great interest in their ongoing development, and suggested he might even attend an upcoming gathering.

However, given the times in which the civil rights' movement was gaining ever more traction and the Vietnam War heating up, it was not long before APP added to their agenda of priestly support and church renewal that of engagement in the struggle for social justice. As Latin American liberation theologian Jose Comblin has written, in the previous model of social action labeled "Catholic Action," lay people took the lead in social engagement, as priests remained in the sanctuary, at most offering lay people training. Now, he writes, it is time for "bishops and priests" to be "out in front projecting the gospel in the world," much as Jesus commissioned the apostles as "missionaries sent to the peoples."[1] Almost from the beginning certain APP members were certainly "out front" in the struggle for justice and equality.

Despite the fact that APP members all had full-time pastoral ministries, mostly in parish settings, and early on began to engage in social activism, they have always been serious about study and research. They rarely pronounced on an issue without serious investigation, whether holding a press conference, writing an op-ed piece, sending formal letters to the hierarchy, including popes, and when producing research documents. In the early years, John Groutt, and to a lesser degree Don McIlvane, wrote and published regularly. Later in the 1970s and 1980s, McIlvane and resident

1. Comblin, *People of God*, 169–70.

theologian, Eugene Lauer, did much of the research and writing. When addressing issues around church renewal, based on the documents of Vatican II, Neil McCaulley and others could also be counted on to conduct serious research. In the early 2000s, after APP altered its membership to include all Catholics, former seminarian and married APP member, Scott Fabian, produced a serious document on Cardinal Bernardin's "seamless garment" pronouncement on a consistent ethic of life, as he (Fabian) reflected upon the 2004 presidential election.

Groutt and McIlvane's writings appeared in such publications as *The Priest, Commonweal,* and the *National Catholic Reporter (NCR)*. In 1971, McIlvane and Lauer published a profound reflection on priestly simplicity and living and working beside the poor, which was published by the *NCR*. This helped put APP on the national map.[2]

In the early 1980s, APP wrote a serious reflection on the role of priests in politics. At the time they were responding and reacting to statements and actions by Pope John Paul II, whom APP considered was turning the clock back on the role of priests in society, i.e., forbidding priests from seeking elective offices—for example, Robert Drinan, SJ, former congressman—or serving in governmental positions—four priests in the Nicaraguan government. Don McIlvane was the primary architect of this document, which had widespread distribution among clergy in Pittsburgh and led to a press conference, but was never published. They followed this up with a direct communication to the pope, applauding him for prophetic words in his visit to the U.S. in 1979, yet challenging him for his attempts at limiting the role of priests in society.[3]

Whenever APP did make pronouncements, either verbally or in written form, they were well prepared and researched, and they took pains to cite official church documents and pronouncements. They "always did their homework."

1992 represented a watershed year for APP, which set them apart from other Catholic clergy groups in the country. Although there were a handful of other independent Catholic clergy groups in the U.S. over the years like APP, most especially in Chicago—Association of Chicago Priests, founded in 1966, the same year as APP—none made the bold move APP did when it altered its membership to include resigned and married priests and their spouses, women and men lay people, and religious sisters and brothers. Although they considered a name change to reflect this new reality, they

2. APP, "Chastity, Yes," 10.
3. APP, "The Priest and Politics."

retained their original designation, Association of Pittsburgh Priests, much to the consternation of the then bishop, Donald Wuerl.

In response to a lengthy proposal by the wife of a former APP member, and after a lengthy internal discussion, which led to a survey sent to all APP supporters, the group voted overwhelmingly to make the change. The significance of this decision was to highlight the notion, reclaimed at the Second Vatican Council, of the common priesthood of all baptized. By this act, APP narrowed the clergy–lay distinction and emphasized the call of all baptized Christians to ministry. The decision had sound theological grounding and, once again, put APP in line with the unfulfilled vision of re-imagining priesthood and ministry in light of Vatican II. But revising APP membership also represented the recognition that the number of canonical priests in the group was dwindling and ageing, and the younger clergy were not attracted to APP's priestly model, either due to fear of retaliation from the bishop, rejection by fellow clergy, or simple disagreement with APP's vision of priesthood.[4] Nevertheless, with this decision to open up its membership, APP became a completely unique priestly organization in the Catholic Church in the United States. This remains the case to this day.

But APP's influence goes beyond Western Pennsylvania. In 2011, long-time APP member, Fr. Bernie Survil, actually a priest of the neighboring diocese of Greensburg, PA, played a key role in initiating a new organizing effort to form a national, independent Catholic clergy group. Since 1968, there has been such a group in the United States, the aforementioned National Federation of Priests' Council (NFPC). APP was a member of the NFPC for over two decades until, in 1999, it resigned, as it judged that NFPC had lost its prophetic edge, and had stopped being an independent voice for church renewal and social justice advocacy, linchpins of APP's vision. In APP's view NFPC had become too close to the bishops. Survil ran his ideas past APP leadership about forming a new, national clergy group that would re-establish an agenda of church renewal based on Vatican II, as well as prophetic justice advocacy. APP was very supportive of such a development, but APP's leadership, now with significant female voices,

4. I had two interviews with a younger clergy member in Pittsburgh about APP. He expressed great admiration for APP's prophetic witness in the diocese, and he especially appreciated its speaker series, which, he acknowledged, he promoted in his parish. "So why are you not a member?" I asked. In his response he used an expression, evidently coined by Lyndon Johnson, while President of the United States. Evidently Johnson and an aide were discussing whether or not to rid themselves of the controversial director of the FBI, J. Edgar Hoover, and Johnson responded that he would rather Hoover "be in the tent pissing out, than outside the tent pissing in." This priest felt APP was "outside the tent," not really in the diocese, and he preferred to offer his criticisms from the inside.

expressed disappointment that Survil's idea would not match APP's vision of the common priesthood of all baptized, thus inclusive of more than just ordained, male clergy. Though disappointed, they encouraged Survil, and the Association of United States' Catholic Priests (AUSCP) was formed in 2011. Several APP priests are currently members. In 2016 the AUSCP voted to offer associate membership to all Catholics. Its agenda of fraternal support, church renewal, based on implementing Vatican II, and social justice advocacy, perfectly mirror APP's vision, minus full membership of all baptized. Clearly APP served as an inspiration for this national network, which counts about 1100 priest members.

"The joys and the hopes, the grief and the anxieties of the men and women of this age, especially those who are poor or in any way afflicted, these too are the joys and hopes, the griefs and anxieties of the followers of Christ. Indeed, nothing genuinely human fails to raise an echo in their hearts."[5] With these words, taken from the document of Vatican II that most inspired the witness and work of APP over the decades, Fr. Neil McCaulley, APP's most dogged and determined promoter of church renewal, began his letter to the entire Catholic community in Pittsburgh. He entitled this letter "The Church of Vatican II" and released it at a press conference in 2012, as the worldwide Catholic Church began to celebrate the fiftieth anniversary of the opening of the Second Vatican Council.

In the letter, McCaulley summarized the vision of Vatican II which had inspired the formation of APP back in 1966. Though a harsh critic of the lack of greater progress in the implementation of Vatican II, McCaulley chose the high road in this reflection and emphasized the many positive changes he had experienced:

> Enormous increase in our exposure to Holy Scripture as well as an emphasis on biblical spirituality . . . the [Church's new] name people of God along with the universal call to holiness . . . called to share in the leadership of the Church . . . [a reminder] that we are all equal in Baptism and the laity have their own call to ministry . . . [furthermore] a more democratic church was called for, with enormously important teaching on collegiality . . . this conciliar model has spread to National Conferences and dioceses and parishes . . . Lay ministry has grown enormously. Tens of thousands of lay people, the majority of them women, have acquired advanced degrees in theology, catechesis, scripture, liturgy and canon law. These same people have entered the parish ministry on staffs as well as at the diocesan level. We have seen the liturgy come alive . . . preaching has become more

5. Paul VI, "*Gaudium et Spes*," 200.

biblical . . . [and] it is important to remember that good liturgy
builds up faith and bad liturgy tears it down . . . [and, finally]
the Council fathers decided to make the logical step of producing a major constitution on the Church and the Modern World
. . . it was a reform Council and a pastoral Council. It made it
clear that the Jews were not responsible for the death of Christ
. . . [and] we began serious dialogue with our sister churches,
the great world religions of the east and the secular world. They
[Council fathers] rejected the notion that "error has no rights"
and embraced the concept of religious liberty.

McCaulley couldn't end his manifesto—if so, he wouldn't be true to
APP's prophetic ministry—without acknowledging that we must "be on
guard against revisionism; an attempt to roll back Vatican II effects. We
should not forget the unfinished business of the documents," pointing out
that "as soon as the Council ended some in the Church began to oppose . . .
and obstruct it." He ends by declaring that these "documents of the Council
stand. Become familiar with them again! Be inspired again!"[6]

No one captured the spirit, the vision, and the commitment of APP
to renewal and justice better than McCaulley. Though retired at the time
of this letter, and in failing health—he was to die in 2014—he captured
beautifully and powerfully what has motivated APP throughout these many
decades since its founding.

Nevertheless, as McCaulley warned, opposition and obstruction to the
vision of Vatican II has been real and there is, to be sure, much "unfinished
business." As liberation theologian Jose Comblin has written in his prophetic book, *People of God*: "The hopes raised at Vatican II for changes in the
relationships between hierarchy and people, bishops and pope, and clergy
and people have been disappointed in practice because the council changed
the theology but left canon law intact. In the subsequent forty years [now
over 50] the Roman Curia has nullified the aims of Vatican II, concentrating
control over doctrine and over episcopal ministry and appointments."[7]

There is likely no better example of this problem of the lack of institutional change and clerical, hierarchical control, than the current clergy
sexual abuse crisis. At the current moment, no diocese in the country is
suffering the effects of the hierarchy's lack of transparency and determination to protect the system more than that of Pittsburgh, in light of the recent
Pennsylvania Grand Jury report.[8] Although APP as an organization has

6. McCaulley, " The Church of Vatican II."

7. Comblin, *People of God*, 178.

8. Office of Attorney General, Commonwealth of Pennsylvania, "Report I of the
40th Statewide Investigating Grand Jury."

been very minimally impacted by the revelations, it lives under the same cloud as all Catholic clergy do at the moment. And it remains loyal—though often dissenting—members of an international organization that has lost much of its credibility. Tragically, there is certainly more to come as other Attorneys General look into other Catholic dioceses across the country.

And, yet, one can only imagine what might have been, if the worldwide Roman Catholic Church had only implemented many more of the reforms of Vatican II, and greatly increased the role of the Catholic laity. Even now it is not clear if the hierarchy understands the need to hand over greater responsibility to the laity, and to hold themselves accountable. Yet, through it all, APP stands as a shining light of prophetic courage for over fifty years, constantly imploring its local bishops and the Vatican to share power and democratize the Church, i.e., fully implementing the intuitions and suggestions of the Second Vatican Council. What if the five bishops who have served the Church of Pittsburgh during the existence of APP had opened themselves to the changes that APP has promoted for over the years? What would the Church of Pittsburgh look like? Might it yet happen or is it too late? Will there be a positive Pope Francis effect, as he frequently decries the scourge of clericalism, and whose election and agenda some in APP have considered a "vindication" of their decades-long vision?

In a positive development in response to the clergy sexual abuse crisis, APP and a number of other lay-led groups are currently meeting to determine a course of action for the Pittsburgh Church. It may well be a new moment, and APP will be a key participant, despite its vast disappointment with church leadership over these past fifty-three years. Whatever the outcome of these listening sessions, I have no doubt APP will continue to promote and live out its original vision, which the current membership recently reiterated in its ongoing mission statement:

The Association of Pittsburgh Priests is a diocesan-wide organization of ordained and non-ordained women and men who act on our baptismal call to be priests and prophets. Our mission, rooted in the Gospel and the Spirit of Vatican II, is to carry out a ministry of justice and renewal in ourselves, the Church and the world.

What follows is the story of the Association of Pittsburgh Priests.

CHAPTER ONE

When the Altars Were Turned Around
APP's Early Years, 1966–1970.

WHEN I FIRST MET Jim Hohman, one of the founding members of APP (Association of Pittsburgh Priests), at his worksite in 2016, it seemed an unlikely place for a former priest to be. After leaving the priesthood in 1967, then marrying in 1968, Jim and three other former priests, Jim Browne, Phil Gallagher and Joe DiCarlo, opened up a financial planning business in 1970 that did quite well, offering advice to people looking to make wise financial investments. By the time I met Jim, he and the others were either fully retired or keeping their hand in the business with old clients on a part-time basis.

Jim was curious as to why I wanted to write about a priest's group in Pittsburgh, formed in 1966, after the reforms of the Second Vatican Council, which ended in 1965. Yet, he also had a desire to talk about his experiences as a priest, some quite negative, others very profound and exhilarating. "Were there other groups like the APP in other parts of the country?" he asked. "Yes and no," I answered. "Has the APP had any impact?" he went on. He had his doubts, but wasn't sure. He didn't know whether APP was important or not, whether or not the group made any difference, but he seemed grateful for his brief experience with the group and he seemed very willing and interested in talking about his experiences. One thing that came out very clearly in the interview was his severe criticisms of the institutional church and its authority structures.

Having been ordained in 1963, Jim was assigned to a working class neighborhood on the Southside of Pittsburgh and began his ministry in the traditional fashion, celebrating the sacraments, saying Mass (in Latin), hearing confessions (in English!), and attempting to meet the needs of his parishioners. Then, something profound happened that became a kind of revelation that altered his view of priesthood and ministry. By its end Vatican II produced numerous documents opening up all kinds of new insights and themes as to where the church of the future should be heading, e.g., regarding the relationship of the church to the modern world, priestly formation, the role of the laity, religious liberty, ecumenism and the relationship between Catholicism and other Christian denominations as well as interfaith concerns, especially with Judaism and liturgy and the role of ritual in the life of the Catholic Church. It was this last one, liturgical reform, which initially altered Jim's his views on ministry.[1]

One liturgical innovation was to begin celebrating the Mass in the vernacular; "Latin made little sense" to Jim. He was delighted when he could celebrate in English. But even more significant, he suggested, had to do with the positioning of the priest and the altar while saying Mass. Traditionally the altar was up against the back wall of the church and the priest celebrated Mass by facing the altar, with his back to the people. Vatican II mandated the turning of the altar around, thus having the priest face the people while celebrating. This took some doing, both physically and financially.

Concerning the latter, a parishioner had recently died and left $3000 to the church for unspecified purposes, which Jim (quietly) arranged to use to create a new, simple, free-standing altar, mirroring the plain table at which Jesus and his followers shared their last meal together, the Last Supper. Jim acknowledged that the deceased parishioner probably never imagined the money being used for such a purpose. The first time he celebrated the Mass facing the people, his ministry began to change. Suddenly the Mass was no longer so much about the priest and God and mystery, a rather solemn affair in a dead language with the people attending as spectators. It became rather an encounter between the priest and the people that still invoked God yet realized a new understanding of church, the so-called "new ecclesiology," which identified the church as "The people of God."[2] Jim's ministry was now about how to serve and be available to God's people staring back at him as he spoke the words of the consecration, changing bread and wine into the body and blood of Christ.

From that time on, Jim realized that priesthood and ministry needed to be rethought; it was time to "get out of the sanctuary" and meet people "in the street," pick up a paint brush and help neighbors restore their houses,

1. Abbott, *The Documents of Vatican II*.

2. Abbot, *Documents of Vatican II* and Comblin, *People of God*. Comblin's book articulates a key understanding of Vatican II ecclesiology, i.e., the church is not the hierarchy and clergy but the people, taken from Vatican II's *Lumen Gentium*.

"pile kids in the car" and head off to the playground, make sure folks have food and medical treatment, get people to their doctors, and, even more importantly for Jim, welcome people back to the church and full participation, i.e., welcome divorced Catholics back to the sacraments, not a Vatican II initiative nor an idea approved by the church authorities, but a pastoral call and one that made sense to Jim, exercising God's mercy, a key priestly charge in his view.[3]

Jim was not alone as he began to rethink priesthood and ministry. After returning from studies in Rome and having been ordained in 1961, shortly before coming home to Pittsburgh, another former priest John Groutt, much like Jim, began to view the priesthood and ministry differently. Even before Vatican II had ended, as early as 1963, Groutt writes, ". . . I began to read the Epistle and Gospel aloud in English at weekday masses—first reciting them, as required, in Latin." Then, by the end of the Council in 1965, he continues: "Some dramatic changes were occurring. Latin disappeared entirely from the liturgy. The altars were turned from the wall where they had been since medieval times. Now, the priest faced the people, as was done in the earliest Roman churches, and used a language they could understand. The ritual returned to a more ancient form with a shared interaction around a communion table rather than conducted at a mysterious altar of sacrifice . . . this was important, but . . . we also needed to help people accept the deeper understanding and '*aggiornamento*' (updating) of the entire theological and moral structure of Catholic beliefs that the council was addressing. I did not see this being done by diocesan leaders or most local parishes."[4]

Regarding this latter point of educating the faithful on the major reforms of Vatican II, Groutt, like many of the early APP priests, was serious about his own ongoing education and, upon his return from Rome, continued studying, taking psychology classes at a local Catholic college, Duquesne University, as well as theology classes at the local Pittsburgh Theological Seminary, a Presbyterian school. It was at Duquesne University where some of the early Post-Vatican II liturgical experimentation took place. Members of the Holy Spirit religious order, priest-chaplains at the university, became known for their creative and informal liturgies and offering communion in the hand, rather than on the tongue, before such changes were instituted by

3. In an interview with Jim Hohman, July 19, 2016, we joked about this practice of a local priest welcoming divorced Catholics back to full participation in the church without hierarchical approval. Such a pastoral call anticipated—by over fifty years!—Pope Francis' "Year of Mercy (2017)" and his overall pastoral compassion, a linchpin of Francis' papacy.

4. Groutt, "The Second Vatican Council," 4.

the diocese. Progressive Catholics swarmed to Duquesne for Sunday Mass once the word got out.[5]

But liturgical reform, though central in inspiring new understandings of priesthood and ministry, was not the only impetus for rethinking the priest's role, as many early APP members were active in the Civil Rights' movement, including John Groutt, who remembers attending marches in downtown Pittsburgh in the early to middle Sixties.

Another early participant in APP, Rev. Don McIlvane, who died in 2014, having remained a priest, was also a key founder and participant in the Catholic Interracial Council in the early 1960s. McIlvane travelled to Selma in 1965 to march with Dr. King, followed, later that year, by early APPers, Mark Glasgow and Don Fisher. Fisher and Glasgow participated a second time in 1966, as they marched and organized in Jackson, Mississippi, meeting up with actor and activist, Dick Gregory. With the growth of the Civil Rights' movement, and, a bit later, anti-war protests, there were, as John Groutt has written, a lot of "restless priests" in the Diocese of Pittsburgh and in many other parts of the country.

Thus, it seems, the time had come for the creation of a new organization. Groutt writes: "In the mid-1960s a group of Pittsburgh priests began meeting, seeking a strategy to bring diocesan officials and other clergy to a greater awareness of the promise and potential of the council that had ended in 1965 . . . The existing *official* Council of Priests was appointed and controlled by the bishop. In our view it was similar to a 'politburo' that rubber-stamped the bishop's decisions. We envisioned, instead, an independent organization serving as a voice of local priests for social justice, church reforms, and public discussion of issues that we believed were not being addressed by diocesan officials . . . Western Pennsylvania had a history of local organizing and a strong union tradition. A 'union' of priests was considered, but it did not seem appropriate for our objectives." Groutt then explains the group's concern that forming such a group might cause difficulties with the "clerical professionals," who only thought in very "hierarchical" ways. These thought the "lower clergy" were expected to merely "pray and obey." They imagined that bishops would be threatened, as tradition suggested priests were not supposed to gather without the 'bishop's permission." Where could they meet undetected, they wondered? Groutt went to his pastor and

---

5. Joe Healey, a Holy Spirit priest on the campus ministry team at Duquesne University in Pittsburgh, an early APP member, with two other priests was suspended by Bishop Leonard for distributing communion in the hand rather than on the tongue, without diocesan approval.

received permission to use the parish hall. The pastor approved of the idea until the following day when his phone began ringing![6]

Hence, the Association of Pittsburgh Priests was launched, one of two such groups in the USA, as the ACP (Association of Chicago Priests), as Groutt mentioned in his memoir, began around the same times as Pittsburgh. They wanted a "voice vs. authority," declared Jim Hohman, "to challenge authority" and "speak our mind."

"Stepping back to the Catholic Church scene in 1966 challenges the memory and imagination almost as would slipping back from the space age into the days prior to train travel. There was virtually no communication across parish lines over mutual concerns . . . there did not exist a structure that called for bringing priests together on their own. Only the bishops had the authority to convoke a meeting of priests," writes Frank Brown, a Catholic priest from Ohio, who in 1987 wrote a short pamphlet documenting the first two decades of APP.[7]

Beyond church renewal and social justice, especially around Civil Rights, many APP members have shared with me that another major incentive for the formation of the group was as a support network. Priests have nightmare stories about rectory life in the 1960s and the many difficult relationships between pastors and assistants (generally young, newly ordained priests). APP offered support: "APP always had your back," mentioned one former priest. Whenever an APP member got called to the chancery to answer to the bishop, APP ensured that that priest was accompanied by at least one or two APP colleagues. I have heard many stories of such meetings over the years. Because of APP relationships, Jim Hohman offered, he likely stayed in active ministry as a priest for two more years than he would have otherwise.

"It [APP] was a Vatican II institution," according to now deceased priest, Don McIlvane, "and we acted with our brother priests as one." Though he couldn't say whether or not the group helped keep him in the priesthood, "it surely kept me active in the church . . . The APP has been a kind of support group. I myself have felt a lot of support . . . if we lost a few [leaving the active priesthood], we might have saved a few, too . . . it widened my perspective. One of the great blessings, as I see it, is that we didn't isolate ourselves."[8]

Although social justice activity and radical, prophetic ministry became early staples for APP, most especially led by Don McIlvane and Jack

6. Groutt, "The Second Vatican Council," 4–5.
7. Brown, "Association of Pittsburgh Priests," 1.
8. Brown, "Association of Pittsburgh Priests," 6.

O'Malley—McIlvane is now deceased; O'Malley minimally active and in his 80s—"blame it [social activism] on O'Malley," joked Jim Hohman, [admiringly], the organization was originally envisioned as a study group, according to Joe DiCarlo, a resigned and married priest and one of the original conveners. The group wished to study the documents of Vatican II to see what they meant for ministry, although DiCarlo admits that once they started meeting, especially after reading "*Gaudium et Spes*: Church in the Modern World," they pretty quickly began discussing war and civil rights, and the responsibility of the priest and the wider church to be involved. Joe has very fond memories of his time as an APP priest and wonders how different the church might have been if Bishop Wright (1959–69) had only worked with the group; "a missed opportunity," he bemoaned. "APP is my idea of priesthood," affirms DiCarlo, "it's an institution, hope it continues, it has accomplished a lot."[9]

On July 15, 1966, in the basement of St. Mary's Church in suburban Glenshaw, PA, north of Pittsburgh, assistant pastor John Groutt pulled together nineteen Pittsburgh priests to begin discussing the possibility of forming an independent priests' organization not under the control of the local bishop, John Wright. "A situation that is recalled with hilarity by the APP pioneers is the short-lived fear that moved the association's secretary to identify members only by numbers in the minutes of their earliest meeting. So number 11 was recorded as having made a motion that was seconded by number 5, etc.," writes Frank Brown. The first meeting was to be a "secret" as "there was a genuine fear of retaliation," according to one of the nineteen, Neil McCaulley.[10]

According to the minutes of the July 15 APP meeting, the group came together "to discuss implications of Vatican II." In order to meet under the cover of darkness, the meeting began at 9:45 pm and lasted until after midnight. Their initial idea, according to the minutes of the first meeting, was to: "Draw up some proposals to eventually be presented to the bishop. Direct confrontation with the bishop is desired, rather than the ordinary channel of the Diocesan deanery meeting. The conviction of the group is that there is not sufficient sympathy on the part of the clergy representatives to bank our interest on their support. Furthermore, the essential idea of communication with the bishop would very much be curtailed. However, it was felt that in the meantime the deanery meetings should be used to air some of the problems discussed by the group, to test the present structure and to enlist support of other priests."

9. DiCarlo, personal interview, July 15, 2016.

10. Brown, "Association of Pittsburgh Priests," 4.

It seems to me somewhat of a curious decision for the secretary to use the words "direct confrontation" in their dealings with the bishop, as I don't think the usual understanding of the word "confrontation" is what the priests had in mind. Rather they simply sought direct access and communication with the bishop, not trusting the usual channels set up through the official priests' council in the diocese. But the word choice suggests to me that they anticipated the perception by the bishop and, perhaps, some unsympathetic priests, would be that by forming such a group it would lead to confrontation. But the more important thought I have about the intention of these original nineteen is that they simply wanted to be in communication with their brother priests and the bishop, i.e., faithfully and loyally working together, yet, at the same time, having the independence to speak directly and with their own truth, not through traditional, and controlled, means. This was their innovation and intention in coming together outside the diocesan structures in my view.

The minutes of the meeting concluded by listing the various themes or matters of concern of this initial group, as well as which priests were interested in which issues—using, of course, numbers rather than names! The categories were: Pastor-Assistant relationships, how assignments occurred, personal life issues and retirement (2, 10, 13, 14, 17); Continuing education for priests and laity, concern about seminary life and relationships between priests and seminarians (1, 5, 6, 16); Parish set-up, administration and structures (3, 11, 15 and 18); nuns (only number 15)—[I tried to discover who that sole priest might be, but no one owned up to it]; church in the modern world, justice, civil rights, ecumenism (7, 8, 9, 12); Schools and birth control (no numbers attached).

The second meeting, also held under the cover of darkness, was convened at St. Richard's Church in the inner city Hill District. Three seminarians joined the original nineteen priests, and Fr. Don McIlvane was elected as the group's "benevolent despot." It was decided at this meeting that the bishop would be informed of the gatherings and why such a group was being formed, and that a letter would go out to all priests in the Diocese, inviting any and all to attend, thus they decided to "surface" from the underground. The general purpose of the group was study, simply to discuss the recent Vatican II documents and their implications for "our present diocesan situation." At upcoming meetings, all themes that had surfaced at the initial meeting would be discussed, as individual priests would draw up statements on each topic to present for dialogue. Subsequently, in late August of 1966, a letter of invitation went out to the bishop and all priests in the Diocese and the decision was made to "out" all nineteen priests, substituting their names for numbers. The group was now public and the APP was born.[11]

The group's initial concerns about "retaliation" by church authorities were not realized and, in fact, in a rather immediate response to the group's invitation, they received an exceedingly cordial letter from Bishop Wright. In it he congratulated them on taking the recently concluded Vatican II Council seriously, and in an entirely affirming and collegial manner offered the following words: "I like to feel that when any one of us meets as a priest with other priests we are all of us represented and somehow present in and through the priesthood of Jesus Christ." Wright went on to express good wishes for the meetings, "welcoming with an open spirit continuing news of them," and since the structure is "informal" and "open," and to be shared with all priests, and "since no structured organization is contemplated there is no need for any official notice on the part of my office . . . [nor do] . . . I see the need to send any representative, though I am grateful for your suggestion that I might do so."[12] Little did Bishop Wright anticipate that the group would become more organized and adopt an official name, Association of Pittsburgh Priests, much to his chagrin of Wright and a succession of Pittsburgh bishops up to the present. Nevertheless, much to its credit, the group despite its independence from the diocese, has had a stellar track record of ongoing communication with each and every bishop over the last fifty-three years!

What strikes one immediately about the early development of APP is that a key motivation for coming together, according to the initial convener, John Groutt, is that there was a sense of crisis, in the world, in the church, and, as a consequence of these realities, in the priesthood. In a preliminary draft of a declaration of purpose for such a group, they spoke of concern that there were "deep rumblings" among God's people, yet no one in the church was talking about the situation, i.e., there was "no structure for open, ongoing dialogue." There was a "crisis" developing with "consequences" for the future of the Pittsburgh Church. "It is an agony to be part of that Church, to have committed one's life to that Church, to love that Church and then to stand back and watch this develop . . . our consciences now cry out to be heard before God and the Church."

11. The nineteen signers were: Gerald Abbott, Mark Glasgow, Neil McCaulley, Robert Jedrzejewski, Raymond Werthman, John Wersing, Christopher Kennedy, James D. Hohman, John J. O'Malley, John E. Bresch, Donald McIlvane, Robert Mueller, Richard Terdine, Andrew J. Tibus, Joseph DiCarlo, Donald C. Fisher, Francis Puskar, John Groutt, Robert Davis.

12. Wright, Letter from August 16, 1966.

Groutt went on to publish three separate short pieces in July, August, and September of 1967 for a journal entitled *The Priest*, a monthly publication of Our Sunday Visitor focused on mostly pastoral and parish concerns of those in Catholic ministry. In these brief reflections, Groutt tried to articulate the nature of the crisis. "Is the parish to adopt and use newer liturgical forms and experiment with others?—or not? Will the local church establish viable church committees where honest disagreements can be aired and decisions made by majority vote? Is the role of the assistant [priest] that of a respected co-worker—or of a servant? Will the diocesan senates be truly representative of the thought and will of priests and laity? Or will they be tools to be manipulated by the bishop?"[13]

Groutt wrote about both the "stress" and "excitement" of the young priests; how "revolutionary" it all could be. But, he warned, if the bishops were "unwilling to be prophetic . . . [then] interesting and imaginative people are being driven from the institutional church in exasperated despair . . . [there will be] a full crisis."[14] He called for "professional proficiency" in the ministry and much more study and training, "team ministries" and lots of "experimentation," thus moving the priest beyond the "doorbell syndrome" [waiting in the rectory to answer the door], and "sacramental syndrome" [confining the priest to dispensing sacraments alone]. He called for more direct involvement in "civil rights, prison reform, poverty programs" and more reaching out to the "most forlorn and desolate of society: the ex-convicts, the hippies, the beatniks, the homosexuals, the divorced, the Negroes, the alcoholics, the insane, the destitute . . . [furthermore] the impersonal institution does not function to give life, but to take it away. Its practices rip at the insides of the man who loves his people, and it tears at the hearts of the people who love their priests. It is deadening. It stops love."[15]

Not long after writing these pieces, in 1968, Groutt asked to go on to pursue doctoral studies in religion and psychology at Temple University in Philadelphia. By then he had one foot out the church door, he acknowledges, in some ways a victim of this crisis he so poignantly described, as he followed his own advice to further his studies and become more professionalized in his work. He was laicized by 1971, but not before having exercised a huge impact on his fellow priests in organizing APP and serving as one of the intellectuals of the group.[16]

13. Groutt, "Crisis"; "The Priestly Priest"; "Of Red Tape," June, July, August, 1967.
14. Groutt, "Crisis," 523
15. Grout, "Red Tape," 720.
16. Groutt, "The Second Vatican Council," 6–8.

Not all of the early APP supporters were recently out of seminary. One older cleric who mentored a number of APP activists, Ed Joyce, pastored a struggling urban church, St. Joseph's, on the North Side of Pittsburgh from 1963–1968. Like Groutt, Gene Lauer and Don McIlvane, Ed Joyce was one of the priests with deep intellectual as well as pastoral interests: "Father Joyce," writes Frank Brown, "a pastor in a declining North Side neighborhood, who died just three years after his colleagues organized the association, would 'do the research, and we'd do the street work,'" according to Jack O'Malley, who served at St. Joseph's with Joyce successively as a seminarian intern, assistant pastor, and in time succeeded Joyce as pastor. O'Malley recalls: "He knew what was happening in the church. He was a prayerful man and an outstanding preacher . . . in the Fulton Sheen style."[17]

Not only a pastor and great preacher, Joyce also gave retreats to seminarians and wrote many position papers, referred to by some as the "Joyce Doctrine," and he also had deep pastoral instincts: he wrote a paper on parish renewal that centered on the importance of "human relationship as the test of Christian parish."[18]

Tragically, Joyce was also seriously flawed. He had a serious alcohol problem and in 1968 was removed from parish ministry after having been reported by Fr. Pat Jones, a resident at St. Joseph's parish, for sexual abuse of a minor. He died in 1969.[19]

Another older cleric who had sympathies with APP, paying dues but without direct participation, was the famous "labor priest," Charles Owen Rice. In a piece in the *Pittsburgh Catholic*, a weekly diocesan paper, Rice spoke glowingly of this new organization upon its establishment, even though he admitted he initially approached the group with a skeptical eye towards the younger clergy. Wrote Rice: "As a member of the older generation, I have trouble establishing empathy with the youngsters. Two recent experiences have helped me. I attended a small session of some of our younger priests . . . who were worth listening to. They turned out to be not a bunch of gripe artists and seekers of personal fulfillment, but constructive seekers of a strong role . . . new and good ideas enter the blood stream of an organization through the young; when the young are totally disregarded, as they are not around here, stagnation triumphs."[20]

17. Brown, "Association of Pittsburgh Priests," 5.

18. Brown, "Association of Pittsburgh Priests," 6.

19. No one in APP was aware of the circumstances of Joyce's removal until the information was reported in the Pennsylvania Grand Jury report (Office of Attorney General, Commonwealth of Pennsylvania, "Report I," 670) on the clergy abuse crisis in 2018.

20. Reported in now closed *Pittsburgh Press*, "Local Priests," January, 1967.

As already mentioned, the initial inspiration of APP was simply to study the documents of Vatican II and consider their implications for the priests' own pastoral work and the work of the wider Pittsburgh Church, although very soon after its inception APP developed a threefold purpose: church renewal, fraternal support, and social justice. One key document they studied out of Vatican II was entitled: "*Gaudium et Spes*, The Church in the Modern World," which challenged the church to go beyond the narrow scope of internal church reform and renewal and support of fellow clergy. But it appears that in the early months of APP the group focused most of its energy on internal church affairs. I say this because of a letter written to the membership by one of its initial participants, Don McIlvane. McIlvane, the famed "benevolent despot" of the group's second meeting in August of 1966, excused himself from the upcoming November, 1966 meeting, but nevertheless wrote to suggest several items for the agenda, seemingly concerned that there was a bit too much attention being paid to internal matters. McIlvane, who along with Jack O'Malley, would soon be seen as the leaders of the social justice, prophetic aspect of APP concerns, wrote his fellow priests: "I think our attention must concern not only problems that deal with priests alone, but those that concern all of the church and the general community." At the time McIlvane was chair of the study committee for the Church and the Modern World Document. He kept repeating in his letter the need to address "broad issues" of the community and the need "to establish a proper balance in our recommendations [to the bishop], even from the beginning. Hence, thanks to McIlvane and O'Malley and others, APP's reform agenda would apply to the wider society as well as the church and its clergy.

APP immediately took McIlvane up on his concerns and at the December 1966 meeting he was asked to present a paper on the Vatican II document *Gaudium et Spes*. In his presentation McIlvane focused on the need for a theology of peace, given the deepening involvement of the U.S. in the Vietnam War. In November of 1967, McIlvane published the first of several pieces on peace and non-violence for the aforementioned magazine, *The Priest*.[21]

But McIlvane was also concerned about strengthening APP membership and was especially sensitive to those in the clergy not of a liberal bent. Like any good community organizer, McIlvane was a great strategist; he understood that to make a real difference the organization needed to be strong, have a deep membership, and represent all clergy. Numbers matter. So in his letter he insisted that the group reach out to all, young, middle-aged and older, as well as liberal and conservative. "If the more conservative priests

21. McIlvane, "Non-violence," 923–28.

do not join our group, it must not be because they weren't invited," he wrote. It was also at the November, 1966 meeting, that the group adopted the official name, still in use fifty-three years later, the Association of Pittsburgh Priests.

As APP was still forming and recruiting from the entire pool of Pittsburgh priests in the fall of 1966, I am particularly struck by three things: (1) Its scope of interest, i.e., its early agenda included committees on parish renewal, continuing education of priests, justice issues and the theme of the relationship between the church and the modern world, priestly (and rectory) life, liturgy, experimentation and reform, and ecumenism. These are all huge undertakings, but they had enough participants to form study committees on each; (2) Their determination to straddle a fine line between independence, outside of formal diocesan structures, yet loyalty as responsible priests in good standing by constantly communicating through formal correspondence with Bishop Wright. This correspondence included detailed letters from Wright, in which he makes every effort to maintain cordial relations with this clearly independent-minded group of clerics; (3) The group was determined to always do its "homework" and not "shoot from the hip," as one member mentioned. Whenever making public declarations or in their correspondence with the local bishop as well as Vatican officials, they always assigned one member or a committee to seriously study whatever issue it was they were addressing, and to bring it to the group for comment and strengthening. Their statements were always thoughtful and researched. They were serious, faithful and loyal priests and they wanted to be taken seriously.

A very significant part of what APP members thought had led the church into a crisis following Vatican II was the whole question of priestly life, especially the relationship in rectory life between the pastor, generally an older priest, and the assistant, often fresh out of the seminary. There was often a deep disconnection between older and younger priests, suggested early APP member, Mark Glasgow, who said rectory life could be "awful." APP offered friendship and support in sometimes difficult moments.

One former priest, Phil Gallagher, an early member of APP, who loved and was inspired by many of his APP colleagues, told me a particularly graphic example of what rectory life could be for a young cleric. Phil had a motorcycle and in the summer he would drive around town on the motorcycle wearing a swimsuit. His pastor clearly didn't approve. Upon returning from a spin on the motorcycle, Phil found all the screen doors to the rectory locked. He rang the front doorbell and the pastor appeared but refused to unlatch the screen. The pastor disapproved of Phil's riding around town in such attire. Phil then pointed to his cycle and suggested to the pastor, a

Monsignor, that if he didn't unlatch the lock on the screen door Phil would get on his motorcycle and drive it right through the "fuckin'" screen and over the pastor's body. The pastor immediately unlatched the screen door and lugged his large frame up the stairs to his room to (presumably) call the bishop. "Gallagher threatened me with physical harm," the bishop was told. Within days a letter arrived on Gallagher's desk re-assigning him. There was no investigation, nor did the bishop ever ask Phil what had happened.[22]

Because priestly life could be so challenging, and the disconnection between older and younger clerics contentious, one of the early initiatives of APP was to recommend to the diocese the appointment of a Vicar for Priests, a position "sorely needed to clear the air about many diocesan misunderstandings," according to a January, 1967 APP newsletter. They went on to propose that along with a Vicar, who would work closely with the bishop, a personnel board should be developed made up of two priests appointed by the bishop, two from a list developed by priests, and two professional lay people, possibly a doctor or psychiatrist, whose duties would be mainly: "assignment of priests, dealing with any personal crises in the life of the priest and develop new personnel structures . . ."[23] Clearly APP had in mind situations like Phil Gallagher's, in which the younger clergy had nowhere to go to discuss problems other than the over-worked bishop who mostly listened to pastors. But, also, and typical of APP, they wrote this recommendation to the Diocese citing key documents of Vatican II which in their minds supported such an initiative. Once again, they were "doing their homework."

As cited earlier, simultaneous with the initiation of APP in Pittsburgh, a group of diocesan priests in Chicago began to meet also to form an independent priestly voice in the diocese. They called themselves the Association of Chicago Priests (ACP). And, in February of 1967, APP received a phone call from the priests in Chicago inviting them to a meeting involving themselves and priests from Atlanta, Fargo, Detroit, and Washington, both to share notes and also to begin discussing the possibility of a national group, which later formed in 1968, the National Federation of Priests' Council (NFPC).[24]

For the next several months APP continued to study and research various of their concerns through the committee structures and produced proposals for discussion and possible implementation in the diocese, e.g., on liturgy, they proposed establishing a "Liturgical Center." They also

22. Private interview with Gallagher, November 9, 2017. This story was also recorded in Trainor, *Unfinished Pentecost*, 264–67.
23. APP, "newsletter," January, 1967.
24. Brown, *Priests in Council*.

submitted proposals related to seminary life, ongoing priestly education, optional celibacy and ongoing relationship with resigned priests. All the while they deepened their bonds of collegiality and support which, as one former member, long since resigned and married, suggested probably helped keep him in ministry for two years longer than if there were no such support group. Many who stayed and continue to function as priests, or who have retired as priests, have said something similar to me.

Another indication of the seriousness with which these priests took the establishment of this new moment of priestly independence in the wake of Vatican II is their creation of a formal constitution. The Association of Chicago Priests was ahead of APP on this score, as they finalized a constitution by November of 1966. However, APP began working on such a document in 1966 and, by the early summer of 1967, forwarded to Bishop Wright such a draft along with a Preamble. Wright responded in a letter to APP in June of 1967. At the time Wright was actually in Taipei, yet he responded to the document within ten days. And typically he couldn't have been more cordial, constantly thanking them for their "courtesy in informing me of this proposed arrangement." Wright went on to suggest it might not be appropriate for him to make any "official comment" on the document as to avoid the appearance of seeking "to influence a voluntary organization which has had and has sought no official status in the structure of the diocese." This fascinates me on a few levels. Firstly, the bishop is acknowledging the right of his priests to form an independent, "voluntary organization." That is, at no point did he seem to want to challenge its existence or exercise any control, at least overtly. But, secondly, it seems obvious to me, he is also making it clear that APP has no standing or "official status" in the diocese. Therefore, whatever they do or say simply represents their own membership and not the diocese of Pittsburgh. That is, they are considered a kind of social club with no clout or authority. This was a very carefully constructed response by Wright.

Having earlier written that he should not make any official comment or attempt to influence the group in any way, Wright then proceeds to make recommendations and subtly suggests "that your Preamble not seem to promise more than your organization can properly hope to attain and that I, as Bishop, could honor in the matter of organized dialogue between your group and the Bishop . . . Informal" dialogue, he writes, is always available between the Bishop and all of his priests, "but," he continues, "there is some ambiguity (or so it might seem) on this point in the third paragraph of your Preamble." And then he writes, cleverly, "I mention this only because you ask my observations."

Then Bishop Wright gets very clear as to the limits of his tolerance for APP when he states: "Pending the establishment of our diocesan *Presbyterium*, plans for the formal structuring of which were announced at the Clergy Conference and will be implemented in the organization of the Synod, I cannot and shall not consider any structure, however large or small, as speaking for the priests of the diocese except their duly elected Council." Of course, the bishop controls that council! The rest of the letter goes on to solidify and reiterate that pretty much nothing will happen regarding priests without the bishop's approval.

Bishop Wright ends his response by, again, offering appreciation for APP's "courtesy and prayerful best wishes," then writing in long hand, he added a more personal note: "excuse my typing. It is over one-hundred degrees here [in Taipei!]."[25]

The paragraph in APP's Preamble whose ambiguity the bishop wanted clarified, follows a paragraph in which APP quotes the Vatican Council about the importance of dialogue between bishop and priests on a regular basis. APP follows this by further quoting the Council encouraging priests to be concerned about "the spiritual welfare of the whole diocese," and adding the following words: "Hence, arises a voluntary association of priests which proposes to work with the Bishop and to work through the Clergy Council and deanery meetings he has established. We are convinced," they conclude, "that such an association is necessary to fulfill the Conciliar injunctions quoted above."[26]

It seems like both APP and Bishop Wright are mapping out their turf, APP announcing its seriousness to be loyal collaborators with the bishop, yet, at the same time, declaring its independence and freedom to speak for their association, and the bishop, in pretty clear terms, reminding the group that they have no official status or authority, and that only the bishop-sanctioned Clergy Council speaks for the diocese. Thus solidifies the beginning of a fascinating relationship between independent-thinking [the group uses the word "voluntary" to describe itself in their constitution], yet loyal clerics of the Diocese of Pittsburgh, and their duly recognized spiritual leader. To my knowledge, or anyone else's in APP, Bishop Wright—unlike the next four bishops—never asked APP to change its name before he moved on from Pittsburgh to Rome in 1969, since they don't represent the diocese or all priests, the organization's official name notwithstanding. It is my understanding that subsequent bishops, Leonard (1969–1983), Bevilaqua (1983–1988), Wuerl (1988–2007) and the current bishop, David Zubick, have all,

25. Wright, Letter to APP, June 30, 1967.
26. APP constitution draft.

at one time or another, asked the group to come up with a new name. To date, after much discernment, the Association of Pittsburgh Priests still follows that original designation despite its current membership, which now includes resigned priests, religious sisters, and lay women and men, since 1993 (more on that in chapter 4). Their initial constitution—revised a few times, first in 1984, then 2017—was finalized at a meeting in July of 1967.

Bishop Wright was a complicated, curious figure, on the one hand a serious intellectual, fairly liberal and open-minded in some ways, yet authoritative and reactionary in other ways. To the former point, APP convener John Groutt, who had been sent to Rome to study in 1957, confirms this impression of Wright whom he met there in 1959 after Wright had replaced Bishop Deardon as Bishop of Pittsburgh. Later, back in Pittsburgh, Wright seemed in the forefront of ecumenical matters, an important issue coming out of Vatican II and one of the early concerns of APP. "Ecumenism was one area that surprisingly did not greatly trouble Americans as much as it did those in some traditionally Catholic countries," writes Groutt, in the *Journal of Ecumenical Studies*, a publication founded in 1964 by a then professor at Duquesne University in Pittsburgh, Leonard Swidler. Furthermore, Groutt continues, "John Wright, bishop of Pittsburgh, invited groups and theologians to the diocese who were in the forefront of interfaith dialogue."[27]

In line with Wright's initiative, in the latter part of 1967, APP's Committee on Ecumenism began working on a proposal to be sent to the bishop on how to develop a program for the diocese. They distributed this proposal in January of 1968. "The role of the priest in advancing ecumenism is one of intelligent activist, he must be a pacesetter, leader and teacher," they wrote. They attached all sorts of suggestions to the document, encouraging the bishop and all Catholic parishes to get involved in direct relationship with Protestants. Wright was supportive.

Despite all of this, Groutt remembers that Bishop Wright, the intellectual with liberal leanings, came back from the Council and slowly "turned the other way . . . [as] he delayed implementing many of the council reforms for as long and as much as possible. It was to this type of intransigence that many of us were reacting to." Former APP priest, Joe DiCarlo, laments the fact that Bishop Wright "didn't work with APP; what a missed opportunity." And in an ironic twist, writes Groutt, Bishop Deardon, a conservative when he left Pittsburgh for Detroit in 1959, thus nicknamed "Iron John, cold and aloof," went off to the Council and returned to Detroit a "changed man," full of enthusiasm for implementing reform. Deardon became the real liberal as time went on. Worse yet, writes Groutt, "Perhaps he [Wright] sensed that

27. Groutt, "The Second Vatican Council," 5–6.

the winds of power at the top had shifted. Following the Council [actually in 1969, several years after the conclusion of the Council], he returned to Rome to head one of the important curial posts in the Vatican: the prefect for the Sacred Congregations of the Clergy. There was little hope that reforms suggested by the Council for the clergy would ever be implemented.[28]

But APP was not yet done with Bishop (now Cardinal) Wright. Sometime after Wright went off to Rome, he returned to Pittsburgh to preach at the annual Labor Day Mass in Pittsburgh's St. Paul's Cathedral. At the time APP had been very active with and supportive of the Black Construction Coalition, which felt excluded from a major construction project at the U.S. Steel building in downtown Pittsburgh. APP, along with the Catholic Interracial Council and others, sent a letter to Cardinal Wright saying that he must address the plight of black construction workers during his Labor Day sermon. Wright responded that "Nobody will tell me what to say," to which APP members replied that if he didn't address this issue, they would walk out in the middle of Mass. He didn't and they did! After walking out at the termination of the sermon, they held a press conference on the stairs of the cathedral. Jack O'Malley, a now retired priest, yet still active APP member, shared this story with me and added: "I don't think Cardinal Wright ever forgave us after that action."[29]

Another deep concern of APP in these early years was that of clerical celibacy. It was an early discussion at APP meetings, perhaps because priests were already beginning to leave active ministry, in many cases due to the celibacy requirement. In the wake of Vatican II, in fact, many clerics across the world were leaving active ministry to marry. So in March of 1967 APP sent a letter to every priest in the diocese, "to try to determine the mind of the Church as revealed in her priests concerning the present discussion of clerical celibacy." Enclosed in the letter were two documents from the leadership of a group called The National Association for Pastoral Renewal. The documents were written by "theologians, church historians, biblical scholars, canon lawyers and men with parochial experience." Besides sending this to all diocesan priests, they also forwarded the letter to Pope Paul, the Apostolic Delegate, the President of the Bishop's Conference, and three Pittsburgh bishops, including, of course, Bishop Wright. Thirty-five APP members signed this letter with a brief statement which read: "We the undersigned priests of or working in the Diocese of Pittsburgh, ask that the

---

28. Groutt, "The Second Vatican Council," 6.

29. Brown, "Association of Pittsburgh Priests," 7. Also, private interview with Fr. Jack O'Malley, July, 16, 2016.

Bishops of the United States study openly and honestly the issue of optional clerical celibacy" (March 11, 1967).

Once again, remarkably, along with their full time pastoral duties in local parishes, APP members were constantly discussing, studying and communicating their concerns to brother priests, episcopal leadership, both at the local, national and international level. And nothing they did was done without serious dialogue and consultation, as well as serious study and discernment.

At the same time APP realized that their strength needed to be in numbers, so they were constantly trying to recruit new members through formal letters to all diocesan priests, as well as personal contact and invitation to upcoming gatherings. They were always transparent about their ideas and activities. One early APP member recalls at least 200 attendees at meetings in 1966 and 1967. However, as best I can tell, the number of dues-paying members never reached more than about 84, the high point being in the late 1960s. Nevertheless, they did enjoy wider support from other clergy who, for various reasons, chose not to become official members. Evidently some still felt intimidated by associating with APP, imagining some form of retaliation from older pastors or the bishop, perhaps. Some of the latter still would send money to quietly support the group and its endeavors.

Remarkably and ambitiously, in the early part of 1968, APP, through an ad-hoc committee concerned about racial integration and housing for low-income Pittsburghers, decided to develop a "plan to buy, rehabilitate and lease houses to the poor." The plan received enthusiastic support and five sub-committees (legal, public relations, rehab, property selection and finances) were set up to implement the plan. Garrett Dorsey, currently a retired yet still active APP member, served as chair of the Housing and Integration Committee, and eventually, landlord!

This was a huge undertaking for a group of priests who had no prior experience in purchasing and renovating property, not to mention playing the role of landlord. So they asked for experts/consultants from throughout the city to help them realize this ambitious plan. And they had to raise serious money: to start, $35,000. They even put together an informational brochure to be circulated across whatever neighborhood they located an appropriate property to quell any fears neighbors might have as to just who was buying up houses and selling them and just what their intentions might be. Might this be the beginning stages of gentrification, for example? They focused on fairly stable neighborhoods where there were lots of owner-occupied properties, not predominantly rentals. Then they would locate one blighted property in an otherwise stable community and fix it up.

By November of 1968, they closed on their first house in an urban neighborhood bordering Brushton (within Pittsburgh city limits) and Wilkinsburg (inner-ring suburb). Initially they wanted to not only lease a house to a low-income family, but also work on the issue of integration, so they targeted predominantly white neighborhoods, knowing that the chosen families would be black. However, the interest in the integration aspect was delayed initially and the neighborhood chosen was mostly black and poor. APP explained this decision by saying: "We have not abandoned the integration aspect of the program. We found that this was a complication which we could best tackle after initial experience in the housing venture itself." In January of 1969, a woman with four children moved into the first property APP had purchased. Later, they purchased a second house in the Beltzhoover neighborhood of Pittsburgh, rehabbed it, and a woman with six children moved in in April of 1970.

Eventually, due to the challenge of constant fundraising, serving as landlord and keeping the houses in good functioning order, the Housing and Integration Committee of APP had to acknowledge that they couldn't carry the project forward. "By that time we felt that we made our point," explained APP priest Warren Metzler, "that small groups could realistically get into the housing market."

However, this attempt by APP to work on housing and integration for the benefit of the marginalized, mostly African Americans in Pittsburgh, was only one example of a much larger issue around their concern for the role of the church in the inner city. In late 1967, they had submitted a proposal recommending a stronger presence of the Catholic Church in urban Pittsburgh, with, among other things, ideas of developing team ministries of priests and sisters and lay folk. Evidently APP was unhappy with the response of the diocese to its proposals for the church's role (or lack thereof) in the inner city. Furthermore, they seemed quite agitated at the weak response of the diocese after the April 4, 1968 murder of Dr. Martin Luther King Jr. and subsequent protests, and on April 25 of 1968, sent a pointed letter to Bishop Wright expressing their concerns and making strong recommendations for diocesan implementation: "We are appalled at the extent and depth of the hate and inhumanity recent events have uncovered within the Catholic community of the Diocese, among priests and laymen alike. While this may be the reaction of the minority of Catholics, more appalling we feel is the even more widespread fear and confusion among so many of our people regarding the recent civil disorders."

They go on to applaud the Bishop's public comments about civil rights, racism and inequality, but suggest that they are not nearly strong enough and must be followed by concrete actions. They ask: "Just where does the official Church of Pittsburgh stand on these matters?" They then make concrete proposals for action: educational programs and the formation of a task force, pulpit letters and sermons, housing initiatives, welcoming blacks into parishes, advocacy for the poor, support for the Poor Peoples' Campaign (which King was about to engage in by marching to Washington, DC), for Catholic schools to welcome poor and black folks, etc. They conclude these strong words with: "Hoping that we have made our urgent, cooperative point, Bishop, we request that you seek to find time as soon as possible to meet with some of our number." Later that year, of course, APP initiated its own housing and integration program, as outlined above. Less than two years from its founding, APP had found and profoundly exercised its prophetic, priestly voice and was beginning to be heard.

Regarding the larger, national stage, Fr. Frank Brown, an early biographer of APP, wrote that APP, along with the ACP (Association of Chicago priests) and other groups, was instrumental in the formation of a national group of priests, founded in 1968, which called itself The National Federation of Priests' Councils (NFPC), as has already been mentioned. Two-hundred eighty-four priests converged on Chicago, in February of 1968, to begin discussing the formation of such a group. "Many of them," writes Brown, ". . . were apprehensive of what would happen to them when they returned home and had to face bishops who actually suspected the Chicago gathering as some sort of conspiracy against them." In truth, Brown continues, their "goals" were simply to create dialogue in their individual dioceses and participate in decision-making on policies that directly affected them.[30]

According to APP minutes of its February, 1968 monthly meeting, the several APP delegates to the Chicago gathering all agreed there was need of a permanent national group. Although the idea of forming a union was considered, it didn't seem to fit the objectives of APP members. Instead they "emphasized the need for coordinated positive action in a professional priestly atmosphere," yet another clear indication that these priests sought a collaborative, mature, cooperative relationship with their local bishops. They were hardly a renegade group. The Pittsburgh participants all supported the idea of joining up with the fledgling NFPC (which officially formed in May of 1968). A new moment had now been reached as post-Vatican II priests were gaining their voices and envisioning a more democratic church.[31]

As has been an important theme of this study, I want to emphasize once again that APP always envisioned itself as not only an action group, but also a serious study group. Thus, before acting they would always do

---

30. Brown, "Association of Pittsburgh Priests," 5.

31. Brown, *Priests in Council.*

research and write position papers on whatever topic of action they were contemplating, and the group was well equipped to take this dual role on, as a number of APP members were also good scholars. Each time an important issue came up for their consideration, they would assign certain members to prepare to speak to the issue.

Only months after their inauguration in the late summer and early fall of 1966, APP produced a paper on liturgical experimentation in January of 1967. They were trying to follow up on, and begin to implement, one of the key documents of Vatican II: *Sacrosanctum Concilium*, Constitution on the Sacred Liturgy. Immediately, after the end of the Council, Pope Paul VI had stated that "the liturgy was the first subject to be examined and the first, too, in a sense, in intrinsic worth and in importance for the life of the Church."[32] What is most interesting to me about this early focus of APP is the aforementioned connection Jim Hohman had made between the turning around of the altar to face the people during Mass and how deeply it impacted his perspective on ministry. After several meetings APP drew up a proposal for the diocese of Pittsburgh to implement. Included in this proposal was the idea to "establish a Liturgical Center . . . [to] be affiliated with a university facility and that its work of experimentation draw on the rich ethnic, racial, cultural, musical backgrounds which exist in the Pittsburgh community." The document/proposal was very well researched, beginning with scriptural citations and mapping out the various developments in liturgy from the early church right up to Vatican II. APP envisioned Pittsburgh as "a center of liturgical studies" and renewal.[33]

In September of 1968, APP organized a panel discussion on the recent and controversial papal encyclical, *Humanae Vitae*, the Vatican statement on birth control, issued by Pope Paul VI and released on July 29, 1968. In this encyclical, the traditional Catholic teaching, prohibiting the use of artificial means of contraception, was upheld. This despite the fact that a papal commission, made up of theologians, priests and married persons, appointed by the pope, had recommended the prohibition be lifted. Frs. John Hugo (spiritual mentor to co-founder of the Catholic Worker Movement Dorothy Day), Garrett Dorsey, and Eugene Lauer, a theologian and professor over the years at a number of Catholic Colleges and Universities, were asked to present papers.

Interestingly, it appears there was not unanimity on the birth control controversy, either among the panelists or the rest of the APP membership; thus, the need for such an informed discussion. The panelists prepared

32. Pope Paul VI, *Documents of Vatican II*, 139–182.
33. APP, "discussion paper," January, 1967.

separately, without collaboration, and spoke to the essence of the encyclical as well as how each saw its pastoral implications. A lively discussion followed the presentations and it was determined to continue at the next gathering. However, it was also determined that they needed a special meeting to consider how to respond to the fallout from the highly controversial teaching. A regional meeting of several priests' associations was to occur in Philadelphia, and each local priests' group could send two representatives to this conference. Two issues were to be discussed: " the stand of the Washington, DC theologians and parish priests regarding the birth control encyclical and the concept of 'due process' in regard to such penalties as 'suspension,' when imposed upon priests."[34]

The delegates were not authorized to speak for APP at the meeting, nor did APP make any public statement at this time as to taking a position on the issue of birth control. However, regarding the "due process" concern, the delegates were authorized to "initiate discussions about priests' rights . . . and help formulate a statement of solidarity about priests' rights and, finally, the delegates were authorized to issue a public statement on 'due process' in relation to the 19 Washington DC priests (who were suspended for their dissent—another 41 across the country were suspended by various bishops—once they obtained the facts of the case."[35] Thirteen APP priests went to Washington to participate in a larger demonstration of over 300 priests who picketed at the national bishop's gathering at the Hilton Hotel.

Then, at the November APP meeting it was decided to ask Bishop Wright to intervene with Cardinal O'Boyle in DC, asking O'Boyle to submit the issue (of priest suspensions) to arbitration at the next meeting of the NCCB (National Conference of Catholic Bishops). Although I cannot document that Wright ever wrote such a letter, the case of the suspended priests vs. Cardinal O'Boyle lasted for three years and was finally arbitrated by a Vatican committee set up by Cardinal Wright, who since 1969, headed up the Congregation for the Clergy at the Vatican. The final decision allowed both sides to save face, according to a priest from the NFPC, and in the mind of NFPC biographer, Frank Brown, this was a very significant decision related to due process and the rights of priests to speak their mind.[36]

34. APP minutes, September, 1968.

35. APP minutes, September, 1968. According to APP priest, Gary Dorsey, a suspended clerical friend could say Mass but not preach or hear confessions. Also, Curran, *Loyal Dissent*, 51–56 & 143–149. Curran was a professor at Catholic University of America and one of the theologians who dissented from the teaching of the encyclical. Also, Brown, *Priests in Council*, 30–32.

36. Brown, *Priests in Council*, "To this day, I am convinced, U.S. priests at the grass roots by and large have no appreciation for the impact the Washington priests' case had

As has been acknowledged previously, yet in my view cannot be emphasized enough, the APP took theological and pastoral reflection very
seriously, they were intellectually curious and seemed always to think and
reflect before they spoke and acted. They grounded themselves in good theology and took the documents of Vatican II very seriously. As Frank Brown
wrote in his 1987 pamphlet about APP, upon reflecting on the early years,
"They (APP) agree that it was their willingness to do needed research that
lent them credibility, perhaps especially to the news media [if not to the
bishops!]." For example, they collaborated with St. Vincent's Seminary in
Latrobe, PA., on the school's curriculum, where many APP members had
studied. When they called for the diocese to institute team ministries, especially in poor areas, they had done extensive research on existing models.
They also conducted a number of surveys on topics such as clerical celibacy,
liturgical experimentation, diocesan and parish structures, etc., "none of
which was on the diocese's official agenda." They operated as if they wanted
to be considered trained sociologists, aiming to be well grounded in their
proclamations. "We have always done our homework, and not gone off
shooting from the hip," one APP member suggested.[37]

In this same scholarly vein, the group's most prominent theologian,
Gene Lauer, and one of its most serious activists and the oldest member of
APP, Don McIlvane, were asked by the group to work on a document on
priestly life, ultimately entitled: "The Priest and Gospel Simplicity." After
submitting the document to the membership, it was approved in late 1970
and published in 1971 in *The National Catholic Reporter*, under the title:
"Chastity, Yes; Obedience, Of Course; but also Simplicity."[38] With the help of
NFPC, this document had wide circulation throughout the country.

Interestingly, I first was made aware of this early document in an interview with Pat Fenton, a resigned APP priest, one of the last priests to join
APP in 1971, who while in seminary in the late 1960s did some summer
internships at a key APP parish on the north side of the city, St. Joseph's in
Manchester. The seminarians referred to these experiences with key APP
activist priest, Jack O'Malley, and Pastor Ed Joyce, as "summers at St. Joe's."
St. Joseph's, where a wonderful collaborative ministry took place between
the parish priests and Sisters of Mercy, was an important training ground
for urban ministry and a great introduction to the concerns of APP. Fenton
told me that this document had a profound influence on his identity with

---

on their lives. Because the case was decided at the Church's highest level, no bishop
anywhere—for any reason whatever—is likely to suspend his priests *en masse*." According to Gary Dorsey, it was rumored that Wright "engineered the decision Roman style."

37. Brown, "Association of Pittsburgh Priests," 8–9.

38. APP, "Chastity," 10.

APP and his deep commitment to priestly ministry. He remembered reading it while in seminary and sharing it with fellow seminarians. It continued to inspire his over twenty-years in priestly ministry and, it is clear to me, beyond that in his current work with a low-income housing program in Pittsburgh.[39]

Fenton's recollection of this document and its impact on his ministry and life is especially fascinating to me because, ironically, its co-author (Don McIlvane was the other), Gene Lauer, recently deceased APP member, didn't remember writing it! Lauer had a long career, much of it spent in academia, including a lengthy tenure in a pastoral institute at the University of Notre Dame. Ordained in 1961, having earned his doctorate in theology at the Jesuit *Gregorianum* in Rome, Lauer was part of that progressive theological world that valued experience over philosophy as the key grounding for theological reflection. A big fan of the twenty-first century English cleric and Cardinal, John Henry Newman, Lauer followed key Vatican II progressives, Karl Rahner, SJ, Edward Schillebeeckx, OP, and Hans Kung, as well as more contemporary thinkers such as David Tracy and Elizabeth Johnson. Over the years, whenever APP wanted to address an important theological issue through its Speaker Series, it would often call on Lauer to do the presentation.

I want to spend a bit of time analyzing the document, as I am of the view that this had a deep significance in grounding some of the key values of APP in its understanding of who the priest ought to be and how he should live out his priesthood.

It begins by acknowledging a major concern of priests after Vatican II, i.e., clerical celibacy. However, that was not its sole concern. Having been drafted and ultimately approved in late 1970, it was also concerned with the question of priestly obedience: it comes on the heels of the suspension of hundreds of priests for their dissent of the papal encyclical on birth control, *Humanae Vitae*. Though the document acknowledges the appropriateness and legitimacy of the virtues of priestly chastity and obedience to their bishops, it acknowledges some disagreements "on the practical application of these virtues."[40]

But while acknowledging the importance of addressing the issues of chastity and obedience, it goes on to regret the neglect of "another basic principle" of priestly spirituality: "that of Christian simplicity in the life of the priest." They grounded this insight in the life of "Christ himself" when he declared, as recorded in Matthew's gospel: "Foxes have holes and the

39. Private interview, July 18, 2016.
40. APP, "Simplicity," 10.

birds of the air have nests, but the Son of Man has nowhere to lay his head" (Matthew 8:20).

Recognizing the ongoing debate on clerical celibacy, but more concerned about simplicity, they write: "Celibacy as a compulsory requirement for ordination is a matter of legitimate debate. Simplicity and detachment are not. Every priest, married or celibate, is called to reflect the simplicity of Christ in many ways." But they go beyond mere lifestyle demands on the priest when they suggest: "Life style alone does not make a priest poor in the spirit of Christ. There must be also a willingness to serve the poor and to be among them in the most literal sense of those words. This commitment to serve the poor must be reflected in the life of every priest, whether he be serving a congregation that is predominantly poor, or one that is not."[41]

This attempt to connect lifestyle commitments to ministry among the poor was part of a key initiative of APP to challenge the diocese to commit to team ministry in the inner-city parts of Pittsburgh, something the group clearly felt the diocese was not sufficiently focused on. This perspective may reflect, although not explicitly stated, the influence of Latin American bishops and theologians who in 1968 had declared the important ecclesial principle of "preferential option for the poor," which has become, right up to the present, a central theological tenet of Roman Catholicism, affirmed over and over by church theologians as well as hierarchical leadership.

The document goes on to decry an attitude among priests that the best and most prestigious parishes to serve in are the most well healed in money and buildings. "This attitude, so easy for priests to slip into, is contrary to the spirit of the Gospel." And, it continues, "Priests should see the poorest parishes as the best parish to serve." Even in affluent parishes the priest should seek out the poorest to serve, they declare, and challenge any negative attitudes towards the poor on the part of middle and upper-class parishioners. Priests are called to be "zealous defenders of the poor" and they decry the sometimes "harsh and repressive attitudes toward public welfare recipients or public housing tenants prevalent among so-called devout Christians."

Furthermore, the authors talk about priests "seeking out the poor . . . the last man to whom the poor should be invisible ought to be the priest." Some might remember that the author of the famous study of inequality in America, *The Other America*, Michael Harrington wrote of the "invisible poor." The priest is called to be part of the "struggle" to help the poor gain "dignity, freedom and decency" with the aim of ending "degrading poverty and injustice," they argue.[42]

41. APP, "Simplicity," 10.
42. APP, "Simplicity," 10.

Accused by some of too much "political involvement," the priests suggest that it is their identity with the poor and their "rightful struggle for justice" that is the real objection of their detractors, who imagine the correct priestly role is one of "healing and reconciliation," not "agitation." To that the document responds with a quotation from the prophet Isaiah regarding their appropriate role: "to break unjust fetters, and undo the things of the yoke, let the oppressed go free and break every yoke" (Isaiah 58: 6–7).

Demonstrating the influence of views from the South American continent, they cite the words of the recently elected—and ultimately assassinated in 1973—socialist president of Chile, Salvador Allende, who in a tribute to priests and bishops—"few, unfortunately, in our nation," declares the document—in Latin America who have shown solidarity with the poor: "Before, for centuries, the Catholic Church defended the interests of the powerful. Today the church, after John XXIII, has become oriented toward making the Gospels of Christ a reality, at least in some places."[43]

Having laid a foundation for a new outlook on priestly ministry, the statement goes on to make very detailed lifestyle recommendations: first, they object to the designation "monsignor" for clergy as a term coined in the middle ages and a sign of royalty, in contradiction to Gospel simplicity and the life of Christ, and they ask "brother clergy" who have accepted this title, to drop it; secondly, they advise, only owning cheap cars, limiting ownership of televisions and radios, traveling simply, vacationing in modest accommodations, refusing membership in country clubs, investing and saving modestly, avoiding tax loopholes that favor the wealthy, living in modest houses and rectories, even simple apartments close to the poor, and donating 20 percent of their income to charity.

The authors conclude the document with a very humble and sincere statement that they do not wish to judge others nor do they condemn any priest who sees lifestyle issues differently, to assure any readers that they understand differing human needs. Then they add a "private letter to the current bishop, Vincent Leonard," applauding him for his simplicity of lifestyle, but expressing unease at the luxuriousness of the bishop's residence and location in an affluent part of the city. They encourage Leonard to leave his residence by citing a decree from Vatican II: "Priests and bishops should spurn any type of vanity in their affairs . . . let them have the kind of dwelling which will appear closed to no one and which no one will fear to visit, even the humblest."[44]

---

43. APP, "Simplicity," 10.
44. APP, "Simplicity," 10. Also, Paul VI, "Decree on Ministry.."

One member suggested rather than sending this "simplicity" document with a special letter to Bishop Leonard, along with their request that he vacate his residence, that he be approached personally by three of the group, Don McIlvane, Gene Lauer (the two co-authors) and Regis Ryan. The meeting did take place and Leonard's immediate reaction was defensiveness and anger, but realizing the three APP priests were not attempting to be accusatory, he eventually applauded their efforts and acknowledged they were likely right, yet he felt it was not something he could do. The house, which had actually been donated to the diocese years before, in his view, served larger purposes than a mere residence and that made it necessary that he stay put.

What is amazing to me regarding this document is just how serious APP members were about shaping their lives and ministry in direct accord with the ministry and life of Jesus and Gospel radicalism. Although diocesan priests, therefore not members of the vowed religious life, where poverty, chastity and obedience were fundamental to the religious commitment, nevertheless, they were committing themselves to the same witness and vision as vowed religious. Interestingly, in this serious reflection on priestly spirituality, they viewed chastity and obedience as serious commitments yet somewhat negotiable. By that I mean that they saw the law of clerical celibacy as not necessary for ministry, and might, indeed, change in their lifetimes, and that obedience to the bishop needed a lot of clarification. However, the group viewed simple living and commitment to the poor as absolutely fundamental to priestly ministry. The latter was, in their view, necessary for living fully the priestly commitment in following Jesus. In their view, it lent credibility and authenticity to their priesthood, if you will, and a clear sign they weren't seeking special privileges as men of the cloth.[45]

At the beginning of the 1970s, APP was pretty well established in the Pittsburgh Diocese as an alternate voice of reform, renewal and social activism, with a keen interest in grounding their thinking and acting in serious biblical, ecclesial and theological research. Besides this deep reflection on priestly simplicity and identity with the poor, Don McIlvane had earlier written a statement articulating a theology of peace, a profound challenge

---

45. As a member of a vowed religious community (Dominican) for ten years, I am very familiar with the commitment of the vows of poverty, chastity, and obedience. I, too, understand the commitment of poverty or simplicity as a commitment to working directly with the poor, a key element of priestly ministry, yet one receiving less attention in many religious communities than chastity and obedience. I was deeply influenced in this vision by religious movements in Latin America, not so much by Salvador Allende as the theologians of liberation, most especially Gustavo Gutierrez, who first articulated the notion of the "preferential option for the poor, in his groundbreaking work: *A Theology of Liberation.*

to the traditional doctrine of just war in Catholic social teaching. So beyond their serious attempts at ecclesial, sacerdotal and local parish reform and updating, they were very active on the social front from the earliest days: besides the aforementioned issues, they worked with Cesar Chavez on the farmworker grape and lettuce boycotts—Cesar and his organizers actually stayed in the rectory at St. Joseph's on the Northside with Jack O'Malley and in the Sisters of Mercy convent next door; draft counseling regarding the Vietnam War; anti-war activity and eventually withholding taxes to protest the war; picketing a local Catholic hospital over worker rights; civil rights through the Catholic Interracial Council (CIC); and many other justice issues of the day.

By 1970 APP numbered some eighty-four dues-paying member priests—with many others who supported from a distance with money and encouragement—and they had several functioning committees assigned to study, research and propose directions and action steps. They were a force to be reckoned with both in the diocese and throughout the city at large. As APP member Gary Dorsey told me the group has been a "constant voice and the diocese has to be aware that APP would analyze whatever it did."[46] In a similar vein, Plowshares activist, mother and grandmother, and co-founder of the peace and justice Thomas Merton Center (1972), and an early member of CIC, Molly Rush, told me in a private interview: APP was an "amazing brotherhood . . . [that] has had great influence on lots of people."[47]

For at least one former Pittsburgh priest, when the altars were turned around, now facing the people, so was his life and priestly ministry as well as the lives of his parishioners. That liturgical change along with so much new thinking that came out of Vatican Council II, ending in 1965, changed the lives of priests and Catholics all over the world. Among other things, in Pittsburgh, it led to the founding of a new priestly organization, the Association of Pittsburgh Priests, which has spent the last fifty-three years attempting to implement this new thinking with the hope of transforming an ancient religious institution.

46. Private interview, June 15, 2018.
47. Private interview, July 18, 2016.

CHAPTER TWO

Some Losses, Some Gains
Deepening the Vision of Vatican II, 1971–78

By THE EARLY TO mid-1970s, APP was going through some changes and growing pains, as some of the early conveners had resigned from the priesthood, a few others went off to study, one went off to Africa to pursue missionary work with the Spiritan religious community for five years, some new faces appeared, and newly ordained joined up. Meanwhile, the Pittsburgh Catholic Diocese was getting used to a new bishop, as John Wright headed for Rome in 1969, and one of his assistants, Vincent Leonard, was named his successor. Leonard wound up serving as bishop from 1969–1983.[1]

In many ways Leonard was the antithesis of Wright. Wright was an intellectual, an early liberal turned conservative after Vatican II, with a large ego, as was demonstrated by his reaction to the demand from the APP he address the plight of black construction workers during his Labor Day sermon, as related in chapter 1. Leonard, by contrast, as Frank Brown records: "... all agree is a mild-mannered, fatherly leader with no bent for disturbing calm waters."[2] Even though initially angered and defensive by the APP's suggestion that he relocate from the bishop's mansion on the east side of the city, after the publication in 1971 of the APP's aforementioned document on "priestly simplicity," he ultimately expressed regret that he couldn't move

---

1. John Groutt received permission to pursue a PhD in Religion and Psychology at Temple University, ultimately resigning from the priesthood in 1971; Tom Harvey began studies for his MSW at Colombia in 1972; Jim Hohman and Joe DiCarlo left ministry and eventually married by 1968 and Don Fisher joined up with the Holy Spirit religious community to volunteer for missionary work in Tanzania from 1975–1980.

2. Brown, "Association of Pittsburgh Priests," 2.

and even agreed with their perspective that it would probably be a better symbol if he did move to a smaller, more modest home. Much like Wright, despite occasional disagreements, he tried to accommodate APP, often willing to meet and dialogue, never suggesting they disband, and sometimes even complementary of their witness and vision, despite consternation with their use of the name Association of Pittsburgh Priests, reasoning the name misrepresented them as speaking for all priests in the diocese.[3]

A number of APP members had humorous anecdotes about their dealings with Bishop Leonard and how unintimidating he could be, even when they were called in to defend themselves for transgressing diocesan procedures or stretching theological and pastoral orthodoxies. One such story involved Phil Gallagher, an early APP member who resigned in 1977, and later married, but who remains an active APP member. Beyond parish duties Phil had a radio program in the early 1970s and on one broadcast explained that he had parishioners in second marriages, many of whom were from other parts of the country, complicating the process of gathering proper documentation in pursuit of an annulment, thus making it very difficult, in some cases impossible, to complete properly. Hence, on this particular evening's broadcast, he welcomed such people to full participation in the church, including receiving the Eucharist, a "pastoral call," he explained, yet still deemed a violation of church teaching. Someone blew the whistle on Phil (presumably Bishop Leonard was not a regular listener), and soon after, he received a call from the diocese: The bishop wanted to see him. He wasn't told why.

Before going to the chancery, he shared his concerns with his pastor, the famous labor priest and great tactician, Fr. Owen Rice. Rice offered the following advice: "You are not going to have a theological discussion with the bishop in his office. Whatever he says you did, agree that you did it and tell him that since then you have learned a big lesson. He will not ask you what the lesson is." Both Gallagher and Rice were correct on what they suspected the issue would be: The bishop had received many letters from radio listeners reporting that Fr. Gallagher was inviting divorced Catholics to the Eucharist. At the actual meeting, Leonard asked if it were true that he said such things on the radio. "Yes, bishop, I said that, but since then I

---

3. In a private interview with Don Fisher, early APP participant who died in 2017, he often remarked how easy it was to talk with Bishop Leonard about pastoral assignments. The following scenario was typical: Leonard would ask about one's interest in a new assignment by taking out a box of index cards, each representing a particular parish. If he made a suggestion and one balked, he'd simply lick his thumb, pull out another index card and ask whether the next one had interest for you. Fisher smiled widely as he recalled such experiences.

have learned a big lesson," to which the bishop responded: "I'm glad to hear that, Father," and the meeting ended with a handshake. Issue resolved; Rice's advice had been brilliant.[4]

After having returned from the annual meeting of the National Federation of Priests Council (NFPC) in the early part of 1972, the same Phil Gallagher, reporting about the meeting in a piece published in the *Pittsburgh Catholic* (March 31), writes: "I become more aware than ever of the gentleness and concern of Bishop Leonard. His efforts at establishing procedures for due process, personnel boards and grievance committees are far in advance of most dioceses."

But there were also tense moments between APP and Leonard over the years. One young priest had been accused by his pastor of stealing money from the church collection. Without any due process, the priest was immediately transferred, much like Gallagher in a incident reported in chapter 1. The priest complained to APP and Jack O'Malley organized a group to immediately meet with Bishop Leonard. A dozen or so priests went to the meeting which surely got Leonard's attention. He agreed to investigate. For Phil Gallagher this was a sign of change; authority could be challenged. "Bishop Leonard blinked and the APP felt empowered."[5]

A painful episode occurred in the latter part of 1974 when Bishop Leonard suspended three priests at Duquesne University—one, Joe Healy, an APP member—for distributing communion in the hand, a post-Vatican II liturgical innovation. Although the practice was in use in other locations, the Pittsburgh diocese had not yet approved it. APP went into action and demanded to meet with the bishop in a letter describing their concerns (letter dated January 22, 1975, signed by APP chair, warren Metzler). APP felt that the three very faithful priests had been slandered as "dishonest, dishonorable and disobedient," and they demanded that their names be exonerated publicly. Secondly, they demanded a review of and possibly change in diocesan policy on the issue, since practices varied across the international church following liturgical changes from Vatican II. Lastly, they suggested that the priests' rights to face one's accuser and to due process had been violated and this violation represented a threat to all priests in the diocese. Not long after this incident and protest, permission to distribute communion in the hand was granted and the priests reinstated!

APP suffered losses during this time. As a number of priests resigned, in most cases to marry, active membership leveled off at about seventy-five,

4. Private interview with Gallagher, November 17, 2017. Also, Trainor, *Unfinished Pentecost*, 266.

5. Interview , Gallagher, November 17, 2017.

even though many more priests in the diocese had at one point or another showed interest, came to gatherings, or sent money. Nevertheless, APP was clearly settling in for the long haul as a volunteer, independent thinking yet loyal group of active clergy, which had a significant hand in helping form a national group, NFPC, which, by 1972, APP joined as a dues' paying member, having attained the NFPC's required 10 percent membership of the overall priest population in the diocese. Most years APP sent out a letter to all Pittsburgh priests inviting them to join their ranks. In their 1971 recruitment letter they tried to make clear they were not a "divisive group" opposed to the (official) Clergy Council in the diocese. In fact they were totally supportive of the Council and wished that the Clergy Council would be the official representative to NFPC, rather than APP. They go on to say in this letter that APP wished to promote healthy dialogue among priests and bishops, and even though there may be tension at times, their aim was to protect every priest's "deepest personal rights."

APP was constantly analyzing and evaluating its purpose and direction, always sensitive to how it was perceived by non-APP clergy and the wider diocese. What was their relationship to the bishop? How did they want to relate to him? At an early 1973 meeting they discussed the perception that there was some resentment by non-APP clergy as to whom the group actually represented; possibly just a few cranks? Some younger priests thought the APP was a clique or exclusive club, involved in groupthink. One sympathetic yet critical member of the clergy I interviewed said he tried to join APP when he was a deacon, one year before ordination. He was told he had to wait until he became a priest. Angered by this response, he never revisited this, despite his view that APP was right on most of the issues. He found the group too "ideological and clerical."[6]

APP members would often review their goals and platforms, helping to remind themselves of their importance to the wider church. To this end, early in the 1970s, the APP adopted an annual brainstorm gathering they referred to (and still do in 2018) as mountaintop retreats, where they would spend two days evaluating the previous year's activities and goals,

6. Private interview with Fr. Lou Vallone, November 17, 2018. Recently retired, Vallone expressed great admiration for APP, especially certain members whom he considered mentors. He acknowledged that APP has been a "prophetic voice in the diocese, its impact very real." Nevertheless, his experience of rejection as a deacon stayed with him and he found certain members of the group personally objectionable. Beyond personal issues, he found the group too "ideological and clerical," and as a priest dedicated to the apostolate with the African American community, he felt APP had a "paternalistic" attitude towards blacks, despite its deep commitment to racial justice. He also felt the group rejected his model of immersing himself in the black community and its culture.

while proposing new goals for the upcoming year. They would often bring in trained facilitators to keep them focused and results-oriented. They rarely went to the "mountain"; more often than not they met in city locations. Nevertheless, it was a time set aside to evaluate and refocus.

Celibacy was a major concern of the APP right from the start, as it was across the nation; it was an agenda item for the NFPC as well. And in a sign of the deep bonds, solidarity and relationships developed by these priests in the post Vatican II world, a pretty consistent theme at APP meetings over the years is what might be the role of resigned priests in the diocese. At a minimum APP priests wanted to be in touch with those who had left ministry, not only to imagine ways their skills and background might be of help to the diocese, but just, on a human level, wanting to support those who had resigned by maintaining ongoing connection and communication.

In the February 2, 1972 minutes of an APP monthly meeting, a very interesting discussion occurred regarding a resigned priest who had received dispensation from his vow of celibacy and wanted to marry in the diocese. In order for a resigned priest to be allowed to marry in the diocese, it was up to the local bishop to set the conditions. The former priest had to be married in a church where he was not known, a diocesan-appointed priest was the only priest allowed to witness the marriage, and only immediate family could attend. The resigned priest objected and declined the diocese's conditions. Jack O'Malley offered his current church, and encouraged him to invite anyone he wanted. In the end, a priest from out of town celebrated the liturgy. Shortly thereafter, O'Malley received a call from the bishop's office and had to go to the chancery to see Bishop Leonard. "Not sure to this day if O'Malley had learned a big lesson," read the minutes, possibly a humorous attempt to say O'Malley didn't follow the Monsignor Rice strategy offered to Phil Gallagher. But the bigger issue of concern for APP members was how resigned priests were treated by the diocese as they made their transition. Money and housing were immediate issues for resigned priests, who often had few resources or job possibilities. Apparently there was no diocesan policy in place to help resigned priests transition to life as a lay person. APP decided to get on the case.

Interestingly, at the next APP meeting in March of 1972, a letter was read from an early APP member who faded fairly quickly from the group, though remaining a priest in the diocese, and who objected to statements he read from APP meeting minutes regarding the marriage of the above-mentioned resigned APP priest. The minutes had suggested that the church's negative and restricted response to the resigned priest's wedding dampened any sense of joy and celebration of two people in love and wanting to be happily married in the church they still loved. APP decried the official church's attitude. The priest, whose letter objected to such a statement in the minutes, wrote that, while he was not condemning his former fellow priest for getting married, he opined that by marrying, this former priest had fallen short of his full commitment to God, since he had abandoned his lifelong pledge to celibacy. The letter asked that a section of the minutes that criticized the diocese for its treatment of the resigned priest be dropped, implying that the diocese was right to imagine it not so joyous an occasion, as the marriage might even scandalize some of the faithful. In response to the letter, and in support of the marriage of the former priest as a joyous occasion, APP members present voted unanimously not to change the minutes and affirm their former priest's happy marriage, thus respecting his own experience. It seemed to me a deep sign of love and affection for resigned brothers and a concern for their happiness and well-being. Nevertheless, the letter from a sympathetic supporter of APP, also served as a sign that priest resignations, at least for some who remained, were upsetting, a kind of failure, thus not a cause for celebration.

But true to their convictions, APP stayed on this case, even writing a letter (dated February 10, 1978, signed by APP chair, John Oesterle) to the National Conference of Catholic Bishops, expressing deep concerns about "the status of priests, deacons, and religious men and women who have re-signed from the active ministry." They have "rights" and "gifts" which APP suggested should be of service to the church. They decried treatment by the institutional church they deemed "unjust" and "unfair" and they suggested revision of legislation that restricts these women and men in their potential future service to the church.

Their former bishop, John Wright, by this time a Cardinal and head of the Congregation for the Clergy in Rome, responded to this request with rather strong, decidedly un-Leonardian, language. In typical Wrightian fashion, he was cordial and gracious in his comments to then APP chair, John Oesterle, but he in nowise entertained their request or perspective. He called their request for opening the avenue to ongoing ministry for resigned women and men as "rash and unreasonable," and went on to argue that current restrictive legislation actually "protects the special dignity of the Roman Catholic Priesthood." Wright continued: "There is no question of the rights and gifts of these ministers; it is simply that they have elected a vocation inconsistent with the mind of the Church."

Wright ended his response to APP, as he often did, with a mix of cyni-cism yet cordiality, by stating to Oesterle, someone he obviously had affec-tion for: "Despite my inability to choose between the Association (APP) and the Papacy, I send you fraternal best wishes and kindest remembrances." (Rome, March 1, 1978.)

On this occasion, Cardinal Wright didn't have the last word. Ever cordial and ever faithful to the strong witness and convictions of APP membership, Oesterle, a very precise and detail-focused fellow of proud German roots, surrounded by a sea of Irish clerics, chose St. Patrick's Day to respectfully challenge Cardinal Wright, and thus the "Papacy," by reminding the Cardinal that many in the church favor optional celibacy. He continued by chiding Wright for implying marriage as a lesser calling, even as he affirms his own deep commitment to priestly celibacy. Oesterle also challenged Wright to clarify some of his statements. He ended his response by thanking Wright for his friendship and wishes him good health, even sharing some personal matters regarding his own mother, whom Wright obviously knew. This was an extraordinary exchange between a cardinal and priests, yet typical of APP: personal, forthright, challenging and unintimidated.

At the same time APP was solidifying its unofficial status as an independent priestly voice in the diocese of Pittsburgh, as it attempted to deepen its implementation of its chosen role as a catalyst for church renewal, to promote the prophetic biblical message of social justice, and to serve as a support group and source of fellowship for brother priests, it was also raising questions about the priesthood itself, i.e., just what is the priest, what is his proper function, and what changes need to happen to priesthood and ministry in light of the Vatican II call for renewal, change and reform.

In 1971 NFPC produced a short document on the current state of the priesthood entitled: "The Moment of Truth," in which they begin by citing a statistic about resigned priests: 25,000 had resigned in the past seven years worldwide. They express dissatisfaction with the lack of hierarchical leadership and the slow pace of needed reforms. They recommend collaboration and shared leadership between bishops and priests. Massive reorganization needs to happen and new forms of ministry need to develop, they propose, such as co-pastorates, team ministries, more lay involvement and "official ministry by women."

They go on to mention the importance of human rights within the church itself.

They strongly recommend disentangling the priesthood from the requirement of celibacy. Though they recognize "celibacy as a precious tradition of the church," they call for married priesthood to be an option. They also suggest inviting back to ministry those who have left and married, arguing that the "charism of celibacy is subordinate to the charism of service."

And in line with APP's document on "priestly simplicity" and commitment to poverty and the poor, they recommend a renewed spirituality in the life of the priest.

They conclude by calling for a "reading of the signs of the times," and courage to institute major renewal and change in a changing world. "The moment of truth is now," they conclude. (Unpublished statement on the priesthood by NFPC, 1971.)

A few years later NFPC followed this internal document by circulating a written piece by Jesuit theologian Walter Burghardt, entitled: "What is a Priest?,"[7] followed by their own working paper in March of 1976: "Serving in a Ministerial Church," in which they discuss "priestly identity, office and person, and functions." As a working paper, the document is interested in creating discussion about how we view the priesthood in light of the calling of all baptized to ministry in the church. Clearly there was a need to understand the unique role of the ordained priest in relation to all others in the church.

Although priest resignations are often related to the issue of clerical celibacy, personal experience in ministry and conclusions drawn from both reading and numerous interviews suggests to me that celibacy has not been the sole factor in priest resignations. That is, there are other contributing factors that lead some priests to resign, such as structures and lines of authority in the church that are stifling and isolating. Phil Gallagher, who after twelve years in ministry resigned in 1977, outlined for me what he called the "three strikes" he experienced in ministry which ultimately led him to resign. One involved a lawsuit filed against him for speaking out against a group he accused of racial discrimination. He asked Bishop Leonard for help and was told, since he—the bishop—hadn't been consulted, Phil was "on his own." Strike two was described above in a dispute with a pastor around his use of a motorcycle in which he was unceremoniously transferred with no hearing or due process. And, strike three involved his interest in deepening his professionalism in ministry by going back to school to study psychology. He asked the diocese for financial aid and was not only denied, but was told it was not his role to provide professional counseling; that should be left to others more prepared. There was actually a strike four experienced in his last assignment before resigning involving a pastor listening in on his "private" phone calls, but by then Phil was pretty much out the door.[8]

APP took very seriously the uneven relationships between pastors and assistants and the lack of more collegial dialogue with the hierarchy, and worked hard over the years to alter such structures and dynamics, which they referred to as "dysfunctions." At a December 1972 APP meeting, Neil

---

7. Burghardt, "What Is a Priest?," 55–67.

8. Private interview, Gallagher, November 17, 2017. Trainor, *Unfinished Pentecost*, 265–67.

McCaulley, now deceased but up until his untimely death in 2014 one of the most active and serious of APP members for nearly fifty years, gave a report describing the often lonely and unsupported role of the parochial assistant, especially in a context in which the pastor was an autocratic tyrant. Neil found that Canon Law offered very little guidance for assistant pastors. He especially focused on the issue of guidance for "working on projects outside of parish ministry." Often, it seems, young, energetic assistants were stifled in "initiative and creativity" regarding "outside ministries" as opposed to "responsibility for primary parochial assignments," an issue alluded to earlier in written pieces by John Groutt. Neil asked whether the assistant can actually make a contribution to the wider church within the diocese. Priests who do seek to make an impact beyond the parish seem often to have been criticized by brother priests for stepping beyond traditional ministerial boundaries, he suggested.

McCaulley went on to provide specific examples of creative initiatives that could enhance one's ministry and priestly life: "liberation of the life-style of the priest, house of prayer for priests during the summer, personnel policy that would see conversations that would prevent false starts in the parishes, professionalization of ministry [a common theme] . . . [in short] define a project for self, interest other priests in that area and work on it, pray over it, and attempt to discern God's will in your life."

The group then engaged in a lively discussion of Neil's report and acknowledged that pushing such envelopes would involve conflict and "active suffering . . . for the sake of change." Ultimately, to push actively for constructive change was viewed by the group as a "spiritual issue."[9]

One of the more extensive proposals made to the diocese by APP regarding structural change and ministry had to do with team ministry, a way, perhaps, to break through this often dysfunctional and unequal relationship between pastor and assistant, generally involving older and younger priests. They submitted an extensive proposal to the diocese early in Bishop Leonard's tenure around 1971—although they had made a prior proposal during Bishop Wright's time in 1967 or '68, specifically for inner city ministry in the Hill District. Tom Harvey, an early APP member, who eventually went on to Notre Dame University before leaving the active ministry in the mid-1990s, wrote this proposal and sent it off to Bishop Leonard.

The aim of the proposal was multifaceted, focused on shared authority in ministry, concentration on each minister's skill set, a desire for more satisfaction in one's ministry, and a sense that lay parishioners would benefit from "exposure to many priests," not just one. Interestingly, the proposal

9. APP minutes, December, 1972.

recognized areas of difficulty in this transition, and it was realistic about how such an initiative needs to be carefully developed, including teams of priests working together on a small, experimental project in order to begin developing relationships and determining complementary interests and skills.

Having been involved in a team ministry approach in the South Bronx in the late 1970s while a Dominican priest, I found this APP proposal very prescient in its detail and awareness of challenges. Two Dominican sisters and I formed a team ministry and went through an evaluation with Fr. Phil Murnion around personality types and pastoral inclinations and skill sets to see how we might fare as a team. The exercise with Murnion was exceedingly helpful as it suggested we had complementary skills and would be successful if we appreciated our differences. One of us turned out to be a visionary, another, a detail person, the last a people/relational type. It was a huge help to find this out, even when our team ministry didn't work perfectly.

APP approached this experiment with eyes wide open. They even proposed certain urban churches for the early stages of implementation. And they suggested a regional approach, not just individual parishes. Finally, when proposing how such team ministries would be arranged, they suggested that priests need not necessarily head up each ministry: trained lay people or religious sisters, properly qualified, could fill leadership roles.

Concerning the internal workings of the institutional church, APP members were constantly trying to open up lines of communication between priests and bishops, but even more importantly, they felt strongly that in all matters concerning how the local church should be structured and should function, open dialogue with all of the faithful was necessary. That is, reflecting upon the model of church referred to earlier as "The people of God," a Vatican II staple, APP insisted that when bishops gathered to discuss matters that affected the faithful, the meetings should be open to all.

Beginning in 1973, the nation's Catholic bishops organized regional meetings. Pennsylvania and New Jersey were linked as Region III. However, Region III was the only national group that held private meetings, inviting neither the press nor anyone other than bishops. As a force for democratization in the church, APP members were outraged. And, of course, they acted on their outrage and prepared to attempt to open up these meetings in 1974.

APP attempted several times, unsuccessfully, to set up a dialogue with Cardinal Krol from Philadelphia, the current head of the national bishop's council, and pretty clearly "the most powerful figure in the Region III church." When that failed, they tried to set up meetings with other leaders, to no avail. So several APP members went to the meeting location, rented a hotel conference room, and set up a press conference to voice their concerns.

In a conversation with Don McIlvane, one of the four priests from Pittsburgh at the meeting, Frank Brown records the following: "The day before the meeting I (McIlvane) received a call from the hotel saying that, sorry, the room would not be available to us, after all. I told the woman calling that I didn't think the hotel would want us to take a room in the hotel just down the street and tell the press that the church in Philadelphia had put pressure on you folks. She said that she would call me back and promptly did. We could have the room. And she added apologetically to me: 'I'm just a poor Jewish woman caught in the middle.'"[10]

McIlvane communicated this to the press and the *Philadelphia Enquirer* reported it on the front page. APP knew how to play hard ball when needed. Ironically, the topic of the closed bishop's meeting was: "The Use of Modern Means of Communication as Instruments of Evangelization." APP priests, Hal Baily, McIlvane, Warren Metzler and Pat Jones, said the event was an "embarrassment and a scandal," and that "it is the right of the faithful . . . to know what their bishops are saying and doing in these regional meetings." And, in typical APP fashion, quite authentically, I believe, they went on to declare: "We are here because we love and respect the church. We deeply respect the apostolic office of the bishops . . . we are (simply) priests who care what happens in the church." Their protest even got the attention of Pittsburgh's Catholic newspaper which issued a scathing editorial criticizing the bishop's closed-door policy. Writing that the bishops "created a serious public relations blunder" by meeting in private, the editorial went on to say that "what makes the situation ridiculous is that the topic of the meeting was 'The Use of Modern Means of Communication as Instruments of Evangelization.'" Citing the fact that this regional meeting was the only one of twelve in the country that was "not open in some way to the press or the public," the editorial concluded by expressing the "hope" that the "public relations *faux pas* will not be repeated next year."[11]

Nevertheless, in 1975, the same closed-door policy remained in place; in fact, APP had to put together a press conference very hastily that year as they didn't even find out where the meeting was until a week beforehand. Once again they had tried to communicate with various bishops ahead of the meeting, to no avail. This time they pointedly accused Cardinal Krol, "a very powerful man," of overruling bishops interested in opening the meeting. "It was almost a CIA operation," said McIlvane.[12] According to Frank

10. Brown, "Association of Pittsburgh Priests," 10.

11. Wallace, "Priests Call Secret Talks"; Editorial, "Communication?," *Pittsburgh Catholic*, May 3, 1974.

12. McCray, "Priests Protest," 1.

Brown, the following year the meeting was open.[13] There were times when APP could be quite effective!

Throughout the rest of the decade of the 1970s, APP continued to press for a more open and participatory church, less driven by the hierarchy, and more decentralized, with encouragement of leadership roles for the laity and a reexamining of traditional church teaching in areas that deeply affected all of the faithful.

Specifically, they promoted the idea of full participation of church leadership in the selection of bishops, full participation of women in "all ministries of the church including sacramental orders," fuller lay participation in decision-making through a "Diocesan Pastoral Council" made up of bishops, priests, nuns and lay folks, continuing education and professionalization of various ministries for priests and lay people, a new look at issues of church teaching concerning birth control, divorce and remarriage, and renewed outreach to disaffected Catholics, etc. And in every case, APP would do research and come up with concrete proposals as to how the diocese might implement such directions.

And, again, all such proposals were generally very well thought out and discussed at annual mountaintop retreats and brainstorming sessions, sometimes held at the Sisters' of Mercy retreat house in the Laurel Mountains. Such proposals were presented to the wider diocesan clergy and, when deemed appropriate, the diocese. It's fascinating to read about their constant attempts to analyze membership in the group (or lack of) and relationship to the rest of the priests in the diocese who weren't part of APP and, also, the hierarchy and laity. Why don't more priests join APP, they often wondered. Too much involvement in social justice? Too closed? Failed communication? Too scattered/unfocused? Too isolated? Too ineffective? "Do we really mean anything to anyone? Just what is our dream?"[14]

Yet each year, it seems, despite their angst and doubts, they would renew their spirit and efforts, concluding somewhat as they did in 1979 at the "mountaintop," that "we are who we are—we believe in social justice and reform (in the church) and even though there's not a lot of organized support we will keep going. There is no other forum for these issues in the diocese. We have to acknowledge the tensions, live with them and say yes anyway."[15]

Having described internal church reform issues in the 1970s, I want now to look at APP's extensive social justice work, as APP becomes more

13. Brown, "Association of Pittsburgh Priests," 11.

14 APP minutes, October, 1976.

15. Mountaintop minutes, Fall, 1979.

established as an independent voice within the institutional Catholic Church of Pittsburgh.

While some APP priests remained focused on church renewal efforts, a number of them were also very active as social justice advocates throughout the 1970s. However, as mentioned earlier, two early APP members stand out in this regard: Don McIlvane, ordained in 1952, and Jack O'Malley, class of 1963. As Frank Brown mentions in his 1987 pamphlet on APP, all agreed that McIlvane was the group's "principal political tactician," a "great strategist."[16] I would say that McIlvane's strength as a strategist applied both to strategy around social justice issues, especially related to civil rights and labor concerns, and to ways to challenge church hierarchy, as witnessed by his participation at the aforementioned closed bishops' meetings in the Philadelphia area.

Although I have heard two versions of the story, there is general agreement on the following account. At some point in the latter 1970s, either then Pittsburgh Mayor Richard Caligueri or City Council President Jeep DePasquale, or perhaps both at different times, was heard to comment publicly on any number of social issues that the city was dealing with, something like Do we know what Fr. McIlvane is thinking? Even if he would call a press conference and be the only speaker, as more than one person told me actually occurred on occasion—McIlvane could be a loner at times—the press would be there and report just what McIlvane—and usually APP as well—was thinking. In community organizing circles one would say that's power.

If McIlvane was the chief strategist, pretty much all the interviewees acknowledge O'Malley was the lead activist. Much as with McIlvane, as well as other early APP members, it was the civil rights' movement that was their initial involvement in social protest. McIlvane, Don Fisher and Mark Glasgow all went to Selma and Jackson in the mid-1960s for freedom marches. But O'Malley had his own experience of racial injustice while a basketball great at St. Francis College in Loretto, PA. He was captain of the team—drafted by the Detroit Pistons, but he chose seminary instead—and, while playing in the mid-1950s on a team with both white and black players, experienced racial discrimination firsthand. Upon arriving with the team for a game in Winston-Salem, North Carolina, the team was told whites will stay in a hotel, blacks in the hospital. The team gathered and decided they would stay together and sleep at the airport instead. The incident received

---

16. Brown, "Association of Pittsburgh Priests," 5–6.

national press coverage and the players an education in social divisions in the United States.[17]

Jim Hohman, who acknowledged he was never overly political while an APP member, said you can "blame O'Malley" for all that political activism! To this day he can see O'Malley carrying protest signs through the streets: against the Vietnam War, for civil rights when Dr. King was killed, grape and lettuce boycotts, etc. By "blame," Hohman reassured me, he was speaking about O'Malley with deep admiration.

APP member Fr. Gene Lauer agreed: "O'Malley was always so quick to see injustice, so clear on message," he said. He remembered an event in which O'Malley was honored by the NAACP for his civil rights work. It was during the farmworker lettuce boycott. When he got up to accept the award, O'Malley gently reminded—and chided—the black brothers and sisters that their brown brothers and sisters needed support as well; don't forget their struggle. As earlier mentioned, St. Joseph's in Manchester, where O'Malley arrived in 1963, was a training ground for young seminarians to be mentored by Ed Joyce, a thoughtful, progressive and scholarly pastor, and O'Malley, who was living out his convictions on the street. St. Joseph's became Pittsburgh headquarters for the grape and lettuce boycotts. In 1972, Cesar Chavez, who had visited Pittsburgh a number of times, sent a letter to APP thanking them for their support in a favorable ruling with the NLRB (National Labor Relations Board), thus allowing them to continue organizing and boycotting. He asked that they continue to boycott lettuce until ultimate victory. "Viva la causa," wrote Chavez.[18]

In his social justice efforts, O'Malley went to jail so often, having been arrested for acts of civil disobedience, that one Presbyterian minister friend said to me after getting arrested with O'Malley, all of the prison guards knew O'Malley and kept asking him if everything was okay: did he need anything while in jail? Upon observing O'Malley's treatment at the hands of his jailers, the minister, Rev. Don Dutton, said to me: "Next time I get arrested I want to make sure O'Malley is part of the group."

As has been previously recorded, APP was always evaluating its actions to determine what effect any particular action may have had, and how it might be done differently next time, an important community organizing exercise. In the area of social justice, there is nothing they have done that is more important over more than five decades of existence than their instrumental role in helping a start-up group, the Thomas Merton Center, a peace and justice organization, named after the famous Cistercian monk

17. Brown, "Association of Pittsburgh Priests," 5–6.
18. Chavez, Letter, June 19, 1972. Private interview, Lauer, June 15, 2017.

and prolific spiritual and social writer, get off the ground. In September of 1971, two Catholic peace activists, Molly Rush, later a Ploughshares activist with the Berrigan brothers, and Larry Kessler, a long-time activist with the Catholic Interracial Council, approached the APP for moral and financial support to open a center of peace activism to protest the Vietnam War and nuclear proliferation. In his request to the group, Kessler noted that the Diocese of Pittsburgh did not see the need for a Commission on Peace and Justice, hence he was turning to APP. Rush and Kessler had a multi-focused approach to their vision: draft counseling, resource center for educational materials, training in non-violence, lobbying for peace, support for the poor, and service as a kind of clearing house in Pittsburgh for social concerns. Between fifty and one-hundred (Rush says fifty, Kessler 100, during separate interviews!) APP members agreed to pledge $10 a month to help Rush and Kessler rent space and begin to implement their vision. Over the years, whenever the Merton Center faced financial challenges, it would return to the APP for support, and the APP would step to the plate. The Merton Center is still in existence and is approaching fifty years of existence. At its fortieth anniversary celebration, I had the privilege, as both a former staff person and board member, to address its membership as a keynote speaker. "If Thomas Merton were alive today, would he be a member of the Merton Center?" I began, emphasizing the need for the interplay of action and contemplation, a must for followers of the famous monk. At the end of my talk, I answered yes, Merton would belong, in no small part due to APP's ongoing support.[19]

In the early years of the newly formed center for peace and justice, the Merton Center focused almost entirely on an anti-war, anti-nuclear proliferation agenda. As a key partner, APP also focused much of its social justice agenda on peace activities. One long term initiative of several of the priests was tax resistance as their way of opposing war funding. Reverends O'Malley, McIlvane, Metzler, Fenton and Glasgow deducted 20 percent of their tax obligations as a formal protest of the Vietnam War in April of 1973. In a statement picked up by the now defunct newspaper, *The Pittsburgh Press*, they declared: "Today by our tax resistance we are protesting in conscience against immoral activities by our government. It is a privilege and duty to pay taxes. It is likewise a duty to resist evil in conscience. When that evil is done by one's own government, the duty is no less. With heavy heart we cry out against this evil by our actions today . . ." (April 16, 1973).

APP also joined the Merton Center in a years-long campaign against Rockwell International, whose corporate headquarters was housed in

19. McDonald, "A Prophet in the Monastery."

Pittsburgh at the time, and who served as the "prime contractor" for the B-1 bomber. Rockwell, located in the middle of the city, was a focal point for anti-war activity for many years, including many acts of non-violent civil disobedience. As usual, the priests, great at getting media attention, and typically led by McIlvane, cited the "vigorous denunciations of the arms race at Vatican II," as well as statements made by the world's Catholic bishops, as they publicly decried Rockwell's participation in the "immoral arms race." As part of their witness, they also met with Rockwell officials, applauding the company's positive contributions to the U.S. economy, manufacturing products "that help us all," while demanding they stop producing weapons of mass destruction.[20]

One very interesting and complex social issue, which actually cuts across both society and church lines, i.e., abortion, was an early challenge for APP to negotiate. At a late 1971 meeting of APP, one Pittsburgh priest and a lay person addressed APP on the "seriousness of the abortion issue." In an interesting anticipation of a later, more official Catholic Church position articulated by the late Cardinal Joseph Bernardin, entitled "Seamless Garment: A Consistent Ethic of Life" (1986), an APP member observed that those who are anti-abortion activists usually aren't involved in other issues dealing with "respect for life," e.g., war, life in prison (death penalty), life in poverty, etc. Warren Metzler tried to remedy this divide in many conversations with antiabortion activists but reported back in a few months, recorded at an APP monthly meeting, that "establishing some kind of bridge between anti-abortionists and anti-war people" didn't seem very "favorable."

Going forward, the issue of abortion has always been the source of much contention between the APP and the diocese and the international church, not unlike what more recently has occurred between Catholic sisters and the Vatican. In the latter case many sisters have been criticized for focusing more on economic inequality and poverty than on abortion. Although APP has always been clear that it is anti-abortion, it has consistently criticized the diocese and the national bishop's organization for focusing too much on abortion and not nearly enough on issues of war and peace, economic inequality, death penalty, etc. When, many years later, Cardinal Bernardin articulated his consistent ethic perspective, APP felt vindicated in their concerns for a myriad of life issues.

Interestingly, concerning the issue of abortion, in the mid-1980s, APP took a public stand in support of two nuns from West Virginia who had publicly declared their support of a pro-choice position and, subsequently, were threatened with dismissal from their church work. Though not directly

20. APP press release, *Pittsburgh Post-Gazette*, December 27, 1974.

supporting the nuns' position on choice, they were objecting to the Vatican's threat as squelching dissent on church teaching. I'll elaborate on this significant event and the ensuing dialogue in chapter 3.

Another of the myriad of social issues APP took on involved a dispute with the local District Attorney over a prison furlough system and prison reform in general. Given that serious prison reform has only taken hold in this country in the last few years, once again we witness APP as ahead of its time in promoting serious and systemic change. And, as usual, they did their homework. Jack O'Malley and Warren Metzler were in the lead in this initiative. At a conference at a "Public Affairs Forum" at the local YMCA in October of 1973, Metzler gave a very detailed and well-researched speech on the "moral issues involved in our changing attitudes about prisons." The thrust of his speech was on treatment vs. "custody" of offenders.

The key issue at the time in the State of Pennsylvania was a newly instituted furlough program. Specifically, prisoners who had served at least one-half of their sentence and were thus eligible for temporary release could apply for weekend furloughs to re-acquaint with family, go to school or work part of the day, and even receive early release to small community treatment centers in lieu of more jail time. In the midst of his talk, Metzler cited numerous studies of the deleterious effects of prison time, especially for young offenders, and the desire to seek alternatives, especially for non-violent offenders. In this vein, APP and others had successfully opposed the building of a proposed County Detention Center.

Suggesting "society's vindictiveness" as the primary impediment to significant prison reform, Metzler and the group encountered strong opposition from the local district attorney, Robert Duggan, as well as the Fraternal Order of Police. The DA and the FOP warned that hardened criminals might be furloughed and that the proposal was "ill-conceived and ill-planned." Maintaining a united front with the DA, the FOP "told the priests, in effect, to stay in parish work and out of police work."[21] APP responded immediately with a press release challenging the DA and reminding the FOP that it often asks for clergy and church support, which the group assured would still be offered! However, said chairman Metzler, "We priests and clergymen will not stay in our parishes; it's not where we belong. Our nation's morality, in fact its greatness, will be judged by how we treat our prisoners. We shall stay concerned about our prison system and press for prison reform because of moral issues that affect our people," e.g., the brutality of prisons, forced sex and drugs, separation of families and spiritual and material suffering. Pleading for compassion towards offenders,

21. "Cops Rap Priests on Con Furloughs," *Pittsburgh Press*, September 21, 1973.

while chiding the DA for offensive language regarding the criminal justice system, APP affirmed: "Justice, yes, and punishment that is within human standards, but vengeance and harshness, never."[22]

Although APP had somewhere between sixty and eighty active, dues-paying members through the decade of the 1970s, there were other priests who were quietly supportive. Some sent donations, but for various reasons did not want direct identification with the group. Among the more notable priests in this category was the aforementioned famous labor priest, Monsignor Charles Owen Rice. Rice was a fierce champion of the worker and the labor movement in general, although he was also a rabid anti-communist and provoked the ire of many secular leftists who felt his outspokenness actually hurt the labor movement. Rice was totally with APP on much of its social justice agenda, but he was often reluctant to criticize the institutional church. He shared this reluctance with many clergy.

But APP, true to form, never shared such reluctance. Focused on justice in society and within its own its own institution—and employer—in the mid-1970s, APP took on directly the issue of Catholic teacher rights, specifically wages and unionization, as well as support for a teacher's strike. This became a very divisive issue within the church, and set APP against Catholic Church leadership in Pittsburgh. One APP member told me he is pretty sure it also cost the group some support among the clergy, who argued it made the institution look bad.

The Catholic school issue first surfaced in 1976 as the Catholic school teachers were deliberating as to whether to unionize, and if so, which of two unions to join. It was an issue APP could not come to unanimity on. A heated debate ensued among APP members: some supported a strong pro-union position, others advocated for a particular union, still others preferred neutrality. The latter group reasoned that the issue was complicated, thus wanted to encourage teachers to freely choose unionization or not. In an unusual decision for APP, the group chose neutrality, encouraging teachers "to vote their conscience without intimidation."[23]

But this was just the beginning of APP involvement in the Catholic school issue. Astutely, because Catholic sisters were so traditionally involved in teaching and administration of the schools, at the next APP meeting the priests invited a number of sisters to help discern the issue.

In the spring of 1977 the elementary school teachers of the Diocese of Pittsburgh voted not to select a union to represent them, and, at the same time, Bishop Leonard organized an ad hoc committee of pastors to discuss

22. APP Press release, September 20, 1973.
23. APP minutes, April 6, 1976.

the needs of these teachers. Then, in the fall of 1977, the Catholic high school teachers, who were unionized, went on strike. At that point APP went into action, and in an op-ed piece published in the *Pittsburgh Post-Gazette*, suggested an "independent mediator" negotiate between the union and diocese. In a very carefully constructed statement APP applauded all sides in the dispute, i.e., teachers, pastors, parents, parishes and the diocese, as good-willed, and acknowledged the financial challenges involved. In collaboration with the National Federation of Priests' Council, APP recommended the establishment of "diocesan pastoral planning" and a "Diocesan Pastoral Council" to help discern the best way forward, as the diocese and union negotiated in good faith.

APP involvement in the school issue actually induced the bishop to release a full financial disclosure of the sizeable contributions the diocese was making to education. He sent this report along with a somewhat defensive letter to APP, suggesting that their advocacy for teachers was partly responsible for the many letters and phone calls that the diocese had received, criticizing its lack of adequate support for Catholic education. Bishop Leonard wanted to set the record straight and "present the facts," asking APP to help disseminate the correct data (letter to APP from Bishop Leonard, September 22, 1977). Then, in October of 1977, John Oesterle, in the name APP, sent a letter to Fr. Hugh Lang, assistant superintendent of schools, thanking him for his role in "reaching a settlement with the Catholic high school teachers" (October 10, 1977). Case closed? Not exactly.

Although the high school teachers reached a settlement, the elementary school teachers were left in a different situation, especially since, unlike the high school teachers, they had voted not to unionize. By the fall of 1978, a committee of pastors, set up by the bishop to determine next steps with the elementary school teachers, recommended that each parish determine salaries of teachers according to their local situation and finances. APP reacted swiftly, in a press release, suggesting such a policy a bad idea for any number of reasons. In their objection APP quoted the U.S. Catholic Bishops who, among other things, recommended "trained negotiators," not pastors, help determine the contracts. The bishops also recommended the formation of "teacher organizations" to help negotiate, in good faith, adequate contracts. Finally, APP strongly advised that the diocese reconsider the recommendation to let individual parishes determine salaries.[24]

APP had actually tried to set up formal meetings with Bishop Leonard to address the issue before going public, but the bishop refused to meet with

24. "Teacher Salary Decision Hit by 30 Priests," *Pittsburgh Post-Gazette*, September 4, 1978; "Priests Rap Parish Setting Teachers' Pay," *Pittsburgh Catholic*, September 8, 1978.

them, suggesting if he did meet it would appear he were recognizing APP as an official clergy group in the diocese, such as is the official Diocesan Clergy Council. Nevertheless, he did agree to meet separately with APP chairman, Fr. John Oesterle, in June of 1978, but Oesterle reported having little effect on the bishop's viewpoint. Leonard did offer to meet with any teacher who felt unfairly treated, but insisted that the new policy was sound and fair. Although the issue greatly divided the Catholic Church in Pittsburgh, pitting teachers and their supporters against the diocese and some pastor-priests, and may well have cost the APP members, especially those serving as parochial pastors with schools, it was yet another moment in which APP sought to speak its truth, soundly based on Catholic social teaching, despite the consequences.

Regarding the issue of the APP losing clergy support over its advocacy and direct action, an APP member resigned from the group in July of 1976, just as the teacher issue was heating up. Although he suggested his resignation was related to other commitments, most especially serving on the official clergy council of the diocese, he chose to add that while he appreciated APP, "I felt that some of our deliberations took the form of big brother helping out a defenseless child . . . The APP has a tenuous reputation as it is, without drawing criticism for helping people or causes that have not taken the proper steps to solve their own problems."[25]

Although much of APP's energy in these early years was concentrated on church reform, especially the Pittsburgh Church, and local social justice initiatives, the group also spent time and energy on national and international issues, consistently commenting on the moral issues of the day. They were never timid about corresponding with the national bishops group or the Vatican on matters that concerned them. In anticipation of a major Bishops' Synod in Rome in the fall of 1971, APP sent a proposal to the bishops as to what should be of concern regarding "World Order and Justice." In this statement they proposed a commitment of 10 percent (tithing) of all church funds be devoted to "world justice and peace." They recommended every diocese set up commissions to implement educational programs around justice and peace, including counselors for Catholic youth regarding war and conscientious objection. They also addressed the issue of corporate responsibility with respect to church investments, i.e., avoiding corporations involved in "military products and services" and investing in corporations that help narrow the economic inequality gap. Finally, they called on the bishops to "condemn the War in Vietnam" and declare "the immorality of Catholics participating in any way in the development,

25. Letter from Fr. Robert Meyer, July 21, 1976.

production, or delivery of nuclear, chemical, and biological weapons of mass destruction."[26]

Putting their money where their mouths were, in the mid-1970s, APP, following the National Federation of Priests' Council, voted to contribute 10 percent of their incomes to organizations working to address world hunger. Initially they focused on sending aid to UNICEF to help war victims from Vietnam and Cambodia.

In October of 1973, APP decided to publicly address the Watergate scandal and in a press conference declared: "As clergy called to be moral leaders we can be silent no longer when the extent of corruption and misdoing at the highest levels of our government is without parallel in our entire history." They go on to suggest that President Nixon was suffering from a "serious moral defect" and called on him "to resign from office." If he chose not to, they advocated for impeachment. Finally, they encouraged "brother clergy of several faiths to speak out . . . [as] religious leaders." Not to do so "would be an inexcusable default in moral leadership," they concluded.[27]

Never fearful of stirring the pot of controversy, yet absolutely convinced and resolute that the documents of Vatican II compelled them as ministers of the Gospel to address the moral, social and political issues of the day, it didn't take long for the group to get pushback from the public, something they became accustomed to. And it wasn't always from local church members. By now APP had a national profile. One reaction came all the way from Homewood, Alabama, from a man who wrote the following: "Gentlemen, I am a Catholic! I've got a belly-full of you priests trying to tell others off, like you are telling the President to resign. You are making asses of yourselves . . . my advice is you stick to your knitting [? hand-written word unclear] and let us lay people take care of you and the government." After suggesting that President Nixon had a stellar record of accomplishments, he went on to write: "For sure Mr. Nixon is acting with responsibility and you clowns are not! I'm telling you, this is a league you are not qualified to play in and you'd better stay out of it. Try the priesthood for a change. You might make a good act of contrition, recite the rosary or go hear some confessions, visit the sick; anything, just keep your nose out of politics!"[28] APP never received a follow-up letter from Mr. Hawkins after President Nixon resigned.

But Mr. Hawkin's was not the only negative reaction to the outspoken priests. Another came from a Catholic sister, this time from Illinois.

26. Sent to bishops on September 30, 1971.

27. APP press release, October 30, 1973.

28. Letter received from Mr. Marvin Hawkins, November 18, 1973.

Evidently APP's statement appeared in the national Catholic magazine, the *The Sunday Visitor*. Acknowledging she was a Nixon supporter, Sister He-derman suggested the priests had a right to their "political opinion," but not a right, as priests, "to promulgate" such an opinion. In defending Nixon, the nun acknowledged she had a nephew who was killed in Vietnam, a war she blamed on Presidents Kennedy and Johnson, who had "escalated" it, and which Nixon "stopped." (Several years later, of course, after his own escalation) Sister Hederman ended her "protest of your protest" with her real problem with the priests: "Harking back to the 'good old days' when the pastor used to come over to the convent to tell the Sisters how to vote in the elections, I seem to hear a little re-echo of the same, same song. Could you now be telling us whom we should 'un-elect' or impeach?"[29]

What these letters bring to light is the perennial issue that religious figures face when making moral commentary, whether in the pulpit or on the street, in letters to the news media or public press releases, on issues of import, whether war and peace, economic inequality, racism, government corruption: the suggestion that mixing religion and politics, for many, is an inappropriate exercise of ministry. Anyone in ministry who has been socially involved has faced this challenge. Once the minister goes beyond charity—collecting food, serving in a soup kitchen, supporting a shelter for homeless, etc.—and into the realm of social justice—lobbying congress, criticizing social policy, demonstrating and marching for a cause, doing civil disobedience, etc.—many opine (s)he has crossed the line beyond the priestly calling.

Facing such criticism, APP drafted a document (untitled) on this topic which, for reasons I haven't been able to determine, they never released. The document clearly stated their beliefs about public commentary on "po-litical" (one might say moral) matters. The document is not dated, but was likely written in the latter part of 1973 or early 1974, not long after they received the above letters. I speculate this because the statement begins with an allusion to Watergate. Seemed like Watergate and the general topic of government corruption and cover-up, and their view of the responsibility or moral and religious leaders to comment, became the occasion to attempt to clarify the whole question of the relationship of religion and politics, as well as the responsibility and role of religious leaders.

They begin the statement by suggesting that in the face of blatant government corruption, the general public remains passive and "cynically" accepting of business as usual. They even suggest such an attitude reflects the public's own lack of moral integrity. Beyond that, they decry the political

29. Letter received from Sr. Paula Hederman, Aurora, IL., November 21, 1973.

"apathy" of so many who didn't even vote in the 1972 election. Related to this, they cite studies suggesting only slightly more than one-third of citizens even know who their local or national representatives are. They take it one step further, something pretty close to home for them as priests, by suggesting that "A sermon on morality in politics is as rare in our churches as an Eskimo in Brazil." The priests considered that to comment on the political is "to preach the Word of God," i.e., there is no conflict in their minds in viewing sermonizing on morality in politics and preaching on the bible, which they view as their priestly duty. Preaching only on "personal morality" is not exercising the fullness of priestly obligations. They also take to task retreat directors, theologians and even bishops who neglect addressing "political ethics," despite the ordinary Catholics desire for guidance on such issues. Only the Pope avoids their criticism, as they acknowledge that he (Pope Paul VI) "from time to time, has dealt with the issue of good government."

Priests do not want to be seen as "partisan," they continue, hence they avoid any immersion into partisan or electoral politics. APP, as a group, does not endorse candidates; partisanship has no place in the pulpit. But commentary on "moral issues in government and on particular pieces of legislation" with moral implications, in their view, is part of the task of proclaiming truth to power. No matter the risk of alienating some, the priest cannot avoid the obligation to offer moral commentary. "Like John the Baptist, he must speak boldly and without fear, perhaps sometimes in the exact manner of the prophet, naming a political leader who has particularly corrupted his high office."

As they often have in their over fifty years of existence, APP criticized so many "Christians," especially Catholics, Evangelicals, and bishops who have ventured into politics on only one issue, namely abortion. Though clearly in support of the so-called "pro-life movement," they decry what they call "one-issue tunnel vision."

And, as is common for the APP, they end their reflections with recommendations. Describing the current situation as one of "great political and moral crisis," they ask theologians to begin working on "formulating a contemporary morality of politics," and bishops to take "moral leadership" in their "sermons and pastoral letters," encouraging the latter to "not fear to offend those in the congregation who may be powerful as the world understands power." And they especially urge bishops to bring the "searing word of God to the newest 18 year-old voter." The latter group they urge to register to vote and consider "entering careers in government."

Beyond speaking to theologians and bishops, they ask that dioceses and local parishes sponsor programs on political issues. Such programs need to be undergirded with Christian principles. There should be "know your candidate" nights, inviting candidates for office to share their platforms.

Though the group did not advocate for "priest-politicians," a situation they consider ed an "extremely rare role to be exercised only in very limited instances" (no indication of their view on Fr. Robert Drinan, an elected congressman from Massachusetts at the time), they did suggest training of certain priests, "political priests," in "political morality . . . who will know their way in government very well and be therefore better able to find out and highlight moral problems for all of us." They go on to argue: "We have had junky priests, labor priests, medical priests, priest-educators, priest-psychologists;" why not "political priests?"

This very powerful and inspiring document ends on a note of "hope" based on "the resurrection of Jesus [which] has proclaimed once and for all that evil, death, corruption, despair shall not prevail." And as priestly ser-vants of a "hope-filled church," they offer encouragement to all Christians to demand of politicians that they act "justly and effectively . . . to promote the common good."[30]

Despite not going public with this statement, I believe it very fairly reflects exactly how certain key APP members, undoubtedly some in lead-ership roles, saw the relationship between religion, priesthood and politics, and furthermore, how they viewed the priestly responsibility to preach the truth to power based on the biblical foundations of the Older Testament Hebrew prophets and of the crucified and resurrected Jesus. My guess is that some members of APP were not entirely comfortable with the content and boldness of the positions, and hence the decision not to publish. Seems a shame, as the content of the document is rich and would have been a wonderful source for discussion and dialogue as to just what are the social implications of the bible and the Christian faith. To this day the relationship between religion and politics is one of the most hotly contested issues in the religious and political worlds. We can all use guidance on the topic.

One of the marks of the APP's frequent press releases, reflective docu-ments and social actions, is that they are always grounded in the social teachings of the institutional Catholic Church. In the period covered by this chapter, 1971–78, when the vision and social implications of Vatican II were still being solidified and implemented, APP constantly referred to papal encyclicals of Pope Paul VI and international statements of the bish-ops. A good example of this is a document entitled: "Distribution of World Resources," authored by a then-Capuchin (OFM) priest and member of the APP, Fred Just. The document begins by stating: "Since the Second Vatican

30. Nine-page APP document marked "Never released."

Council, 85 percent of the papal documents that have been issued have dealt with the Church's teachings on social justice." In it, Just cites the "growing gap between rich and poor," and goes on to ground this four-page document in several of Pope Paul VI's and Pope John XXIII's encyclicals, the statement of the 1971 Synod of Bishops, and an "apostolic letter" of Paul VI, entitled "Call to Action."

I chose to end chapter 2 in 1978 because that is the year Pope Paul VI died. The election of his successor, Pope John Paul II, began a very different post-Vatican II era, in which the new pope and his key theologian, Cardinal Joseph Ratzinger, who became head of the Congregation for Doctrine and Faith—and the future Pope Benedict XV—slowly put the reins on John and Paul's attempts at de-centralization and collegiality and more local decision-making, and began implementing a much more centralized, pope-centered perspective, in which decisions, especially on church doctrine and discipline, were more and more made at the Vatican rather in regional bishop's conferences.

Pope Paul VI is a somewhat curious figure. He is viewed by many as putting the brakes on this new era instituted by Vatican II, ending in 1965, most especially, in my view and that of many others, due to his decision not to follow the recommendation of his appointed committee on church teaching regarding artificial contraception, hence re-affirming the traditional prohibition on the use of artificial means of birth control in his encyclical, *Humanae Vitae*, in 1968.[31] But in actuality, Paul VI is responsible for guiding an extraordinary period of very progressive hierarchical statements on social issues, beginning with "*Gaudium et Spes*: the Pastoral Constitution on the Church in the Modern World," and continuing with *Populorum Progressio, Octogesima Adveniens*, and *Evangellii Nuntiandi*, as well as "Justice in the World," the 1971 Synod of Bishops document. APP has made ample use of these documents to ground many of its statements and actions over these many years.

Not only was Paul VI—then Cardinal Montini—a close collaborator of Pope John XXIII, as he served as John's Secretary of State, and John's personal choice to succeed him in the papacy after he made him a Cardinal, but, according to Allan Figueroa Deck, SJ, in taking the name Paul VI, Montini "signaled that his pontificate was to be profoundly activist along the lines of Paul the Apostle's tireless activities on behalf of proclaiming the gospel message."[32] Figueroa Deck goes on to write that Pope Paul VI worked with the poor as a young priest, and as Bishop of Milan focused his ministry

---

31. Bauman et al., "An Unhealed Wound," 9–24.

32. Figueroa Deck, "Commentary on *Populorum Progressio*," 295–96.

on the working class and traveled widely in the Third World. As pope he "goes further than ever before in proposing 'solidaristic egalitarianism' as a fundamental principle for political economy."[33]

Beyond Pope Paul VI's vital role in implementing Pope John XXIII's social vision, he also began to implement "key collegial reforms in the teeth of opposition by some in the Vatican old guard." He initiated meetings of the "synod of bishops" beginning in 1967, which were to meet every two-three years, and instituted collegial bodies of bishops both "nation-wide and continent-wide." The shining example of such regional organizations of bishops was the Latin American Bishop's Conference, CELAM, responsible for the ground-breaking conference of bishops at Medellin, Colombia, in 1968, in which the sociological and theological notions of structural injustice and preferential option for the poor surfaced so profoundly and prophetically.[34]

And most interestingly for me and this study, I have become persuaded by Pope Francis' biographers, Austen Ivereigh and theologian, Allan Figueroa Deck, SJ, that Francis sees his role since his election in 2013 to basically leapfrog back over Popes Benedict and John Paul II, to pick up the implementation of the reformist vision of Pope John XXIII and, more especially, Pope Paul VI, in an effort to complete the implementation of Vatican II. Ivereigh quotes Francis as describing Paul VI as his "great light," and considers Paul's *Evangelii Nuntiandi* as "the greatest pastoral document ever written."[35]

And, according to Figueroa Deck, a Latin American specialist, "A rather notable feature of Pope Francis' Petrine ministry is his predilection for the teachings of Pope Paul VI . . . it is as if Pope Francis emphasizes the Second Vatican Council call for reading the signs of the times and its repeated calls for reform that came to a head during Pope Paul VI's papacy . . . Pope Francis wants to focus on Pope Paul's and the Second Vatican Council's unfinished business."[36]

Finally, according to Vatican II specialist, Richard R. Gaillardetz, "The full reception of the teaching of Vatican II remains incomplete. The more decentered and contextual character of Pope Paul VI's approach to the formulation of Catholic social teaching stands in tension with the often sophisticated and perceptive but fundamentally papocentric social analysis of Pope John Paul II."[37]

33. Figueroa Deck, "Commentary on *Populorum Progressio*," 295–96.

34. Ivereigh, *The Great Reformer*, 256–57;. Gudorf, "*Octogesima Adveniens*," 323–25.

35. Ivereigh, *The Great Reformer*, 122 & 369.

36. Figueroa Deck, *Francis*, 29–30.

37. Gaillardetz, "The Ecclesiological Foundations," 86.

In the end, as we consider the legacy of Pope Paul VI, he exercised a "moderate . . . incrementalist and reformist attitude" toward the implementation of Vatican II reforms, writes Massimo Faggioli, a theologian and historian of Vatican II. He was deeply concerned about church unity, writes Paul Collins, thus he sought to "appease" those who opposed changes, making him "indecisive and wavering" to some.[38]

For APP, going forward, the decade of the 1980s will represent new challenges as a new pope takes over in Rome and, eventually a new bishop in Pittsburgh assumes leadership. And 1979 represents a kind of watershed moment in the life and development of APP as the last Pittsburgh priest to join its ranks, Fr. Dennis Kirk, is ordained that year. After Kirk, no ordained Catholic priest from the Pittsburgh diocese has joined APP. Could this foreshadow the beginning of the Pope John Paul II effect?

The decade of the 1970s was an incredibly vibrant one for APP, despite the resignation from ministry of some early members. New priests came on board, the group solidified its message and vision, and it became recognized in Pittsburgh and beyond as a force for transformation in the Catholic Church as well as in the City of Pittsburgh. And, remarkably, though it never received official recognition by the diocese and its bishop, Vincent Leonard, it gained acceptance as an independent, volunteer group of loyal priests, faithfully serving the diocese, but also challenging the diocese and the wider church to faithfully implement the teachings of Vatican II as, in their own way, the priests of APP tried to "read the signs of the times." And despite criticism, locally and nationally at times, it made a difference in the lives of so many in the Catholic Church in Pittsburgh and in the wider community.

38. Faggioli, *Vatican II*, 24; Collins, "Pope Hamlet," 16–17.

CHAPTER THREE

New Challenges, New Strategies
Priests and Politics and the Pope John Paul II
Effect, 1978–1992

1978 REPRESENTS A WATERSHED year in the life of the international Roman
Catholic Church as Pope Paul VI, who both guided the last three years of
the Vatican II Council as well as first thirteen years of the implementation
of the Council's teachings, died. As was pointed out to in the last chapter,
Paul VI is most infamously noted for his controversial encyclical on birth
control, *Humanae Vitae*. Based primarily on the reaction to this document,
many would view Paul VI as a less than progressive light in the Church, one
who would incline toward traditional positions and make sure that in the
implementation of Vatican II documents, there would be great continuity
between the past and present. Yet, as I also stated in the previous chapter,
during his pontificate some exceedingly progressive statements were made
regarding the Church's social teaching.

In the year before he issued the encyclical on birth control, much to
the dismay of many theologians, pastors and ordinary Catholics, he issued
a social encyclical, *Populorum Progressio*, On the Development of Peoples,
which Jesuit theologian Allan Figueroa Deck refers to as Pope Paul VI's
"magna carta on development," which "gave renewed impetus to the strong
social justice concerns of Pope John XXIII's pontificate and of Vatican II."[1]

Following this, in 1968 at a conference in Medellin, Colombia, the
Latin American Bishops Conference (CELAM), in an attempt to put into
words and practice in their own context the teachings of Vatican II, the

---

1. Figueroa Deck, "Commentary on *Populorum Progressio*," 292.

bishops articulated the notion of God's "preferential option for the poor," and, at the same time described their Latin American reality, in which too few had the majority of wealth and power and the poor were marginalized, as a situation of "institutional violence" and "structural sin." "The 1968 assembly at Medellin was a unique experience in the global reception of Vatican II and the largest effort of a continental church for a creative reception of the council," writes Massimo Faggioli.[2] These were revolutionary insights at the time, as the bishops, although not directly supporting the notion, acknowledged that given the structural violence the poor experience due to man-made social arrangements, it would not be surprising that the people would rise up in violent revolt. Most notable about these declarations is that the theological insight of God's "preferential option for the poor" has become institutionalized in Catholic social teaching right up to the present. Remarkably, the Latin American bishops proclaimed a need to develop new social structures, including an endorsement of a preference for socialism over capitalism as part of the solution for Latin American poverty. These pronouncements are among the key elements of the revolutionary theological innovation known as liberation theology which emerged in the early 1970s.

Then, in 1971, at the Roman Synod of Bishops gathering, a statement entitled: "Justice in the World" was issued in which the bishops stated clearly the now famous words in justice circles: "Action on behalf of justice and participation in the transformation of the world fully appear to us as a constitutive dimension of the preaching of the Gospel."[3]

Also in 1971, Pope Paul VI issued an apostolic letter, *Octogesima Adveniens*, to the Pontifical Commission for Justice and Peace, marking the 80th anniversary of Pope Leo XIII's encyclical, *Rerum Novarum*, which "initiated the body of papal encyclicals referred to as social teaching."[4] It was in this document that Paul VI began the institutionalization of the Latin American theological innovation—some would say simply a reclamation from the Bible—of God's "preferential option for the poor." Furthermore, writes theologian Christine Gudorf, both John XXIII and Paul VI, unlike any of their predecessors, acknowledged, along with the Latin Americans, that Marxist social analysis and certain forms of socialism could be useful in the struggle to overcome "domination and exploitation," and attain some level of "social justice."[5]

2. Faggioli, *Vatican II*, 54.
3. O'Brien and Shannon, *Catholic Social Thought*, 306.
4. Shannon, "Commentary on *Rerum Novarum*," 127.
5. Gudorf, "Commentary on *Octogesima Adveniens*," 325.

Finally, in 1975, Paul VI issued a document on evangelization, *Evangelii Nuntiandi*, Evangelization in the Modern World, in which he "makes clear—in line with Medellin—that there can be no proclamation of the Gospel without also attending to the liberation of people from 'concrete situations of injustice.'" Notably, according to one of current Pope Francis' biographers, *Evangelii Nuntiandi* is Francis' "favorite church document (and) the greatest pastoral document ever written."[6]

In the final analysis of the impact of the papacy of Pope Paul VI, writes theologian and historian of Vatican II, Massimo Faggiolo, Paul VI was an "incrementalist" and "reformer," a "moderate" who tried to maintain "the unity of the Church" in the face of a growing conservative backlash against the majority, more liberal sentiment of the participants of Vatican II.[7]

With the election of Pope John Paul II in 1978, the first Polish pope, the international Roman Catholic Church enters a new era with regards to the reception and ongoing implementation of the teachings of Vatican II, what Faggioli describes as his "complex and sometimes contradictory orientation toward Vatican II." Under John Paul II, Faggioli sees a clear development of the Church's social teaching, a deepening interest in ecumenism and interfaith dialogue, yet a "more conservative approach" to internal church affairs. Most especially, he argues, John Paul II gradually limits the "scope of collegiality" and the "role of episcopal conferences."[8]

Stating the case a bit more pointedly, another theologian and historian of Vatican II, Boston College professor Richard Gaillardetz, suggests that, after a beginning with "great promise," and despite "his many considerable achievements," John Paul II's use of "authority" was a throwback to the pontificate of Pope Pius XII. "Like his pre-conciliar predecessor, John Paul II had no patience for theological disagreement with authoritative church teaching . . . and . . . greatly enhanced papal authority."[9]

Echoing similar sentiments, Fr. Charles Curran, prominent Catholic moral theologian, who in 1986 was declared by the Congregation for the Doctrine of the Faith (CDF) under then Cardinal Ratzinger unfit to teach in a Catholic University—he was terminated at The Catholic University of America—refers to the time of John Paul II as a "restoration movement." Much like Gaillardetz, Curran applauds the accomplishments of John Paul II in the area of social teaching on "peace and justice in the world," but argues he was quite different "at home in the church," as he centralized

6. Ivereigh, *Great Reformer*, 122.

7. Faggioli, *Vatican II*, 24.

8. Faggioli, *Vatican II*, 13 and 83–90.

9. Gaillardetz, *An Unfinished Council*, 14.

authority and minimized the role of "national and local churches," and took steps "backward" on "issues of human sexuality and the rights of women within the church."[10]

It didn't take long for APP to engage directly with the new pontiff. Always high on the agenda for APP since its inception was the issue of on-going support for priests who left active ministry. Early on in the papacy of John Paul II there evidently was a suspension of dispensations (laicization) from priestly ministry. Getting wind of this from resigned priests, APP sent a letter to the new pontiff asking for clarification. As always, APP wished the pope well in his new ministry and sent blessings, but, at the same time, they raised questions about the process. Acknowledging that "this is a sensible reaction to gain a perspective on the situation as you come into this new position of overwhelming responsibility," nevertheless, they go on, how long will this suspension last? "Is your intention to make it much more difficult for priests to laicize," they asked, pointing out to John Paul II that their former fellow priests are "anxious and suffering" with these "indeterminate delays" in the resolution of their cases. They conclude by thanking the pope "for considering this request for a clarification."[11]

Shortly after the letter to John Paul II concerning laicization applications for those leaving priestly ministry, chair of APP's social action committee, Jack Brennan, authored another letter to the pope. Written shortly after the papal visit to the United States by John Paul II, Brennan thanked the pope for his strong words at Yankee Stadium on human rights and social justice, yet expressed discouragement "at your apparent lack of openness to the needs and hurts of American women," urging the pope to maintain an openness to women going forward and to take opportunities to applaud women as they do ministry "to us men."[12]

Though I found no record of a papal response to APP, the pope issued new criterion for laicization sometime in the latter part of 1980, and in response the APP, along with the National Federation of Priests Council (NFPC), of which APP member Neil McCaulley was now acting national president, passed a resolution, later sent on to the pope, denouncing the "harsh, rigid and demeaning nature of the new regulations." In it the NFPC suggested such new procedures would effectively eliminate former priests from "active life in the church." They concluded their resolution by encouraging "American bishops to voice their opposition," appealing to them to interpret the regulations in a "generous manner," and asked them to gather

10. Curran, *Loyal Dissent*, 113.

11. APP letter, September 7, 1979.

12. APP letter, December 21, 1979.

a group of bishops, priests and laypersons to look seriously at priestly life and make new recommendations, hopefully leading up to a synod on such issues.[13]

At the same time that the APP was adjusting to this new pontificate, it continued deepening its commitment to reflection and analysis on their priestly ministries. The annual "mountaintop retreats" allowed them to analyze the past year, while also recommending new thrusts for the coming year. The facilitated retreats, which began in 1976, always started with a series of questions, e.g., at the 1979 gathering they asked: "Why exist?" Is there too much "tension" around our "prophetic" witness? "Is it easier to stick with social action rather than struggle with our own church?" Where are new members and how do we recruit? How to support "hurting" members of the ministry? What is our relationship with the Diocesan Clergy Council. At one point in the retreat the group wondered "What change in strategy" might be needed to accomplish our primary goals, e.g., maybe we should generate "fewer shithead letters?" This latter suggestion never seems to have taken hold going forward.

As part of these reflections, APP membership was always questioning why more brother priests were not drawn to the group. The last priest to join APP was Denny Kirk in 1979. Like many others, Kirk, while still in the seminary, was mentored by APP through spending summers at St. Joseph's Church on the Northside, where APP had a long and strong presence, thanks to Ed Joyce, but more especially, Jack O'Malley. Although many priests have offered financial and moral support to the APP over the years up until the present time, no others joined after Kirk, now some forty years later. Curiously, this was only one year after the ascendance to the papacy of Polish Cardinal Wojtila, now John Paul II. Could this lack of new members going forward, coincident with the long papacy of the Polish pope, which began in 1978, be in any way a John Paul II effect?

Whenever APP discussed this issue there was always an attempt to talk with non-members, sometimes during membership recruitment gatherings. In one such meeting in 1980, one active member actually admitted that he was sometimes "intimidated by the priests present," especially when it came to "social action." This priest often felt "left out" and unsure of the issues. Though he saw the need for social justice work, agreeing that it was "essential to priesthood," he wasn't himself drawn to it. He suggested more sensitivity to potential new members.

Others suggested that the overall morale of clergy was low and that APP only offered more work and action, but nothing that would help priests

13. Resolution passed, January 20, 1981.

"personally." Some didn't understand why priests would be doing social justice when they were ordained to focus on pastoral ministry. Furthermore, at
times APP seemed "elitist" and "self-congratulatory," creating controversy,
thus projecting a "bad image." For some working with APP would seem
to conflict with regular parish work. APP members took these comments
seriously, prayed about them and tried to discern the best way forward. In
the end, in a statement that came out of the 1979 mountaintop gathering,
they concluded:

> The consensus surfaced that we are who we are. We believe in
> social justice and reform and even though there's not a lot of
> organized support we will keep going. There is no other forum
> for these issues in the diocese. We have to acknowledge the ten-
> sions, live with them and say yes anyway. In short, it was decided
> we go the risky route, live with the tension, support each other
> and remember we're not in the business of antagonizing people;
> that may be an effect but not a purpose. Numbers may not be
> forthcoming. Rugged individualism prevails among the priests
> of Pittsburgh. If you have a good situation you pour all of your
> energy there; if not you bite the bullet or get transferred. Living
> that way all the energy goes into work or survival. We can chal-
> lenge that as perpetuating a system and style of living that lacks
> a broader vision but we must also be realistic about the impact.[14]

Hence, they re-affirmed their threefold focus as social justice outreach,
including bridge-building with other social justice organizations, support
for fellow priests, including retired and resigned priests and, finally, diocesan reform.

As is recorded in the short history on the APP by Frank Brown, the
group came up with a new "strategy" regarding its relationship to the official
Diocesan Clergy Council. For its first ten to fifteen years, APP tried to influence the council to get serious about social justice issues as well as opening up the whole process of diocesan "decision-making." Up to this point it
seemed APP's many attempts at influencing the council had very little effect.
One of APP's key leaders, Neil McCaulley, decided to put more energy into
the NFPC and got himself elected as national president for a two-year term,
1980–82. But, declining a second term, McCaulley decided to return to
Pittsburgh and serve on the local clergy council in 1982. He not only got appointed, but was elected chairman. Hence, APP's "new strategy" regarding
the clergy council was to work on reform from the inside. As Bishop Leonard was set to retire in 1983 at age seventy-five, McCaulley's first effort was

14. Mountaintop minutes, September, 1979.

to push for wide participation in the selecting of the new bishop by calling together a diverse group of Pittsburgh Catholics for consultation. This was not new in the U.S. as, according to Brown, several dioceses had done exactly this only a few years previously with Vatican approval. And the current bishop, Vincent Leonard, gave his "tacit approval" by his silence. However, now, in the John Paul II era, McCaulley received a warning from the "pope's representative in Washington prohibiting 'group consultations, canvasses or referendums.'" Despite the warning and to promote his initiative, McCaulley took part in a public debate, sponsored by the *Pittsburgh Press*, along with a diocesan canon lawyer, Adam Maida, arguing that the APP position was a "by-product of Vatican II's Constitution on the Church."[15]

On July 5, 1983, five days after Bishop Leonard's "announced retirement," in a press release, APP, ever committed to doing its homework, cited a letter written by priests of the Pittsburgh diocese in December of 1920 to Pope Benedict XV, requesting that the next bishop be chosen from among Pittsburgh priests. There was precedent. They even produced the letter signed by six hundred Pittsburgh priests! APP called the Apostolic delegation in Washington to inform them that there would be letters coming from Pittsburgh about the selection of the next bishop. But APP heard nothing from Washington or the local diocese.[16]

All APP efforts to help select the next bishop went for naught, as Anthony Bevilacqua from Brooklyn was appointed by the Vatican as the new bishop of Pittsburgh with no local input. Never deterred, APP tried to set up a meeting with Bevilacqua upon his arrival, but was rebuffed. APP president, Regis Ryan, was told by the bishop he saw "no reason for the APP to exist." Furthermore, shortly thereafter, the new bishop decided that the official Pittsburgh clergy council would not be attending a statewide meeting of priests, even though every other diocese would be represented. Furthermore, a new directive from the Code of Canon Law had recently made the local bishop head of the clergy council, meaning the bishop, not the priests, would now be setting the agenda for the council. APP asked Bevilacqua to reconsider the decision not to send council priests to the statewide gathering. He never responded, so APP sent its own representative to the statewide gathering. Eventually, Bevilacqua agreed to meet with about a dozen Catholics from the diocese representing various groups, including two representatives from APP, Don Fisher and Jack O'Malley. They met twice, after which the bishop announced there would be no more meetings, as he didn't have time to devote to such a process, imagining that if he

15. Brown, "Association of Pittsburgh Priests," 11–12.
16. APP press release, July 5, 1983.

did submit to ongoing meetings, others would also want to meet with him. As APP representative Don Fisher acclaimed after this experience: this was "the new emerging face of the church."[17]

As was mentioned earlier in this study, the "old face" of the Church, at least in Pittsburgh, was a benevolent, kindly presence, of Bishop Vincent Leonard, "Vince" as many APP members referred to him, who led the diocese for some fourteen years. Wanting to acknowledge their affection for Leonard even though they had many challenging encounters with him, and often saw things differently, APP member Don Fisher wrote a letter to Leonard upon his retirement in the name of the group. It reads as follows: "Thank you for your many years of dedicated ministry as Bishop of the Diocese of Pittsburgh and best wishes on the occasion of your retirement. We know that over the years the activities of the APP have not always brought joy to your heart; likewise, we have often been in disagreement with some of your activities and policies. Underneath it all was our abiding respect and affection and hope that it was a struggle for the Kingdom [of God]. We hope that God's abundant blessings will fill your life for the days ahead."[18]

Concerning Bishop Leonard and his relationship to APP, Frank Brown tried to interview him after retirement and recorded that Leonard declined an interview but responded by letter that he had decided upon retirement to "make no public statements on matters pertaining to the activities of the diocese during the time I was bishop or during the episcopate of my successor." Nevertheless, he went on to say that since APP represented "less than one percent of the priests of the diocese" (to APP, a gross underestimate[19]), he never worried much about their actions or impact. But he acknowledged that "every priest has the right to express his opinion" and, as bishop, he also had the right and obligation to let all priests in the diocese know that he "did not necessarily approve what they expressed."[20] Despite their disagreements with Leonard, once Bishop Bevilacqua settled in and displayed his rather authoritarian colors, APP longed for the days of "Vince" Leonard, a man they could always approach and whom they always respected, as Fisher's letter declared.

---

17. Brown, "Association of Pittsburgh Priests," 13.

18. APP minutes, November 15, 1983.

19. Although no one in the group had a clear recollection of how they counted membership, since there were dues' paying active and non-active members, when APP joined NFPC they had to declare that they represented 10 percent of the diocesan clergy. At the time, Pittsburgh had approximately 600 priests, so APP's membership was certainly at 10 percent, if not more.

20. Brown, "Association of Pittsburgh Priests," 105.

Typical of APP, they didn't give up on Bevilacqua, despite his clear lack of interest in collegiality and open dialogue. Leading up to the 1984 Presidential election they sent him a letter (September 28, 1984) requesting a meeting to discuss multiple issues; APP always had a big agenda. They expressed the desire to develop a "good working relationship" and sent along a recently revised constitution and vision statement. They then described some of their recent activities, citing social justice concerns as well as priestly life matters. They referred to the U.S. bishops "Peace Pastoral" of 1983 and expressed concern that it wasn't getting "vigorous" attention in the diocese. They wondered how to have more input into diocesan peace and justice initiatives, especially suggesting more lay input. And, an ongoing theme, especially related to election year concerns, they decried the "one-issue" focus on abortion and reminded the bishop that "pro-life issues" include "hunger, unemployment, interracial justice and peace." The meeting never took place.

But what is most noteworthy about Bishop Bevilacqua's somewhat short tenure in Pittsburgh (1983–88) involved liturgical practice, specifically the participation of women in Holy Thursday's washing of the feet ritual. This issue received both local and national press attention. Deciding to take on what had become a fairly common practice in the diocese and beyond, namely women's feet being washed on Holy Thursday, Bishop Bevilacqua had one of his diocesan officials send a letter to all priests prior to Holy Week to remind them that only men could participate in the foot washing ritual. The rationale, of course, was that "Christ washed the feet of His apostles who were men." The letter concluded with the rather astounding directive that "if no men are available, the washing of the feet is simply omitted," even if this rite is celebrated in a convent of sisters! Both APP and a gathering of religious superiors and the Tri-Diocesan Sister's Leadership Conference responded to the bishop's directive in public press releases, citing that the inclusion of women in the practice of foot-washing was accepted practice in the Pittsburgh diocese, as well as many other dioceses across the country. Furthermore, they argued, excluding women from this ritual was yet another hurt inflicted upon so many "faithful servants of the Gospel." APP slammed the "superficial and pietistic" theology behind the teaching and demanded a rethinking and, in a press release to the *Pittsburgh Catholic*, urged "Bishop Bevilacqua to look beyond narrow interpretations of various laws to the wider pastoral concerns which will announce much more clearly the attitude of Christian love and service by and for all to which the Diocese of Pittsburgh must be committed."[21]

21. APP press release, 1986 (unknown date).

Remarkably, the bishop responded in a very "pastoral" and careful attempt to assuage hurt feelings, yet suggested he had no option but to enforce church teaching. Nevertheless, the following year Bevilacqua sent a letter to all priests acknowledging that he asked for a "clarification" on this rite from The U.S. Bishop's Committee on the Liturgy. In this letter he attached the bishop's response, which states that, despite the teaching that only men can have their feet washed, "it has become customary in many places to invite both men and women to be participants in this rite." Thus, writes Bevilacqua, "prudent pastoral judgment . . . in your own community" can determine what represents the best practice.[22]

Although Bishop Bevilacqua seemed, in general, to indeed reflect the "new emerging face of the Catholic Church" during his tenure in Pittsburgh, as Don Fisher had suggested, even he seemed to realize that his directive had created a public relations' disaster and that he needed to exercise some "prudent pastoral judgment" to quell the controversy. There was no going back. As one religious woman had said some years earlier, in response to the question of the liberalizing trend of women religious wearing secular clothes, "you can't put the toothpaste back in the tube."

Early in 1984 APP, after one of its mountaintop retreats, decided to update its constitution. Although most of the early constitution from 1966/67 was left in place with minor alterations, they did rename what was "The Preamble" to "Our Vision," and in the vision statement there were some additions to put a decidedly stronger orientation than the original to a focus on issues of justice and peace. To emphasize this change, APP added the following paragraph:

> The association responds to the call of Jesus Christ and the Catholic Church to work for the coming of God's Kingdom in our world. The bishops in synod have said: "Action on behalf of Justice and participation in the transformation of the world fully appear to us as constitutive parts of the Gospel." (Justice in the World, par. 6, 1971) . . . The prophetic dimension of the Church's ministry will be our central concern.

And in one final new wrinkle to this revised constitution, they go on to say: "Our vision is that all the baptized in the Church are empowered to minister as Christ asks us. As an association, we will attempt to call forth the gifts of all the baptized." Such a statement is nowhere to be seen in the original document, which focused entirely on the relationship between APP and the bishop, and suggests to me a new consciousness about ministry shared with the entire "people of God," close, I think, to Luther's notion

22. Letter dated March 2, 1987.

of "priesthood of all believers," a notion also resurrected in the documents of Vatican II, though never really addressed fully. This statement actually begins to lay the groundwork for a decision by APP in the early 1990s to open membership in the group to all the baptized, married priests, religious sisters, and lay women and men, but I am getting ahead of myself and the APP story, so more on this later.

In 1986 APP also got involved in a few internal church issues on the national level; one in a relatively minor fashion, the other in a pretty serious manner involving one of its own auxiliary bishops. The first issue compelled them to write yet another of their "shithead" letters to the editor, in August of 1986, circulating it to both the religious and secular press. The issue was the firing of Fr. Charles Curran from Catholic University of America over his theological writings, particularly on moral theology and sexual ethics (earlier we wrote about Curran's dissent in the birth control issue in 1967, in which Curran maintained his teaching position). In this public statement, APP took direct aim at Cardinal Ratzinger, who since 1981 had served as Pope John Paul II's theological point person as head of the orthodox watch-dog office, The Congregation for the Doctrine of the Faith (CDF). "Is the theologian merely the mouthpiece of the pope and bishops," they ask, "Or is the theologian called to probe more deeply into the mysteries of God, creation and human life so as to help us develop a deeper understanding of these mysteries?"

A gifted theologian and teacher, APP suggested that Fr. Curran's students would have been exposed to the complexities of serious moral theology and how Curran would have been very clear as to church teaching, as well as his own carefully reasoned reflection on that teaching, and accused Cardinal Ratzinger as simplifying Curran's position as "completely opposed to official church teaching." They characterize this as "erroneous and counterproductive," suggesting Curran's viewpoint is "much more nuanced" than we are led to believe from his condemnation. They further argue that "dissent" on "non-infallible teachings" is quite legitimate and allowed according to the U.S. bishops in a pastoral letter after the birth control controversy. They conclude their statement by citing many instances in church history of theologians being silenced, only to be vindicated at a future date and suggest that responsible theological questioning of church teaching "in order to understand it better can only strengthen, not weaken, the faith."[23]

A few months later in 1986, APP took on another national church issue a bit closer to home. The issue involved Pittsburgh priest and seminary classmate of a few APP members, Donald Wuerl. It also involved an APP

23. APP press release, August 19, 1986.

episcopal favorite, Archbishop Raymond Hunthausen, leader of the Diocese of Seattle, WA. Hunthausan was an episcopal leader on many social justice issues, most especially that of peace and nuclear disarmament. In fact, The Thomas Merton Center, the peace and justice organization that APP had initially helped start with financial donations in 1972, honored Archbishop Hunthausan with its annual Merton Center award in 1982, so Pittsburgh had a deep connection to the activist cleric.

However, Hunthausan ran afoul of the Vatican in a number of areas and was under scrutiny by church authorities. APP believed that it was actually U.S. bishops who complained about Hunthausan to the Vatican. Among the concerns were: use of contraceptives in Catholic hospitals, controversy over liberal annulment procedures, offering communion to non-Catholics, permission for general confession and absolution vs. individual confessions, affiliation with "homosexual" groups who challenged church teachings, use of resigned priests, teaching and in liturgy, and unsound theology courses for priests and seminarians. Interestingly, these "charges" were all of an internal church nature and implied no criticism of his social activism around nuclear weapons and his support for withholding taxes in protest of war. However, NFPC and APP priests were suspicious that his social stance was, in fact, part of the motivation for the investigation, since they felt "many of the pastoral practices in the Church of Seattle are common throughout the Church in the U.S., why was Seattle targeted?"[24]

Enter Fr. Donald Wuerl, Pittsburgh priest with impeccable Vatican credentials, having studied in Rome for many years, earning his doctorate in theology at the Pontifical University of the Angelicum in 1974. He also served as Bishop John Wright's secretary after ordination in 1966 and followed Cardinal Wright to Rome, where he served as his secretary from 1969–79. While back in Pittsburgh, Wuerl served as rector of St. Paul Seminary from 1981 to 1985.

I briefly met Fr. Wuerl in a radio studio while waiting to do an interview on issues of religion and politics in Central America along with my wife, Melanie, and friends Ed and Donna Brett. All of us were activists opposing U.S. foreign policy in Central America. Ed, Donna and I had all traveled to Central America with activist groups and Ed and I were there to be interviewed. Fr. Wuerl was also in the studio waiting to be interviewed, on an unrelated matter, on a weekly diocesan program facilitated by a diocesan spokesperson, Fr. Ron Lenguin. Although none of us knew who Fr. Wuerl was, Ed and Melanie got into a fairly heated disagreement with him over the legacy of slain Archbishop of El Salvador, Oscar Romero. Ed argued

24. Memorandum of NFPC, November 4, 1986.

Romero was a martyr and should be canonized; Wuerl suggested he was imprudent and acted inappropriately in the face of grave danger and conflict. Wuerl's perspective seemed to reflect the Vatican's response to the murder of Romero: he had gotten too politically active. For those of us who had been so active in those years in support of human rights in Central America, and who saw Romero as a courageous hero in the midst of frightening violence and structural injustice, it was astonishing to meet a clergy person who seemed so unsympathetic to the Salvadoran struggle and the challenge Romero faced. Was Fr. Wuerl a representative of Catholic Church leadership, in those times, we wondered? How such a perspective has changed in the past thirty or so years, as Oscar Romero has recently been canonized.

Not long after our encounter with Fr. Wuerl, on December 3, 1985, he was appointed auxiliary bishop of Seattle to work with Archbishop Hunthausan. Apparently Hunthausan didn't realize right away why Wuerl was sent to Seattle, although the new auxiliary bishop had responsibility and decision-making power over the Archbishop on various aspects of Church life, e.g., liturgy, annulments, priestly formation, laicization and ministry to gay folks ("homosexuals"). The purpose of Wuerl's appointment only became clear to Hunthausan by mid-1986, and it wasn't made public until Hunthausan himself gave a public speech in September of 1986. Not long after this public declaration Hunthausan went into action in his own defense. In November of 1986, he gave a major address to his fellow U.S. bishops, vigorously defending his pastoral practices and objecting to the entire process, clarifying misunderstandings, and finally asking for restoration of his full responsibilities. Then, a few days after this address, he celebrated a public mass in a school gymnasium with over five hundred Washingtonians, declaring: "It hasn't been easy. I've struggled every day with what I ought to do. I have found myself a stronger person spiritually because of all of this." It was a kind of protest liturgy calling for a restoration of authority, but also a mass of reconciliation and healing. At the Mass, a concelebrant (priest of the diocese) declared: "No matter where you are on the political spectrum, we love you as an Archbishop," as the congregation prayed "for Archbishop Hunthausan, Bishop Wuerl and the Church of the Northwest."[25]

At this point APP went into action. Given the personal relationship a number of the priests had with now Bishop Wuerl, as fellow Pittsburghers and classmates in the seminary, as well as its love for Archbishop Hunthausan, one of its episcopal heroes, on November 19, 1986 APP sent a private letter to Wuerl. In the letter, they acknowledged they considered Hunthausan a "true prophet." Then, expressing their respect for Wuerl, they

25. *New York Times*, November 17, 1986, A16.

urged him to immediately resign his "present position" in Seattle and return home, thus "restoring respect to the Archbishop, relieving the concern of the people of the Archdiocese and enhancing your own respect." The letter, on APP stationary, was signed "Fraternally in Christ, Donald McIlvane," for APP. They followed up this letter with a press release, which was read aloud by Fr. John Oesterle (in the rain with a dozen priests and a few lay folks) in front of the diocesan headquarters in downtown Pittsburgh on December 2, 1986. In the press release APP played hardball, as they suggested they were "scandalized by the injustice done to Archbishop Hunthausan" and charged that "the process used to discredit him and severely limit his authority was secretive, arbitrary and unjust . . . protecting his accusers while denying rights to the accused." They suggested that he is only guilty of being pastoral and prophetic, attempting to "renew the church in the spirit of Vatican II." They concluded by asking, now publicly, for Bishop Wuerl "to resign from his position in Seattle" and for "full authority to be restored to Archbishop Hunthausan."[26]

On December 4, 1986, APP received a letter from Rev. David Jaeger, Director of Seminarians in Seattle, on official diocesan stationary, thanking them for their "vision, courage and wonderful sense of strategy illustrated in your recommendation that Bishop Wuerl resign . . . the best news we've gotten out of Pittsburgh in a long time . . . [and] it is heartening to know of your existence and your work—extended over the last 20 years—in service of a more just church."[27] This letter, from a diocesan official in a major diocese, is an amazing affirmation of the significance of the APP in the life of the Church in the United States.

Lastly, APP actually received a brief letter from Bishop Wuerl, on December 11, 1986, sent directly to Don McIlvane, acknowledging his letter of November 19, expressing appreciation for APP's "concern for the local church in Seattle." He concludes his letter by stating: "Would that the solution to this problem were as simple as you indicate." Though he doesn't respond to their recommendation to come home, he does acknowledge their "expression of fraternal concern and promise of prayers" as he wishes them well in their ministry.

I have no evidence to suggest that the APP's powerful public witness influenced the outcome of this unfortunate case in U.S. Catholic Church history, and it seems clear their witness had little effect on Bishop Wuerl himself, at least based on his reply. Nevertheless, in February of 1987 the Vatican appointed a commission of U.S. bishops, headed up by Cardinal

26. Bergholz, "Priests Ask Wuerl to Leave Seattle."
27. Letter received from Rev. Jaeger, December 4, 1986.

Benardin from Chicago, to conduct a thorough investigation, after which Archbishop Hunthausan had his full authority restored by Pope John Paul II in May of 1987. Wuerl was sent back to Pittsburgh to await another assignment, while acknowledging in a statement printed by the *New York Times* that the arrangement in Seattle had been "unworkable."[28]

APP (and many others) got their wish! Hunthausen was restored and Wuerl came back home. He didn't have to wait long for his new assignment; he was appointed bishop of Pittsburgh in February of 1988 and installed on March 25 of 1988. Although APP didn't imagine that asking him to come home would open the door to his being appointed bishop of the Pittsburgh diocese, the prospect of working with a bishop so well known to many of them at least provided an opportunity for a very personal relationship with the leader of the diocese. And they were not sad to see Bishop Bevilacqua move on.

Though I could find no record of any earlier meeting, as was their practice APP asked for and received a meeting with the new bishop in July of 1988, attended by Neil McCaulley, Regis Ryan and Gary Dorsey. At that meeting, lasting nearly one and one-half hours, congeniality reigned, and the participants felt it was "constructive," giving them "optimism" going forward. They discussed ministry in the black community and a number of peace and justice concerns. And, in a very interesting development, they "considered past and future efforts of APP to dialogue with the bishop before using public confrontation and criticism. There should be forums to work out differences instead of using the press to call attention to abuses."[29] Clearly it seemed a new moment after APP's rather strained relationship with Bishop Bevilacqua, who terminated meetings after determining he was too busy to have dialogue with the many requests he might receive and, shortly after arriving in 1983, taking control of the official diocesan clergy council—Vatican directed—thus ending any hope of open serious dialogue between him and APP.

Early on in his episcopacy, Wuerl was confronted with a number of major issues, e.g., a serious diocesan deficit, shrinking number of priests to serve too many parishes, and thus the need for major reorganization, and, probably the most serious, a clergy sexual abuse scandal often involving children and youth. According to a 2003 interview with Ann Rodgers-Melnick, a religion reporter for the *Pittsburgh Post-Gazette*, shortly after his installation as bishop of Pittsburgh, Wuerl "decided he would not return a priest who had ever sexually abused a minor to ministry." Rodgers-Melnick

28 *New York Times*, June 24, 1987.
29. APP minutes, August 16, 1988.

goes on: "During the 1970s the now-late Bishop Vincent Leonard had transferred offenders to other parishes. In the 1980s Bishop Anthony Bevilacqua
sometimes put them in non-parish ministries on the recommendation of
treatment centers. Wuerl's policy was shaped not by attorneys and canon-
ists, he said, but by asking the Holy Spirit to show him how a bishop should
act." Upon his arrival as bishop, he learned that "three priests were on administrative leave for having molested the same two altar boys. Later that
year the boys' parents decided to press charges and sue the diocese. (The
diocese settled out of court, and two of the priests went to prison)." Although lawyers suggested Wuerl not contact families, with the local pastor's
permission he reached out and was invited to the family's home. "I had been
a priest long enough to say, what else do I bring to this if I don't go and see
them . . . Isn't that what a priest does in any situation? You offer to be present
. . . not as a canon lawyer but as a priest."

In speaking with a number of people who met with Wuerl, Rodgers-
Melnick reported that Wuerl seemed "morally outraged" by what happened
to their children and he went on to say: "you can't help but . . . say, This is
not going to happen again on my watch."

As of 2003, reports Rodgers-Melnick, "By all evidence, he has stuck to
that decision" to the point where he got into a disagreement with the Vatican over keeping an accused priest out of ministry. Though Wuerl hoped
to keep the issue quiet, not wanting the Vatican to look bad, the supporters
of the accused priest, Anthony Cipolla, went public and accused Wuerl of
being a "tyrant persecuting an innocent man." Although the accused priest
"had never been convicted of a crime," Wuerl believed him to be guilty. As
a consequence, writes Rodgers-Melnick, Wuerl became a "poster bishop for
zero tolerance" after the sexual abuse scandal went viral in 2002, thanks to a
major investigative report in the *Boston Globe*.[30]

Although totally supportive of Wuerl's "zero tolerance" policy toward
abusive priests, APP—to my knowledge from speaking with a number of
members—never has taken on this issue directly or issued any major statements. They are horrified and shocked that it has all happened and express
amazement how fellow priests were able to do all of this so clandestinely.
However, in a few interviews I've had with current and former APP members, they have expressed frustration with some members of the episcopacy,
whom they now perceive to have gone from one extreme, i.e., protecting or
transferring accused priests, to suspending accused priests with zero evidence or obvious credibility to the charges, without any due process. Such
a swing, some have suggested, makes all priests vulnerable to charges that

30. Rodgers, "In 15 Years."

have no basis in fact. All of this has led to a serious morale problem, as it appears some bishops are now mostly interested in "covering their own asses," as a few APP members have suggested.

On a personal note, reflecting upon a somewhat larger context of seminary training in preparation for ministry, having been in a vowed religious community for ten years from 1972–82, and serving as an ordained priest for four years, I can attest to the fact that the whole question of sexuality and healthy sexual development were never adequately or even minimally addressed. The only time I remember sexuality or sexual orientation being addressed during seminary years occurred one evening when a superior suggested that any student brother who was discovered to have visited a "gay bar" would be immediately expelled. Beyond that one brief encounter, the issue was never again addressed.

APP members would affirm this experience. Although I found almost no evidence of sexuality or sexual orientation being addressed at any APP meetings, in a 1981 mountaintop retreat one of the priests did raise the issue by suggesting encouraging "support groups" for any priest who had a "homosexual orientation." However, concern was expressed that such a "suggestion might not be received well within the structure." It appears that a very healthy discussion ensued, in which members wondered "how we could do something to facilitate development [sexual] among priests. Some seminary changes seem necessary," they affirmed, and they went on to speculate, interestingly, that "rectory lifestyles may cause a person to regress." This discussion led them to affirm, once again, the need for the institution to address the issue of "optional celibacy," implying that they considered mandatory celibacy a part of the problem of sexual dysfunction and potential abuse among the clergy.[31]

On the social action front, many of the same issues received APP attention in the late 1970s and into the decade of the 1980s, e.g., peace and nuclear proliferation, accompanied by tax resistance related to war spending, worker rights, especially as it relates to Catholic schools, ongoing concern over the institutional church's singular focus on abortion vs. a whole slew of justice issues around life, the role of the priest vis-a-vis politics, the role of the church regarding elections, and, as we enter the decade of the 1980s, the growing wars and violence in Central America and the role of the U.S. government in supplying arms to reactionary forces.

As has been mentioned previously, one of APP's major initiatives was to help fund the starting up of the Thomas Merton Center for Justice and Peace in 1972. In 1980, one of its co-founders, Molly Rush, a serious

31. Mountaintop minutes, May 19–20, 1981.

Catholic activist on racial justice and anti-nuclear and peace activities as a staff person at the Merton Center, took part in a direct action with several others as part of a movement called "Plowshares," by breaking into the General Electric Plant in King of Prussia, PA., damaging nuclear nose cones with hammers. The wider group, formed by, among others, Philip and Daniel Berrigan, was motivated by biblical passages from the prophetic tradition of the Hebrew Bible suggesting "They will hammer their swords into plowshares and their spears into pruning knives" (Micah 4:3). Although Rush's action and fairly brief incarceration was a difficult experience for all, certainly her family but also the Center, APP issued a press release on September 19, 1980, ten days after the action, leaving no doubt as to their support: "We commend these seven Christians for their courageous and creative response to the madness of the nuclear arms race. Daily the U.S. Government spends millions of dollars at plants like G.E., an affront to the poor and a bitter waste." They decried the buildup of these weapons and suggested they will never provide us with "safety and security," and they declared Rush's action "an act of love for the human family," which beckons us all "to become Gospel-inspired peacemakers." They offered total support for this action of civil disobedience.[32]

For so many activists in the U.S., the decade of the 1980s was consumed with events in Central America, as the U.S. Government's foreign policy was supporting oppressive forces throughout the region, most especially the brutally violent regime in El Salvador and a counter-revolutionary group in Nicaragua known in Spanish as the "*contras*," a group opposed to the newly-elected revolutionary government, the *Sandinistas*. Interestingly, in the case of the new Nicaraguan government, several Catholic priests served in cabinet positions, including Maryknoll priest, Miguel D'Escoto, who had become Foreign Secretary of State.

In the 1970s there was a horrific civil war going on in El Salvador, with the U.S. sending aid to the repressive government. Many U.S. activists were sympathetic to the rebellious movements. In 1979, Archbishop Oscar Romero actually wrote President Jimmy Carter, asking him to suspend military aid to the government because the aid was being used to massacre the Salvadoran population, particularly those sympathetic to revolution or significant social transformation. The next year Romero was assassinated by right wing elements related to the government, and that tragedy was followed later in the year by the brutal rape and murder of four U.S. church women, three nuns and a young lay woman. A massive national movement

---

32. APP press release, September 19, 1980.

developed in the U.S. to counter U.S. policy, and Pittsburgh became a hotbed of such activity and resistance.

The Thomas Merton Center, since its inception in 1972, was primarily
devoted to anti-war, anti-nuclear resistance. In 1982, I moved to Pittsburgh
and took an organizer's job with the Merton Center and, despite some opposition from a few of the old guard of the Center, I was asked to devote
some of my time to developing initiatives in opposition to our government's
Central American policy. This involved organizing a "Witness for Peace"
delegation to Nicaragua in 1983 for the purpose of visiting embattled areas and returning to offer eye witness accounts to our elected officials. We
also became part of a burgeoning modern church sanctuary movement, in
which refugees from war-torn El Salvador were being housed and protected
from arrest and possible deportation in houses of worship all across the
country. In Pittsburgh the local Mennonite Church declared sanctuary, and
a husband and wife from El Salvador came to us through the underground
railroad of activists. APP was totally supportive of these initiatives. APP
member and then pastor of a Catholic Church in the East End of Pittsburgh,
Don Fisher, in offering public support for the refugees and the Mennonite
Church, said: "It is because of a love of God and neighbor that we, the members of the Pittsburgh Interfaith Sanctuary Movement, publicly support the
Mennonite Church in their courageous act of offering sanctuary for these
two refugees."[33]

Harboring undocumented refugees and offering public support was
a federal crime. At an APP meeting in May of 1983, APP voted to publicly support the sanctuary movement and take it to the official Pittsburgh
Clergy Council for its support—Neil McCaulley was then chair of the clergy
council. Beyond this action, several members of the group participated in
various resistance activities, including many acts of civil disobedience all
through the 1980s. Also, on the Witness for Peace action in Nicaragua, Frs.
Jack O'Malley and Don Fisher represented the APP. They and others also
went to jail a number of times during ongoing civil disobedience actions,
usually at the downtown Federal building in Pittsburgh. One APP priest,
Mark Glasgow, actually got arrested unintentionally while objecting to the
rough treatment some of the police were employing during the arrest of
those doing civil disobedience.[34]

Protests of U.S. foreign policy in Central America lasted throughout
the 1980s. Finally, by the late 1980s, U.S. policy changed. In the case of

33. *Pittsburgh Press*, August 17, 1983.

34. In that particular action fifty-seven Pittsburghers were arrested protesting U.S.
foreign policy in Central America.

Nicaragua, the "Iran-Contra" scandal put an end to U. S. covert support to the anti-revolutionary "contra" movement, and in the Salvadoran case, Congress voted to end support of the government in 1989 after the brutal murders of six Jesuit priests and their housekeeper and her daughter. Leading up to this change in policy, a priest, Michael Drohan, then a member of the Holy Spirit religious community, which operates Duquesne University, a prominent Catholic school in Pittsburgh, resigned from a research post at the Institute for World Concerns at Duquesne in protest of the University's invitation to speak to a U.S. State Department official involved in providing aid to the "contra" rebels. Drohan was also a member of APP and a number of APP members participated in the protest at Duquesne, holding crosses with the names of murdered Nicaraguans written on them.[35]

Besides acts of civil disobedience with many other Pittsburgh activists, APP members did frequent lobbying with federal officials, most especially the two Pennsylvania Senators, Arlen Specter and John Heinz. Also, APP letter writer extraordinaire, Neil McCaulley, constantly kept the lobbying pressure up with well-crafted missives until Congress finally acted.

One of the key point persons for the ultimate success of the cessation of the aid to the government of El Salvador was then Speaker of the House of Representatives, Thomas "Tip" O'Neill. When asked why he lobbied so hard for so many years to end this aid, despite putting him in opposition to his friend, President Ronald Reagan, he said he received his information from his ninety-one-year-old aunt, Eunice Tolan, a Maryknoll nun, who had many sister friends in El Salvador who experienced first-hand the effects of U.S. foreign policy. "I have a lot of friends in the Maryknoll Order and they keep me highly informed," said O'Neill, "Our policy is wrong. I told the White House that, but they think I get my policy from the little old ladies there, the nuns. And in part I do. They are women of God who are doing His work."[36] Catholic resistance to the U.S. government during the 1980s was a huge part of the eventual change in U.S. foreign policy in Central America, though it took nearly ten years to accomplish.

It was in this period, with the election of Pope John Paul II in 1978 and the emergence of Latin America and the role of the Catholic Church in society in that region, that a process of clarification began for APP as to the appropriate role of priest in relation to society and politics, including political elections. We have previously mentioned the Latin American Bishop's Conference in Medellin, Colombia, in 1968, as a very major post-Vatican II example of the empowerment of regional bishop's conferences. As was cited

35. *Pittsburgh Press*, October 29, 1986, A6.
36. Farrell, *Tip O'Neill*, 612.

previously in this study: "The 1968 assembly of Medellin was a unique experience in the global reception of Vatican II and the largest effort of a continental church for a creative reception of the council."[37] The Latin American bishops then organized another assembly in 1979 in Puebla, Mexico, basically reaffirming "Medellin's theological interpretation of Vatican II"; but the new wrinkle was the presence of a new pope, John Paul II, who, with the help of Cardinal Ratzinger, appointed as head of the Congregation for the Defense of the Faith (CDF) in 1981, would gradually alter this progressive theological and ecclesial drift, thus slowly halting the progressive possibilities of implementing Vatican II. However, it was not yet obvious that such a direction was about to happen directly after the Puebla Conference.

In a lengthy press release issued in February of 1979, APP suggested that Pope John Paul II at Puebla gave a "popularly interpreted . . . directive to Catholics to stay out of politics." In his speech the pope emphasized the "spiritual nature of the priesthood and religious life" and "warned priests and nuns to stay out of partisan politics and condemned the use of violence." APP picked up on an initial report from the *Pittsburgh Press* (January 28, 1979) that headlined a piece about the Pope address with the words: "Pray More, Politic Less, Pope Tells Catholics." Next, a report from the *Pittsburgh Catholic* (February 9, 1979), portrayed a cartoon of the pope admonishing Catholics that "The Gospel message is more important than politics," thus subtly warning folks "to stay out of politics." But APP begged to differ with such an interpretation. On the contrary, proclaimed APP in a press release, encouraging people to "re-examine" the pope's words: "A deeper look at the Pope's address, as well as the concluding statements from the bishops, indicate a renewed commitment to the struggles for human rights and welfare of the poor, particularly in underdeveloped nations." They go on to say that the pope spoke of "a transforming, peacemaking, pardoning and reconciling love . . . and to make systems and structures more human."

The statement went on to affirm that "No human activity is foreign to the Gospel," including involvement in the political realm. Even more radically, in the eyes of APP, the pope went on to say in his final address at Puebla, alluding to the problem of the ownership of land and private property in Latin America, that "Private Property always carries with it a social obligation, so that material possessions may serve the general goal that God intended. And if the common good requires it, there must be no doubt about expropriation (of property) itself, carried out in the proper manner." (This is actually a long-standing tenet of Catholic Social teaching on the relationship of private property and the common good.) The Latin

37. Faggioli, *Vatican II*, 54.

American bishops concluded the Puebla Conference with these words: "In Latin America the gap is increasing between the few who have much and the many who have little. Our cultural values are being threatened . . . It is high time we tell the developed nations that they must cease to block our progress, to exploit us." And, finally, they write: "We are further shaken by the armaments race which does not stop manufacturing tools for death . . . We invite all responsible persons in political and social circles to reflect on these words."

APP ended its press release with the affirmation: "We of the APP find these words addressed to committed Christians everywhere and whole-heartedly support and encourage further involvement in the political arena for the welfare of the peoples of the world."[38] The press release was signed by several APP officers, including Jack Price, a former missionary in Peru, South America, where the Pittsburgh Diocese had a mission. This declaration represented a beginning salvo of APP in the slow clarification of its perspective on the relationship between religion and politics, priesthood and the social implications of the Gospel, a deeper dive into this question than their previous, "never released" document of 1974.

Despite APP's take on and disagreement with the "popularly interpreted" press version of the pope's words in 1979 regarding the role of priests in the political realm, that interpretation was closer to the truth of what John Paul II was intending than the APP's interpretation. This became a bit clearer after a 1980 visit by the pope to Rio de Janeiro, where he addressed a group of Brazilian priests with these words: "The priest's service is not that of a doctor, of a social worker, of a politician or of a trade unionist . . . the priest has his essential function to perform in the field of souls, of their relations with God and their interior relations with their fellows" (July 2, 1980). Also, many of us remember, a few years later in 1983, in a famous encounter on the tarmac at the airport in Nicaragua, the pope wagging his finger in a disapproving manner at Fr. Ernesto Cardenal, Minister of Culture in the revolutionary Sandinista government, as Cardenal kneeled down to receive the pope's blessing.

At this time APP had been deeply analyzing its own position of the relationship of priest and politics, and felt it was time to make yet another serious attempt at articulating a reasoned, well-researched position paper on this most pressing issue. We remember that in 1974, APP had issued a statement on priest and politics for internal consumption. Now they wanted to further develop that perspective. Hence, after months of deliberation and with unanimous approval at their May, 1983 monthly meeting, APP

38. APP press release, February 24, 1979.

prepared a press conference to release their latest document entitled: "The Priest and Politics."[39]

They began by expressing serious misgivings about "repeated warnings from John Paul II against 'priests in politics.'" They challenged both his "words" and "actions" as "inconsistent with our priestly tradition." And they worried that his perspective will discourage any "priestly involvement in the wider community." They decried the pope's "public rebuke" of Cardenal as "ill-timed and most ungracious," and they seemed to acknowledge now a very different take on the pope's views on the matter from their early interpretation after Puebla. They also challenged the pope on his 1980 demand that Jesuit priest and lawyer, Robert Drinan, who had served several terms in Congress from Massachusetts, not run for re-election in 1980. They then proceeded to make a number of clarifying "distinctions," since they judged that the relationship between priests and politics may well have a number of understandings.

For example, this relationship can mean becoming an elected official in order to serve government, either full or part-time, paid or unpaid, in some cases not involving any other pastoral duties and in other cases permitting a priest to continue exercising more traditional ministry. Another understanding of "priests in politics" could be a priest accepting an appointed position in government, either full or part-time, paid or unpaid, again, in some cases allowing a priest to perform other ministries. A third possibility would be a far more common one of a priest's involvement in neighborhood or community issues leading to sermonizing on the moral aspects of certain community issues or visiting public officials to influence community decision-making or even speaking out at public meetings. Part of the latter might be participation in a public demonstration or even involvement in an act of civil disobedience as a protest, anti-war protests or civil rights rallies, as when some APP members went to Selma and Jackson in the 1960s.

In each case the APP document offered specific examples, such as the case of Fr. Drinan. In the third instance they cite historic Pittsburgh cases: one, in which Fr. Albert Kazincy supported a steelworker in a strike in 1919, and was acclaimed in Thomas Bell's famous novel, well known to Pittsburgh labor activists, *Out of This Furnace*; and another, in 1932, in which Fr. James Cox went to DC with over 20,000 unemployed workers to demand legislation to put folks back to work, and who, on his return to Pittsburgh, addressed over 50,000 people at a local stadium and proclaimed this struggle was against "Wall Street and Smithfield Street [City Hall]." They brought their examples up to date with their own involvement in various community

39. APP, "Priest and Politics."

organizations, specific to certain neighborhoods, despite criticism from some for meddling "in politics." They even mention the general support, even if sometimes done quietly, of any number of Pittsburgh bishops over the years.

On a national level, besides referring to the few priests who have served in Congress until the pope's most recent declaration against seeking elected office, they cite a number of examples, one recent, a few distant, of clerics playing significant roles in the so-called public square, e.g., Bishop Mahoney of L.A. who in 1975 was chairman of the newly formed "California Agricultural Labor Relations Board," and who helped negotiate the settlement of the grape boycott strike. They also cited historical figures like Fr. Damien, who in the nineteenth century worked with lepers in what is now the Hawaiian Islands, and who had to fight with the Board of Health to ensure adequate supplies for the lepers, and Fr. Pierre de Smet, who in working with Native Americans in the early part of the nineteenth century helped negotiate peace between the Indians and the U.S. Army and traveled to Washington, DC, to demand the Superintendent of Indian Affairs fight for their rights and for adequate funds for their survival.

In summing up, APP suggests in its document that the pope doesn't really understand the important role of the "priest in politics" in the U.S. in the several ways APP has outlined possible avenues. He doesn't know our experience, they proclaim. Furthermore, haven't priests and bishops (including the pope) in Poland, the pope's native land, in various ways been involved in politics against Communism, they ask. "In Poland, a Marian procession can be a political event," they argue. In the U.S., "where the practice of religion is (generally) free from government restrictions, priestly involvement in political matters is quite different." While they salute "the brave priests of Poland" who have spoken up for worker rights and human rights and have even "died in Nazi concentration camps during World War II," and who bravely "worked and died for justice," we in the West "work for justice in another set of circumstances."

They ask the pope: "as a good pastor, [to] support his priests in their work for justice, decency and human dignity." They intended their statement to open a "dialogue" with John Paul II as they quoted the then President of the National Conference of Catholic Bishops, John Roach, who in August of 1982 said: "As a church we are political practitioners because we have to be. It is important to understand what is appropriate in that position and what is not. It is even more important to understand why it is essential that the church use the methods available to it to influence public policy, because it is by that policy that the moral order is frequently established." They end by expressing in a very powerful statement their convictions:

The priest cannot love the poor in the abstract but must love them in the flesh. The priest cannot seek justice and righteousness in a theoretical way but in the circumstances of the time and place where he fulfills his ministry. Work for justice is an essential part of the priestly ministry, as it is essential for every Christian man and woman. This work for justice takes different forms in different societies. We suggest that when Pope John Paul better understands the traditions of American priests and of other nations, then we will have a better, more constructive, less negative dialogue on how the quest for peace and justice is worked out in priestly ministry.[40]

Once again, APP did its homework, historically, theologically and ecclesially, and, once again, it spoke truth to power. But, as we shall see, they were fighting an uphill battle in their struggle to bring their views on social justice to the church and the public square, both against the pope himself as well as certain members of the American hierarchy, as we'll see as we briefly look at tensions and disagreements that occurred between APP and church hierarchy in the Presidential elections of 1984 and 1988.

Although APP, quite appropriately in my view, has never endorsed a party or a specific candidate, it frequently weighs in on issues important to Catholic social teaching. And, as we've seen over and over again, they are never reluctant to take a stance on an issue and, when necessary, offer a prophetic critique of church hierarchy in the process. To this point when Geraldine Ferraro, a practicing Catholic and Vice-Presidential candidate for the Democratic Party, came to Pittsburgh in September of 1984, it became an opportunity for APP to challenge two bishops, John O'Connor of New York and James Timlin of Scranton, PA., who openly opposed her candidacy because she was pro-choice. APP member, Pat Fenton, actually received a call from Bishop Timlin asking him and the APP, "why are you taking on the Church?" However, APP felt it was on pretty solid ground as it accused the bishops of both violating "longstanding Catholic tradition" of not publicly endorsing or opposing particular candidates, but rather simply reminding voters of church teachings on certain issues. APP pointed out that O'Connor and Timlin's open opposition to Ferraro directly countered the declarations of fellow bishops, who six months earlier, in the run-up to the election, issued a statement that they would not tell Catholics how to vote, merely reminding Catholics that they should "examine the positions of candidates on the full range of issues, as well as their integrity, philosophy and performance." Both Pittsburgh newspapers picked up APP's

40. APP, "Priest and Politics," 1–10.

press release and at a press conference, Pat Fenton, Gary Dorsey and Don McIlvane reminded the public that we priests don't endorse or oppose particular candidates, as these bishops obviously did, even though, at the same time, the priests encouraged political participation by all Catholics. They also used this opportunity to remind Catholics that abortion was only one among "14 key issues" that the Church is concerned about, alongside "human rights, arms -control, energy, etc."[41]

In the mid-term elections of 1986, APP geared up again, this time adding to their critique of church hierarchy their own Bishop Bevilaqua, who along with Cardinal O'Connor of New York again violated church tradition. Both bishops acted in ways that made clear statements about certain politicians and their pro-choice views. Once again, in a press release, APP made clear that church leaders are free to express views on social issues, but not to target particular (Catholic) politicians, who APP suggests "must follow their conscience and the guidance of their constituents (not to mention the leadership of their political party) in voting on the various pieces of legislation to come before them." APP goes on to say that legislators are in a very challenging position and do not have "an easy task" when it comes to voting on specific legislation. And they remind Catholics in their statement that a particular bishop's position on an issue is not "morally binding" on Catholics.[42]

Then, in 1988, another presidential election year, APP went public once again and held a press conference in front of the diocesan building in downtown Pittsburgh, in anticipation of an upcoming primary, reiterating the importance of freedom of conscience for Catholics as they approach the ballot box. But this time APP took a stronger, clearer stand in their criticism of certain bishops for their almost complete focus on one issue, i.e., abortion, a very consistent theme of the APP for many years. "Abortion strikes at the deepest respect for human life. It also touches on the issue of women's rights . . . abortion should always be addressed with restraint and without extremism. We believe, for instance, that to call a 'murderer' any candidate who has voted for public funds for abortion is extreme and intemperate. The same would be true if a candidate who voted for a particular nuclear weapons' system were consequently to be called a 'war monger.'" They go on to again advocate that respect be given to legislators' individual consciences and to remind how difficult that can be to balance. They also reiterate their oft-mentioned challenge for Catholics to become politically active and

41. Private interview with Pat Fenton. The *Pittsburgh Press* (September 28) 1, *Pittsburgh Post-Gazette,* and the *Pittsburgh Catholic,* all reported on this press event.

42. APP draft of press release, unknown date in October, 1986.

become informed about the issues. They recommend "no public endorse-
ments of political candidates . . . [and] no distribution of political literature
or of endorsement lists . . . in church vestibules, church meetings or in parish publications." Finally, they point to the now famous document issued
by Chicago's Cardinal Bernardin known as "the consistent ethic of life," in
which Bernardin advocates for a consideration of any number of issues as
issues of life, e.g., abortion, death penalty, war and peace, poverty, etc.[43]

A month and one-half later, after receiving heavy criticism for their
April 5th statement on elections as demonstrated by many letters to the
editor in the *Pittsburgh Catholic*, APP responded with its own letter to the
diocesan paper. In it they make clear that "The APP condemns abortion as
evil and a morally unacceptable solution to the problem of unwanted preg-
nancies," thus acknowledging agreement with "anti-abortion groups" and
official Catholic Church teaching. But, they continue, "We differ from many
of them [anti-abortion groups] in also seeing abortion as a sensitive women's
issue and value communication with the victims who, in the case of abortion, are not only the unborn, but often the mothers too." As they commend
antiabortion activists for their "courage and dedication . . . concerning the
fate of the unborn," they take such groups to task for not having concern for
the "full spectrum of other life and death issues" and they acknowledge that
the "political choices of many APP members" will "favor candidates who
support that wider thrust," suggesting a concern for "the dignity of human
life from conception to the grave." They end by acknowledging the "tension"
involved in this debate and encourage understanding and dialogue.[44]

It is remarkable to me how consistently well APP and its leadership
have negotiated the moral issue of abortion, a landmine issue in the Catholic world. Each time they have been challenged, most especially around
elections, APP has taken a position that is intelligent, thoughtful, measured
and, it would seem, faithful and theologically sound. And, in the process,
while they have proclaimed their clear opposition to abortion, in keeping
with current Catholic teaching, they have consistently raised the complexity
of the issue, insisting on concern for both the life of the unborn and the

43. APP press conference, April 5, 1988. Also, Bernardin et al., *Consistent Ethic
of Life*. What is noteworthy about APP's stance here all through the 1980s is that
there is currently criticism, once again, of the Catholic Church as individual states are
passing legislation to severely restrict abortion. A reporter in the *Boston Globe*, a self-
proclaimed, practicing Catholic, has found statements in parish bulletins that greatly
distort what pro-choice advocates actually do support. Eagan, "The Church's Dismaying Anti-abortion Rhetoric," A8.

44. APP letter to editor, *Pittsburgh Catholic*, May 23, 1988. Many progressive
Catholics are presently criticizing antiabortion or anti-choice folks as not authentically
pro-life but rather merely pro-birth.

human rights of the woman, a position not often raised in Catholic circles, especially more traditional Catholic circles. I remember studying in a moral theology class in graduate school at Catholic University of America about the concept of conflict in moral values, that is, there are times in life, as we face complex moral dilemmas, we must acknowledge that there is ambiguity because of conflicting values. Applied to this particular case, APP has consistently recognized this moral conflict of competing values between the protection off unborn, nascent life in the womb, and women's rights and the freedom to make decisions that affect them most directly and uniquely.

APP applied the same perspective while commenting on a dispute between Catholic nuns in West Virginia and the institutional Catholic Church on the question of abortion and a woman's right to choice. APP tried to maintain a balance, of both supporting the nun's position on freedom of choice, recognizing women's rights as a moral issue, yet reiterating their own opposition to abortion as a moral evil.

Nevertheless, its position had never been more under attack than during this particular incident in 1986 when two Catholic nuns from Charleston, West Virginia, whose primary ministry was with Charleston's homeless population, took a public pro-choice stance. Evidently the two nuns, Sisters Barbara Ferraro and Patricia Hussey, were part of a group of twenty-four nuns who signed a "statement challenging the Roman Catholic Church's doctrine equating abortion with murder."[45] In all, ninety-seven Catholics signed the statement calling for dialogue on the issue. Of the twenty-four nuns all but two, Ferraro and Hussey, "recanted" when pressured by the Vatican, although half of those suggested that was a mischaracterization of their position. The nuns called for dialogue and the right to dissent from church teaching.[46]

Always up for a good fight, especially when the group feels issues of truth and justice are at stake, APP sent a letter of support to the two nuns commending them "for your stand on behalf of women's choice on abortion. We find the Vatican's effort to prevent any dissent from this teaching to be contrary to the spirit of Christ and the tradition of the Church." They went on to say, in a beautifully strategic, but also heartfelt, manner, "We recall the original context of the New York Times' advertisement when the bishops were trying to make the '84 election a single-issue campaign and applauded the efforts of you and others to challenge this. Even more, we commend you for the day-to-day ministry to God's people you share, and

45. Catholics for a Free Choice, "A Diversity of Opinion," *New York Times*, October 7, 1984.

46. Sherwood, "The Right to Disagree," C-1.

we hope and pray that the confrontation with the Vatican does not stop this. We also hope that you can find the support you need to carry on"[47] Later APP made public their letter to the nuns. The nuns deeply appreciated the support of APP, and in reply to this support, stated: "It's about time that many priests who feel the way they do make their feelings public . . . We applaud the action of the Association."[48] A firestorm ensued.

Shortly after making their letter to the nuns public and reading subsequent reports in the local news about their letter, APP sent letters to Bishop Bevilacqua and the local papers, including the *Pittsburgh Catholic*, in an attempt to make sure their letter of support was properly understood. In the letter to Bevilacqa, they focused on the right to dissent in the Church, citing the cases of Charles Curran at Catholic University of America and of Bishop Hunthausan in Seattle, whereas the press focused mostly on the issue of abortion. They reiterated their adherence to the Church's teaching on abortion, i.e., that it is "morally wrong," but they also returned to a consistent theme that abortion is one among many life issues. They concluded that they strongly objected to the tenor of Church's response to the nuns, one of "threats, punishment and rejection," whereas it should be one of "sensitivity and concern," always seeking "a deeper understanding and appreciation of the truth." They support the right of conscience and dissent to Church teaching, both for the nuns and themselves.[49]

APP was not alone in the Pittsburgh Catholic community in calling for a mature and open dialogue about diverse positions and dissent from Church teaching when dealing with complex moral issues. Sister Patricia McCann, a Pittsburgh Sister of Mercy as well as a professor of church history at the college and seminary level, weighed in on this controversy in a brilliant piece published in the monthly newsletter of the activist Thomas Merton Center. Sister McCann also emphasized that the main issue of concern here was not abortion but rather conscience and the right to dissent. She cited the teachings of Vatican II and the notions of "development of doctrine, collegiality, and subsidiarity" (issues should first be resolved locally if possible), as well as "the way in which authority functions within the Church." She acknowledged tensions that arise in such a context of moral complexity and disagreement, but also spoke to the role of women, both in the Church and outside. In this vein she applauded the bishops of the U.S. for their seeking input from the faithful on matters of war and peace and the economy, a very collegial approach, yet, went on to state that "Ironically

47. APP letter of support, August 31, 1986.
48. Gigler, "Priest Group Backs W. VA. Nuns."
49. APP letter to Bishop Bevilaqua, September 11, 1986.

the bishops find it much more difficult to move out of the authoritarian model when working with questions like the ERA or the role of women in ministry." And she reminded her readers that one can be strongly anti-abortion and, at the same time, seek serious dialogue about differences. Only collegiality and serious dialogue can overcome the current impasse, she concludes.[50]

APP was barraged with bad press and any number of personal letters from outraged Catholics. One letter accused chairperson of APP, Regis Ryan, as being a "half-assed priest" who the "Church would be better off without . . . Apparently you fellows [APP] aren't as familiar with the fifth commandment as you are with today's trends." One other letter criticized APP's stance on dissent by stating: "While you believe that dissent in conscience is a right, we believe that the right to be born is a greater right. Any activity on your part that gives even the slightest support of or suggestion of there being a choice in taking the life of an unborn child is unacceptable."[51]

Early in the previous year, shortly after the 1984 elections, attempting to put the issue of abortion in the much wider context of Catholic social teaching, APP member Neil McCaulley had written a powerful and challenging letter in the name of APP to U.S. bishops, nearly two years before this above-reported controversy over abortion, women's rights and dissent took place. At the time McCaulley was offering "testimony" after a first draft appeared of an upcoming bishop's pastoral letter on the economy, which was eventually issued in November of 1986. As Sister McCann had suggested, in this case the bishops asked for commentary ahead of publication. In the commentary, McCaulley states that he was skeptical that such a pastoral letter on the economy would make any real difference, despite its "beautiful vision," since an earlier pastoral letter on war and peace (1983) rests now in "the graveyard for church statements." Will the economic pastoral experience the same fate, he wondered? Despite the power and clarity of the 1983 peace pastoral, writes McCaulley, when it came time for elections in 1984 only abortion mattered among the bishops (he specifically cites Cardinal O'Connor, Archbishop Law, and the bishops of PA). He also cites the attempt by the same bishops to publicly oppose Vice-Presidential candidate for the Democrats, Geraldine Ferraro, as well as their disparagement of a statement made by "Catholics for a Free Choice." McCaulley concludes his letter by warning the bishops that there are "signals" from Rome that the Congregation for Doctrine and Faith head, Cardinal Ratzinger, is interested in marginalizing the teaching ministry and authority of local bishop's

50. McCann, "Call for Pluralism."
51. Letters received in September of 1986.

conferences. He implores the bishops not to be "intimidated" by Rome and asks them to "commit the time and money and personnel necessary to implement [the pastoral's] vision."[52]

Related to McCaulley's comments above that the U.S. bishop's pastoral letter on peace represented a "beautiful vision," and the APP's ongoing interest in promoting and educating around Catholic social teaching, McCaulley, Fenton and other APP leaders had earlier organized a national meeting of the National Federation of Priests Council in Pittsburgh in October of 1983, entirely focused on the recently published pastoral letter on peace. The gathering attracted a large national and local audience and Pat Fenton served as point person to bring in national figures, among them keynote speaker and former congressman and Jesuit priest, Robert Drinan, Bishop Tom Gumbleton, Dr. Helen Caldicott from the Physicians for Social Responsibility, local Plowshares activist Molly Rush, John Carr of the Social Concerns Office of the Catholic Diocese of Washington, DC, and Fr. Bryan Hehir, representing the United States Conference of Bishops Social Concerns Office. Sister Patricia McCann, aforementioned church historian, was asked to address the gathering about the relationship between U.S. bishops and U.S. foreign policy in history. Unfortunately, she was not able to participate, and suggested the group ask me to tackle the assignment. Neil McCaulley called to ask if I would do it. After several disclaimers that though I was interested, I felt inadequate to the task as not an historian, thus I would have to do lots of research. McCaulley responded: "You sound like an overachiever, just the kind of person we want, we accept." This was my first exposure to the entire membership of APP, having previously known only a few of its key leaders. And it represented the real beginning of my now thirty-six year interest in the group's prophetic witness.

The NFPC office in Chicago was greatly pleased with the conference, once again demonstrating that the Pittsburgh chapter of priests was one of their key national players. One outsider (non-Pittsburgh priest) to the conference commented that it was great to see "the church of Pittsburgh at work." But despite this great national acclamation, APP, even with McCaulley serving as chair of the official clergy council in Pittsburgh, received a rather tepid response to the conference from local clergy as well as the clergy council itself, even if the latter "did cooperate" to some degree. It seemed an indication that while APP had great national press and was a key participant in the NFPC, the group still had little impact with local clergy

52. McCaulley, Letter to bishops, January, 1985.

not sympathetic to their agenda, and a new bishop of the view they had no reason to exist.[53]

McCaulley chose not to continue as chair of the official clergy council in Pittsburgh after serving a two-year term from 1982–1984. His and APP's new strategy of attempting a revolution from within, by working directly with the council, was thus abandoned. He shifted his focus beyond the local once again. It was mentioned above that McCaulley expressed concern in his 1985 letter to the bishops, as they began the process of gathering input for the eventual publication in 1986 of a pastoral letter on the economy, that Rome was slowly undermining the authority of the bishop's conferences, raised up by Vatican II, in an attempt to consolidate central authority in the Vatican. Furthermore, in 1985, as a result of the special synod called by John Paul II, to discuss the significance of Vatican II for the church, according to Massimo Faggioli, "many notions developed by Vatican II were suppressed or silenced," including the notion of the church, central to APP's vision, as "people of God." Although Faggioli acknowledges that the reception of Vatican II at this synod was certainly more positive than it would be later, in the early part of the twenty-first century, there was still a clear sense that Vatican II's optimism about the church's relation to the world had gone too far, and this synod was the beginning of a much more skeptical and cautious view toward this relationship. Faggioli points out that Cardinal Ratzinger was especially critical of the Vatican II document, *Gaudium et Spes*, suggesting it was guilty of "astonishing optimism." Of most concern, Faggioli goes on, this synod "represented the first major attempt of John Paul II's pontificate to steer the reception of Vatican II in a direction that he desired." His reception of Vatican II was complex, writes Faggioli, as he views John Paul II as continuing to develop the social message of Vatican II, what he calls "issues *ad extra* (social teaching, ecumenism, interreligious dialogue) and a more conservative approach to the issues *ad intra*." Finally, "the role of the episcopal conferences . . . was decisively reduced to a mere tool and deprived of real ecclesiological meaning." In Faggioli's analysis such a development reflected "the theological views" expressed by head of the CDF, Cardinal Ratzinger, in his 1985 publication "The Ratzinger Report."[54] McCaulley's concerns back in 1985 seemed completely validated by Faggioli's more recent historical analysis.

Another key social justice issue for APP has been its ongoing work with the anti-war, anti-nuclear arms race group, the Thomas Merton Center.

---

53. APP minutes, November, 1983. Private interview with APP convener of the conference, Pat Fenton.

54. Faggioli, *Vatican II*, 73–74, 84–87.

APP was instrumental in the founding of the Center and has maintained a strong relationship to the present day. As part of the APP's peace strategy, along with many other Pittsburghers, a number of priests have a history of tax-resistance, i.e., withholding taxes in protest of excessive military spending by the U.S. Government. Throughout the 1980s anywhere from six to nine priests withheld from 37 to 50 percent of their taxes in this protest. They participated as part of a wider coalition called the "Pittsburgh Tax Resisters," involving many lay people, some Catholic, some not. As always, APP would issue a press release with the names of the resisters, always citing key church documents on peace and justice issued by the hierarchy.

In 1983 APP drafted a resolution on tax resistance to be adopted by the NFPC, thus attempting to have a national impact on the issue. APP had always been one of the most active clergy groups in NFPC, especially on issues of social justice. Disappointingly for APP, the national group voted the resolution down. This was one of many disappointments with NFPC, which slowly led to frustration with the lack of a more prophetic posture on the part of the national group, eventually—later 1990s—leading APP to withdraw from official membership in the NFPC.

APP most always added ritual to their public tax protests, starting with a prayer service at a downtown Catholic Church, then processing to the Federal Building for a press conference, reading a prepared statement, peppered with biblical passages and quotes from Catholic social teaching, finally hand-delivering to the IRS office the percentage of their taxes they agreed to pay, minus, of course, what they determined went toward military spending. In 1985 they highlighted their protest by focusing attention on a submarine with nuclear capabilities named after the city: U.S.S. Pittsburgh. In 1988 they held their witness by meeting at a local soup kitchen for the poor, which was located across from a military recruitment office near the lower Hill District, reminding themselves and all those listening of the country's "misplaced priorities." They went on to cite the U.S. bishop's pastoral letters on peace (1983) and the economy (1986), quoting from each.

One year, Fr. John Oesterle suggested during a press interview that he expected the "IRS will ask the diocese to withhold the unpaid taxes and penalty from the priests' salaries, explaining that their superiors 'agree with our goal, but not the strategy.'"[55] The next year Oesterle acknowledged that, so far, the IRS had not requested the diocese to withhold taxes. To date only one priest, Don Fisher, had a personal bank account raided to cover his unpaid taxes. In Pat Fenton's case, he received a phone call from the IRS, threatening to do the same. Fenton decided to pay the taxes due.

55. Bradley-Steck, "Catholic Clergy in Nuke Protest," A-2.

The tax-resisters also appeared in a film produced by the religious order of Maryknoll Fathers and Brothers, *The Gods of Metal*, an anti-nuclear war documentary. Former Maryknoll priest, Roy Bourgeois, a great peace activist and founder of the "School of the Americas" protest, annually held at Ft. Benning, Georgia, or more recently at the Mexican border with the U.S., was co-producer of the film. The film was nominated for an Oscar in 1983. Regular tax resisters among the APP in the 1980s were: Pat Fenton, Don Fisher, Denny Kirk, Don McIlvane, Jack O'Malley, John Oesterle, Jack Brennan, Robert Schweitzer and Mark Glasgow.[56]

Also, in the mid-1980s, APP once again stepped up in support of striking Catholic grade school teachers, who were looking to negotiate for higher wages. Supporting Catholic school teacher strikes was always a controversial issue in Catholic circles. These schools were part of the diocesan parishes and the diocese, as previously reported, in the 1970s argued that such disputes needed to be settled on the parish level. APP disagreed, of course, arguing the issue of teacher wages ought to be diocesan-wide issue and should be settled at that level, since there were parishes where finances could be very tight. Their stance directly pitted APP against the diocese. This struggle was a priority for APP, most especially because church social teaching so clearly supported worker struggles for just wages and decent health care. As they often did, APP appeared on the picket line with the striking teachers in front of the diocesan building which housed their employer.

In a letter APP received from the President of the Federation of Pittsburgh Diocesan Teachers, he acknowledged that, while on the picket lines, the teachers were accused by some parents of "violating the Catholic faith." He went on: "The fact that teachers were better versed in Catholic social doctrine was of little comfort to many." But the main thrust of President Scuglia's letter to Regis Ryan, APP chair in 1985, was to say: "Of all the support that our organization was fortunate enough to receive in its recent strike action the support of your group had to be the most appreciated of all . . . the presence of your members at the rally on September 6 was like a drink of water to or members . . . [and, finally] your support was responsible for relieving a faith crisis for many of our members."[57] According to John Oesterle, "APP did lose some active members over that issue."

To the question, does APP make a difference in the lives of ordinary people through its actions, this letter seems to be another clear indication that they most certainly do, even if and when it costs them support from their own brother priests and the diocese. When the strike occurred, Regis

---

56. Atzinger, "Protest"; Tobias, "A Maryknoll Film."
57. Letter received by APP from Bruno Scuglia, September 19, 1985.

Ryan wrote the official clergy council in Pittsburgh expressing frustration that they had not taken a position on this issue of pay equity and justice. He received a response from the chair basically acknowledging the new direction of the hierarchy under Pope John Paul II and Cardinal Ratzinger by stating "The Bishop [Bevilacqua], as [now] President of the Priests' Council, decides what he wants on the agenda . . . He alone decides . . . what he wants for discussion.[58]"

As mentioned earlier, in 1988 APP entered what could be a positive turning point in its relationship with the diocese as Don Wuerl, a Pittsburgh priest, known to many APP members, became the newly appointed bishop. Of course, he had also been the target of APP discontent when he went off to Seattle to, in their minds, undermine Bishop Hunthausan. Nevertheless, especially with the positive resolution of the "Hunthausan affair," APP wiped the slate clean and imagined a much better relationship with Wuerl than with Anthony Bevilacqua, who left for Philadelphia in the early part of 1988. Bevilacqua would not be missed. APP felt they could dialogue with Wuerl. He expressed much more openness to meeting with APP than Bevilacqua. It was a fresh start in their view.

However, it didn't take long for an issue of contention with Wuerl to surface. Wuerl made a decision to close the Diocesan Justice and Peace Office in favor of a Justice and Peace Commission. Although the commission chair, Sister of St. Joseph, Janet Mock, was an APP friend and serious advocate for the church's social teachings, nevertheless, APP was concerned about the closing of an official office "with staff and decision-making power and replacing it with a commission without staff, with advisory power only and whose members were volunteers with other full-time jobs." They asked for a meeting with Wuerl but, at the same time, attempting to set a positive tone, commended Wuerl for setting up a commission and choosing Sister Mock.[59]

But even larger issues soon took over concerns of APP regarding both the local and national church, and so they began a dialogue with Bishop Wuerl in June of 1989. The dialogue began by APP sending yet another very well organized document/reflection on the state of the Pittsburgh church, asking Wuerl to read their agreed-upon thoughts in preparation for such dialogue. They entitled their document "Reflections on a Long Walk Together."

In the document for dialogue, they opened by emphasizing the "new beginnings in the Diocese of Pittsburgh," recognizing the arrival of Wuerl.

58. Letter cited in APP minutes, October, 1985.

59. APP minutes, December, 1988.

The reason for this dialogue, called for by APP, was, in part, due to APP's awareness that Bishop Wuerl was initiating a major discussion around diocesan re-organization of parishes. Under the heading of "Priests," APP cited a recent study by a bishop's committee acknowledging "a serious and substantial morale problem among priests in general." Among other things, they pointed to "the present shortage of priests and sisters." How will the diocese train new lay leaders to deal with the shortage, they wondered; Could a resident pastor be a lay woman or man, sister or couple; What about married priests, since "over 50% of all priests in the U.S. under 60 years of age are married?" (The document is referring, of course, to ordained priests who resigned and married, thus no longer exercising official ministries in the church.) What about peace and justice activities? Will they get short shrift? The document ends by expressing concern that "wealthy, powerful conservative Catholics and Vatican bureaucrats" are already working to undermine "renewal" instituted by Vatican II. Where will the Church stand?[60] Conversations with Wuerl followed.

The following year, 1990, APP once again sent a letter to Wuerl in preparation for another dialogue. This time it was sent by John Oesterle. He had recently returned from a national meeting as APP's representative to NFPC. In the letter to Wuerl he reported that the most energy at the meeting was around the topic of "priestless parishes." The vast majority of participants favored "married priesthood, the ordination of women, and the systematic formation of lay ministers." Oesterle sent some of the contents of this letter to Bishop Wuerl on to the *Pittsburgh Catholic*, who had agreed to publish the report.[61]

Later in 1990, another international synod in Rome was called by Pope John Paul II. The primary topic of this synod was "priestly formation," yet, astoundingly to APP, there was a total ban on even discussing the issue of "mandatory celibacy," as the Pope issued a statement, according to press reports, that read as follows: "Pope John Paul II has said that the vow of celibacy (and the ordination of women) are not to be debated at the synod. However, the bishops may discuss how to help priests live up to their vow of celibacy." In a press release to the editor of *The Pittsburgh Press*, APP chair Neil McCaulley sharply criticized both the pope and the participating bishops.[62]

In March of 1991, at the annual mountaintop retreat, held at Cardinal Wright Center in the city, among other things APP participants continued

60. Letter and document sent, June 28, 1989.
61. Letter sent on May 9, 1990.
62. APP press release, October 8, 1990.

to discuss reaching out to resigned priests, specifically citing Denny Kirk, who had recently left active ministry; but the group also spent time discussing an issue eventually to be implemented, namely, expanding APP's membership to include "resigned priests and their families." How would this effect the organization? What about including "wives," they asked? One member suggested that such a move would likely make "feminist and women's ordination issues" more prominent in future meetings.[63]

And in April of 1992, again in anticipation of a meeting with Bishop Wuerl, APP sent a letter to help prepare for the latest dialogue around parish reorganization. APP had concerns about the process, especially around the lack of participation of lay members of the parishes. It seems that the Executive Committee for the reorganization was made up primarily of diocesan officials. APP feared lay people would perceive decisions were already made without their input. Who is setting "parameters" for discussion, they ask? They also expressed concern that urban parishes, slowly losing members, would wind up on the short end of a diocesan formula for assigning priests, referred to as "priest/parishioner rationing." In this process of simply counting numbers of active parish members, APP felt that most clergy would be assigned to suburban parishes and urban churches would be deprived of adequate clergy presence, since their membership numbers were in decline. Advocating for more clergy in the city, APP described urban churches as "signs of hope and islands of service fostering trust with many who are not Catholic, [thus] numbers are not always the paramount issue." In this vein, they cited the post-Vatican II theological expression of "preferential option for the poor" as often central to urban church ministry. Merely counting numbers of parishioners does not honor this theological and ecclesial perspective. And what about "small Christian communities," another development from the Latin American experience: Is there a plan to develop these, especially in the inner city, they asked? Finally, they call for serious lay ministry training, thus the need to increase professional staff to properly implement a healthy reorganization.[64]

As our story moves into the 1990s, APP is full of questions as to the future of priesthood, direction of the institutional church, the role of resigned priest and the laity going forward, the seeming retrenchment and centralization of power in the papacy, and the rolling back of Vatican II's attempt at greater collegiality. APP was also concerned about its own organizational future and whether APP should consider becoming part of a

63. Mountaintop retreat, March 19, 1991.
64. Letter to Bishop Wuerl, April, 1992.

wider, more national organization of progressive Catholics. What will be the APP's response to this new moment? What will be its next, bold direction?

CHAPTER FOUR

What's in a Name
Priesthood and Prophethood of All Believers,
1992–2012

IN A LECTURE ON his own vocation to ministry as well as his theological education, the Unitarian Universalist minister and Christian social ethicist, James Luther Adams, writes: "the vitality of the church . . . depends on what Luther called the *ecclesiola in ecclesia*, the small church in the large. In this involvement of the laity we are ideally led not only to the priesthood but also the prophethood of all believers." Adams goes on to affirm, in a prayer he used at an ordination of a former student, that ministry is both about "service" and "responsibility . . . directed to both the world and the church, critical of both, yet also of the vaunted spirit of the age" and he prayed that this student would be able to develop "a balance between the priesthood and the prophethood of all believers, endeavoring to bring them together, the priest offering the gentle balm of mercy to those who are discouraged or are ill in body, mind, or estate, the prophet under the covenant rightly dividing the word of truth about us and our society."[1]

In a similar vein, Dutch Catholic theologian Ruud Bunnik, in a book entitled *Priests for Tomorrow*, has written about the loss in the Catholic Church of what he calls the "common priesthood" (priesthood of all believers, all baptized). According to Bunnik, the "common priesthood," a central notion of the early church, which was reclaimed by the Protestant reformers, also found its way into the documents of Vatican II. However, over the centuries and, more recently after Vatican II, this notion has given way to

1 Adams, *An Examined Faith*, 53–54.

an ever more "hierarchical structure of the Church and the special ministry [ordained male celibate priesthood]." This latter development, he argues, accelerated "since the Middle Ages," became a key criticism of Martin Luther's call for reforms against "strong clericalism" and for "scriptural theology," specifically a return to the notion of common priesthood, "a gift," writes Bunnik, "bestowed on every believer, including the minister." Furthermore, like Adams, Bunnik also affirms that "every Christian participates not only in the priestly but also in the prophetic and royal office of Christ."[2]

Bunnik goes on to write that in reaction to Luther's perceived attack on the priesthood, first at the Council of Trent, then deeper into the Counter Reformation and Vatican I in the latter part of the nineteenth century, "it was argued that the 'special priesthood' differs both in 'rank' and 'nature' from the 'so-called common priesthood,' and it was further reasoned that 'a priesthood of the laity is a concept that cannot be entertained seriously by anybody. It shows very poor taste and exegetical confusion to deduce anything like it from 1Peter, 2:5 and 9.'"[3]

Fast forward to Vatican II and we receive a very different message from Pope Paul VI, who in his encyclical *Ecclesiam Suam* declares: "The Christian realizes with joy that he is endowed with the dignity of the common priesthood, the characteristic of the people of God." In comparing the common priesthood with the special ministry of priesthood, Bunnik writes that "the common priesthood is more important than the special ministry since it is a basic category of God's people, while the special ministry is 'merely' a functional one." Bunnik continues:

> Insofar as there can still be talk of an authentic priesthood and real sacrifices in the New Testament, it is one that is granted to all believers. Strictly speaking, it is only by virtue of the common priesthood that the ecclesiastical minister may call himself in a true sense as priest, *hiereus-sacerdos*, together with all his fellow Christians . . . The priesthood of the laity is not a secondary participation in that of Christ, but precisely a primary one . . . [lastly] Hardly any fundamental difference of opinion seems to exist at present [1969] between the Reformation and the Catholic theology as regards their respective understanding of the common priesthood . . . [due to] the Catholic 'rediscovery' of the common priesthood . . . [ecumenically speaking] the common priesthood is a source of unity at all levels.[4]

2. Bunnik, *Priests for Tomorrow*, 39–42.

3. Bunnik, *Priests for Tomorrow*, 42.

4. Bunnik, *Priests for Tomorrow*, 43–44.

Finally, Bunnik suggests that with the central theme of Vatican II of a new emphasis and opening to the modern world, the priesthood/ministry in the Catholic Church is moving away from a primary focus on the cultic dimension of ministry, "ecclesiastical worship and celebration of the sacraments," to be much more inclusive of the importance and centrality of preaching and prophesying; thus the importance of the notion of priesthood and prophethood as it relates to ministry, both special and common. Furthermore, he suggests distinctions between "minister and layman should be stressed as little as possible." He cites St. Paul (1 Cor 12:12–31) who writes about different ministries and charisms in the community and that no one aspect of the ministry should be considered above any other. But he then goes on to offer a somewhat cautionary note about the implementation of this Vatican II "rediscovery" when he writes:

> The implications of the people of God ecclesiology of Vatican II have by no means yet been established [again, he is writing in the latter part of the 1960s]. The declericalization of the idea of the special ministry, which is primarily functional, will take some time, not only because it involves a theoretical theology, but also because it means abandoning an existential situation in which many put great faith. One can only say that it is required by the service of the minister to both the Church and the world.[5]

Bunnik was prescient when he stated that such change "will take some time." In writing about ministry in a 1985 book entitled *The Church with a Human face: A New and Expanded Theology of Ministry*, Dominican theologian Edward Schillebeeckx offered a lengthy analysis of what the special Bishop's Synod of 1971 said about the priesthood as it followed up on Vatican II. In a section entitled: "the crisis of the apolitical, celibate priesthood," Schillebeeckx writes about the deep polarization among the bishops at this synod on the priesthood, between what he calls "supernaturalism," the perspective of bishops tied to a pre-Vatican understanding of priesthood, wanting to emphasize the "distinctiveness" of the special priesthood vis-à-vis the common priesthood of all baptized, and "horizontalism," the perspective of those adopting a Vatican II vision of priesthood with its reclamation of the notion of the common priesthood of all believers and the prophetic focus of priesthood emphasizing the social and political dimensions of the faith. This "obsession" on the part of the bishops with maintaining such distinctions or "clear dividing lines" between common and special priesthood was of "little concern" in the New Testament, despite its recognizing "the particularity

5. Bunnik, *Priests for Tomorrow*, 93–94.

of each member's charisma and service," writes Schillebeeckx. The Counter Reformation, solidified through the Council of Trent, emphasized a priest-hood focused on the sacramental and cultic, specifically the Eucharist and confession, whereas the Vatican II elaboration emphasized preaching and community-building. After much deliberation at this 1971 Synod, sadly, no unanimity was reached; thus the status quo prevailed, despite the great clamor by many bishops about the pastoral crisis of a shortage of priests, poor morale, and the concern for the community's access to the Eucharist.[6]

According to Schillebeeckx, the "impasse" could have been bridged if the bishops had been willing to recognize and empower the local church to respond appropriately to its own pastoral needs. They weren't "brave enough" to do that, he goes on, thus missing an historical opportunity to address a deep pastoral concern. "Subsequent history" might deem this de-cision "as the great refusal," opined Schillebeeckx. He thought that Peruvian Bishop Damert Bellido "hit the nail on the head" when, in a speech at the Synod, he declared: "Any attempt at changing an infrastructure (in this case the priesthood) within a greater structure (the church) without changing this greater structure is a utopia." Schillebeeckx suggested a better word might have been not "utopia" but "ideology."[7]

Another backdrop for some of the concern of the more conservative bishops at the Synod was the emergence of the Latin American liberation theology movement (of which Damert-Bellido was an important hierarchi-cal supporter), which had political implications for the priesthood and the church that clearly scared some of the participants. Vatican II and, later, es-pecially the Latin American bishops conference in 1968, reflected in certain documents, "were opposed to any division between the process of human-ization and the growth of the kingdom of God," and Schillebeekcx went on to argue that any purely apolitical perspective on the church and priesthood would certainly overlook the deep suffering of God's people as they struggle with oppression and poverty.[8]

One other issue of import that surfaced during this 1971 Synod was that of married priesthood. According to Schillebeeckx, more than half the Synod bishops advocated for a married priesthood, based on the deep pastoral needs in their own contexts. Some argued that change could be al-lowed in those regions where the Christian community deemed it necessary due to pastoral considerations. Furthermore, one African bishop pointed out that only a married priesthood had full legitimacy in his context, i.e.,

6. Schillebeeckx, *The Church*, 209–13.
7. Schillebeeckx, *The Church*, 218–19.
8. Schillebeeckx, *The Church*, 220–21.

people presumed that priests and bishops were married and had families. Despite the declaration in the final documents of the Synod that married priesthood was certainly "theologically possible," and that celibacy needed further investigation and understanding in a modern context, going forward the status quo prevailed, yet another historic opportunity lost in the view of Schillebeeckx.[9]

Although the initial impetus for the founding of APP in 1966 was to study assiduously the documents of Vatican II and attempt to live out the Council's teachings as well as challenge the institutional church to follow suit, I have no clear indication that the group spent a lot of time analyzing this notion of common priesthood or seriously considered its implications for their own ministries, at least in the early years. On the other hand, their consistent call for married priesthood and women priests may actually be a pretty clear sign that they imbibed this Vatican II teaching quite well. Certainly, though, they immediately put into practice the prophetic (political) charism as a central role for the priesthood and the Catholic Church as the state of the modern world became a serious concern. But the early 1990s seems to me to represent a new moment in the group's evolution. As two of their most active as well as youngest members, Pat Fenton (ordained and joined APP in 1971) and Denny Kirk (ordained and joined APP in 1979), resigned from active ministry, Kirk in 1989, Fenton in 1991, both eventually to marry, the group was not adding members. Also, of course, those remaining were aging, a few approaching retirement age. One of their original and oldest members, Don McIlvane, retired from active ministry, though not from participation in APP, in 1994. Furthermore, vocations to the priesthood were diminishing and parish closings and consolidations were well underway. What would be their future, they wondered, and what would be the future of the priesthood?

9. Schillebeeckx, *The Church*, 224. "In the name of the Ghanaian bishops, Mgr. P.K. Sarong said that in accordance with the social ideas of his people a (spiritual) leader of a community needed to be married, because among them marriage was the sign of adulthood and potential leadership. This was so obvious that after a round trip another African bishop found that when he said goodbye to those whom he had visited they spontaneously sent greetings to his wife and children. He added, 'Only the catechists smiled. For the others, there was nothing unusual about it.'" In a similar fashion, a former nun who left and married, later having three children, shared with me that when Fr. Jack O'Malley was serving St. Joseph's parish on the Northside of Pittsburgh, she lived next door with her husband and family in the former convent, which they had purchased. One day as she was walking the neighborhood with her children a neighbor (an African-American neighbor, not a member of the Catholic Church) greeted her matter-of-factly, as "Mrs. O'Malley," reflecting the presumption that Fr. O'Malley was married and actually lived next door to the church and rectory with his wife and kids. Of course, most of the black clergy in the city would have been married.

Hoping that the wider church and their own diocese would begin addressing some of their major concerns about ministry and the future, APP drafted a letter to the diocese and all brother priests in anticipation of the annual Pittsburgh priests' gathering in Oglebay, West Virginia, in September of 1992. They were hoping to get APP concerns on the agenda. In their letter they raised a number of serious issues: the stance of the institutional church regarding discrimination against "homosexuals" (which the APP considered "egregious"); the change in retirement age from 70 to 75 without consultation; concerns about lack of consultation on reorganization and clergy assignments; lack of open dialogue and reporting on major issues in the diocesan newspaper, *The Pittsburgh Catholic*; refusal to take seriously their own proposals around team ministry; the question of married clergy and women priests, especially in the face of clergy shortage and related issue of the possible lack of availability of Sunday Eucharist in areas without priests.[10]

At the same time APP was trying to get its own diocese to address some of these challenging issues, the group had received a proposal for the APP to consider from the spouse of a resigned priest. Kathy Grabowski, married to a former priest, Giles Grabowski, having been warmly welcomed into parish life by APP member and pastor, Don Fisher, wrote a lengthy proposal asking APP to consider altering its membership to include resigned and married clergy and their spouses, as well as resigned priests who might in the future marry. "Each active priest within the APP who is committed to a married clergy would make their assigned church a (safe house) place of worship to take place within a parish community," the proposal read. Grabowski imagined that Pittsburgh could "create a model with plans to influence the associations nationally and internationally." Finally, she wrote, although there were risks for both APP members (discipline by diocesan officials) and resigned priests and their wives (rejection in the parish and new wounds), "The gains include a revitalization of APP, a connection for married clergy and alienated, wounded Catholics, and an opportunity for spiritual growth for all."[11]

After reading Grabowski's proposal and spending many hours in deep discernment, APP decided to conduct a major survey about the future with current APP members, "non-canonical priests" (resigned and married,) and some lay supporters. In an introductory letter to the survey, APP Chairperson Greg Swiderski wrote that on its celebration of twenty-five years of existence (actually twenty-six): "In order to broaden its vision, ministry,

10. The letter was signed by APP's steering committee.
11. Proposal to APP by Kathy Grabowski, July 24, 1992.

and support system, The Association of Pittsburgh Priests is considering extending its membership to include all those who wish to embrace its mission of renewal and reform of church and society . . . priests who have left the active ministry (non-canonical priests), their wives, (when applicable), women and married men who wish to be ordained, and other laity."[12]

The survey included questions about membership in APP, church renewal efforts and a myriad of social justice concerns. The respondents were asked to rate how important each of the concerns was. Across the board there was support for married and women clergy, making celibacy optional, "breaking down barriers between clergy and laity," and deep affirmation for social justice work. There was great support for opening up membership, raising the question among a few as to the possibility of a name change for APP. Among current APP members—all priests, of course—a few dissented on the question of opening membership. A few others suggested founding a totally new organization. Another was a bit more pointed: "I would keep the APP as it is, to be for priests. I believe this new concept should be another distinct organization which I could support and belong to. Former priests, yes, but not their wives or women in general. I think the new idea would bring the APP to an end." Others complained that APP had lost its direction, purpose and relevancy and had become too "adversarial." On a somewhat crankier note, amazingly, one complained the group met on his "day off," another that "Tuesday is bad for me." Ever respectful and inclusive of all viewpoints, APP included such comments in their results.

Although I cannot document the exact date when APP decided to open its membership to those beyond canonical priesthood, and no members I interviewed could remember exactly, they did update their mission statement sometime in late 1993 or early 1994 to read: "The Association of Pittsburgh Priests is a diocesan-wide organization of ordained and non-ordained women and men who act on our baptismal call to be priests and prophets. Our mission is to carry out a ministry of justice and renewal, rooted in the Gospel and Spirit of Vatican Council II, in ourselves, the Church, and the world." Hence, APP had embarked on a new understanding of itself, raising up the early church notion, reclaimed by the Protestant Reformation, and rediscovered by Vatican Council II, of the common priesthood (and prophethood) of all believers/baptized. By this decision APP was calling all to priestly ministry, understanding its vision as fully implementing the teachings of Vatican II, which over the preceding decades seemed to have been thwarted by a reactionary, hierarchical leadership. APP made a bold stand for their notion of a future church, a remarkable development.

12. Survey distributed on October 14, 1992.

As mentioned above, some of the survey respondents suggested that if APP opened its membership, a name change should follow, to reflect the new reality. Over the years, the issue of a name change has surfaced many times. Sometimes it came as a request from the local bishop. This time it came from the survey as APP altered its membership. Subsequently, every few years, the issue would re-emerge, and each time the group voted not to do it.

Throughout its fifty-three year history, every bishop has at one point or another requested that APP change its name, suggesting it was confusing to Catholics who presumed whenever APP went public they were speaking for the official group of Pittsburgh clergy, i.e., the clergy council. At one point, as was noted earlier, APP decided to "infiltrate" the "official" clergy council, thus promoting change from within. Amazingly, APP member Neil McCaulley became chair of the clergy council for two years, 1982–84, while, at the same time, maintaining membership in APP. But that strategy was abandoned after two years, as it was clear the clergy council and its agenda was controlled by the bishop, after a new Canon Law was promulgated in 1983 giving total control to the local bishop. The clergy council's agenda thus became the bishop's agenda.

APP's vision was always to have an independent voice, free to support or challenge the institutional church. Each time the group was asked to change its name they respectfully answered they would pray about it and consult the wider membership; each time they respectfully declined the bishop's request. Remarkably, despite multiple requests over the years, and the sometimes tense relationship between APP and these various bishops, a respectful and open relationship has always been maintained for over fifty years. Though Bishop Bevilacqua (1983–1988) was clearly the least interested in dialogue and the most antagonistic toward the group, questioning their very existence, he never attempted to shut them down in his relatively short tenure. His posture was to ignore the group as best he could.

Although the issue of name change did come up occasionally in the first twenty-five years it became more of a concern for some in 1993 when APP opened its membership to non-ordained people. In this period APP developed a proposal for discussion, outlining the issue as follows: "Reasons for changing the name, reasons for not changing the name and reasons for putting off the whole matter till later." With a new open membership policy and the aforementioned new mission statement emphasizing "baptismal priesthood," not the canonical priesthood, maybe the wider public would be confused with the ongoing name, imagining it was still only a group of ordained clergy. On the other hand, "the APP has a proud history . . . changing the name would disconnect that . . . and cause us to move away from our heritage . . . our name gives us a certain clout with the diocese (and) many in the media . . . count on the APP for some juicy pronouncements. Groups do not develop this relationship with the media overnight." In the end, they decided on option #3, i.e., "putting off the whole matter," since with fewer and fewer clergy going forward, the group acknowledged that it might eventually "merge with a group like Call to Action."

At a regular meeting in January of 2001 the group once again voted to keep its original name. A month prior, in December of 2000, a former seminarian, Scott Fabean, now married with three children, wrote a passionate letter to the group advising them to maintain their traditional name. He had a few compelling arguments for maintaining the APP name, e.g., "any illegitimate pronouncements from Rome are most assuredly met with an equally reasoned response from the APP," reassuring for Fabean. But his most convincing reason was his final statement: "The APP has earned a lot of clout with our bishop and clergy of the diocese, the press, other peace and justice groups, and the laity. I think it would be a little short-sighted to let all that go. In fact a terrific reason to keep the name of APP is the fact that the hierarchy of our diocese and the Church would feel more relaxed if the APP wasn't around. Please keep their feet to the fire. After all, I've heard it said: 'the best place to sink a ship is from the inside.'"[13]

APP and its name remained on the radar of the bishop and official clergy council in 2004. APP's steering committee received a letter from the Rev. James Young, Episcopal Vicar for Clergy, acknowledging that there was discomfort among many diocesan priests that the APP, especially since it is now no longer merely a group of ordained clergy, was sowing confusion as to who they were speaking for in their public pronouncements. The letter even suggested a lack of "honesty" in "continuing the use of the name when the vast majority of your members are not priests . . . [though] we note the theological subtlety in your mission statement ('baptismal call to be priests')." Finally, the letter suggests, "we wonder if continuing to use this name is really an exercise of the justice we seek in 'truth in advertising.'" As often has been the case over the years, despite the somewhat subtle attack on the APP's integrity, invoking words like "justice" and "truth," the Rev. Young ends the note on a theme of "fraternal communication . . . (merely) sharing with you concerns raised by brother priests and others." Of note, the letter was sent not to the entire APP membership but only to "brother priests."[14]

13. Letter to APP from Scott Fabean, December 21, 2000.

14. Letter received from Fr. Young on November 12, 2004. In an interview with Fr. Lou Vallone, November 19, 2018, a diocesan priest and member of the diocesan clergy council at the time. He shared with me that Bishop Wuerl wanted to force APP to change its name, to which Vallone responded that they had every right to the name and,

As far as I can tell, or that any current member can remember, APP politely responded that they had decided to maintain their original name. However, one APP member, Fr. Warren Metzler, had a very pointed and slightly cynical answer to the letter and made a few suggestions to APP membership. In a letter to APP leadership, Metzler encouraged APP to publicize the letter from Fr. Young, "Since nothing should live in darkness." Also, he had heard from another priest with the following suggestion, echoing a sentiment held by many APP members: "They want you to change your name to more honestly reflect who you really are? In that case the Catholic Church in the U.S. should more honestly change its name to The Republican Party!" Ultimately, Metzler suggested no response would be most appropriate, writing: "The letter hardly merits an answer. Action merits reaction. Childishness merits none." The name survived yet another challenge.

In its most recent encounter, and last, I believe, with a bishop who had requested a name change, sometime in 2008, current Bishop David Zubik asked the group to consider the change. I was told anecdotally by several members that after a period of "discernment," the group's steering committee met with the bishop to say that after "prayerful reflection" they had decided to keep the name. In this face to face encounter the bishop responded that he was deeply disappointed by their decision, to which APP member Jack O'Malley replied that now the bishop knew how the APP had felt all these years.

Shakespeare wrote: "What's in a name? . . . a rose / By any other name would smell as sweet" (*Romeo and Juliet*, II, ii, 43–44); evidently, for APP, quite a bit! Quoting Shakespeare in a 2008 missive to the group, long-time APP member, Neil McCaulley cautioned against a change as he wrote: "We think there is a lot of important history in our name, The Association of Pittsburgh Priests."[15]

Some might consider I've belabored this issue of the name APP, spending too much time reporting the various conversations and challenges from the official church. Who really cares? Is there that much at stake in a name? Is the diocese right that the name confuses people and misrepresents their membership? My thinking, not unlike the rationale of former seminarian, Scott Fabean, is that the name is quite vital to what APP has stood for over fifty years, i.e., a unique group of clergy, and since 1993, clergy, married

---

in fact, were on solid theological grounding by referencing the notion of priesthood of all believers, as Fr. Young acknowledged, by referring to the call of all baptized to the priesthood as a "theological subtlety." Furthermore, they had a right to exist, argued Vallone. He thus claimed he dissuaded Wuerl from doing anything about APP, reasoning that it was less and less significant and would eventually fade away.

15. Letter to APP from Neil McCaulley, May 13, 2008.

priests and spouses, nuns and laity, women and men, consistently standing for reform in the church and society and showing the way for what the
future church could look like if Vatican II were fully implemented. Their
witness is, among other things, to re-emphasize and elaborate on the notion of common priesthood, or better, "priesthood and prophethood of all
baptized," a notion reclaimed by Pope Paul VI but, as of yet, not fully (or
at all) embraced by the institutional church. In this vein, I've been told by
several members, that Anthony Padavano, theologian and spiritual writer,
a former priest now married and in the leadership of a pro-married clergy
association Corpus, has over the years in his many visits to Pittsburgh as a
guest speaker, strongly suggested they maintain the name Association of
Pittsburgh Priests as a vital symbol of where the church should be headed.
Although to this day there is still talk of a possible name change, or more
especially the merging with some other Catholic reform movement such as
Call to Action, to date APP has resisted calls for such a change.[16]

Though APP's mission statement has continued to emphasize mutual
support, church renewal and social justice outreach, I do have a sense that
since the change in membership instituted in 1993, the group has devoted
somewhat more energy to church renewal, and a bit less to social justice, in
part, perhaps quite appropriately, allowing other groups such as the Thomas
Merton Center and Pennsylvania (originally Pittsburgh) Interfaith Impact
Network (PIIN) to carry the social justice banner more consistently and
coherently. An indication of this subtle shift was articulated in a letter to
the steering committee from a lay woman member of APP. In June of 1994,
Karen Gorham wrote to express "disappointment" about the "focus" of a
recent APP meeting. She expressed frustration with a lengthy discussion
at the meeting over Pope John Paul II's recent letter suggesting the Church
was in no position to consider ordaining women, while "reports on peace
and social justice" lasted only about fifteen minutes. She then listed a myriad
of critical issues the group should have addressed but didn't. What about
"prophetic witness" to justice, she asked? "I am still trying to figure out why
so many people put so much of their time and energy into what one man,
who lives in a big house in Italy, has to say or what he thinks."[17]

One long term APP priest member tried to defend the concern with
internal church matters by responding to Gorham's criticism "that we must

16. In the same interview as above with Fr. Vallone, he opined that he thought APP
lacked a good public relations strategy. That is, when APP changed its membership to
reflect the notion of common priesthood, they needed to explain this shift publicly,
thus educating the diocese, clergy and laity, on the legitimate theological notion of the
baptismal call of all to priesthood. Thus, Vallone argues, confusion still reins.

17. Letter to APP from Karen Gorham, June 21, 1994.

deal with justice inside the Church in order to have integrity in addressing justice issues in the broader community."[18]

An internal church concern that has been there from the beginning with APP, i.e., the question of mandatory celibacy and married clergy, as well as the role of women in the church, especially around ordination, seemed to me to become an even deeper concern as the membership of APP changed.

In May of 1994, Pope John Paul II issued a pastoral letter, *Ordinatio Sacerdotalis*, in which he stated: "The Church has no authority whatsoever to confer priestly ordination on women and this judgment is to be definitively held by all the church's faithful." Case closed, it would seem. Not so, responded APP. It immediately issued a press release and, along with forty or so others, women religious and lay people, gathered at outside the downtown chancery building both to challenge the Pope's statement and call for an open dialogue on the issue. They followed this public witness, some months later, by sending off a letter to the pope, "their elder brother, Bishop of Rome," agreeing not to openly defy him by preaching against the ruling, but rather declaring they would continue to openly and publicly discuss women's ordination. At the same time they challenged the pope to place women in leadership positions in the church, suggesting that the lack of female presence in such roles "is a scandal and weakens your credibility in this whole area of women's role in the church."

Described as "maverick priests" by the Greensburg and Pittsburgh newspaper, the *Tribune-Review*, for their position vis-a-vis the pope, APP leader Don Fisher responded by explaining APP's dissent, distinguishing between "tradition and divine law," pointing out the former can be changed and in the course of church history has been. Not ordaining women is simply a church tradition, he argued. When quizzed on APP's position, diocesan spokesperson, Rev. Ron Lenguin, responded that the group had little standing in the church and had "no basis to question traditions," a very curious position as Fisher was a priest in good standing in the church and was well-read enough to know that historians and theologians question church tradition all the time.[19]

In November of 1994, following up on this perspective, APP had a letter published by the liberal Catholic newspaper, *National Catholic Reporter*. The letter elaborated on Fisher's point on tradition and criticized the pope for attempting "to stifle dissent and end discussion," for by doing so "he sends signals that demoralize those who are trying to serve the church with fidelity and creativity. He also misrepresents his own authority. Tradition

18. McIlvane, minutes of APP meeting, September 19, 1994.
19. Seate, "Rogue Priests."

is just that; tradition. It is not, and can never be confused with, divine law." Though respecting the "authority of the Bishop of Rome," they insist on their "own search for truth, our own right to speak and discuss with others." They reject "blind obedience" to such teachings.[20]

Interestingly, not all APP members and sympathizers supported the group's actions around women's ordination. Aforementioned Pat McCann, an APP friend, Sister of Mercy and church historian, weighed in by writing APP a lengthy letter in December of 1995 expressing reservations about ordination being the key issue for women in the church at the current moment. Rather, she suggested, the question of "women's leadership in all of the ways now possible" is more pressing. Specifically, she wrote, we need: "women on parish teams, as pastoral administrators, as education leaders, as lectors and Eucharistic ministers, as parish/diocesan business managers, as chancellors in dioceses, etc." McCann reasoned that once such roles for women were common, "then ordaining men and women, married and celibate, will follow." She alluded to a letter from the pope in May of 1995, suggesting "clear signs of a major evolution in thinking" on women's issues. Furthermore, she opined that "newspaper ads are a useless strategy," expressing a preference for "education, empowerment and dialogue."[21]

Another APP woman friend had expressed similar hesitation on women's ordination in the previous year. Suzanne Polen argued that, despite her long term interest in the ordination of women, the pope's current position might be "providential," i.e., "It prevents, for a while, a top-down solution, and allows time for a further de-clericalization to the Church . . . My hope is that by the time women are openly ordained, bottom-up liberation forces will have purged much of this structural sinfulness (sexism)."[22]

In 1998, APP member Sarah Wellinger attended a conference in Milwaukee on "women and men seeking equality" in the Church. 3500 participated. A bishop, Ray Lucker, presided over the final liturgy and was "assisted by several women, including Mary Ramerman," who had been recently fired as an assistant pastor in a church in Rochester, NY. The pastor in the Rochester church, Jim Callan, was also removed for, among other things, allowing Ramerman "an active role in the celebration of the liturgy." Corpus Christi was an urban parish that grew from two-hundred members in the 1970s to 3500 by the latter 1990s and had developed all sorts of ministries for the marginalized and economically challenged; a model church, one might suggest. However, the local bishop was forced to remove Callan

20. APP, "Priests Retain Right."

21. Letter to APP from Sr. Pat McCann, December 3, 1995.

22. Letter to APP from Suzanne Polen, July 11, 1994.

and Ramerman at the direction of then Cardinal Ratzinger, who deemed Callan "an untrustworthy priest." Wellinger reported back to APP about this moving experience of women and men celebrating together, a dynamic and exciting example of future church, yet she also expressed discouragement over the news of the termination of the co-ministries of Callan and Ramerman, realizing the difficulties that lie ahead in trying to create such a church, given current church leadership.[23]

I actually visited this church while at a conference in Rochester earlier in 1998, while Callan and Ramerman were still in leadership. It was a truly extraordinary experience, imagining that this was exactly what church renewal ought to be about. After experiencing a very lively and participatory liturgy, I made an appointment to meet the priest the next day. I was amazed at what had been accomplished in his twenty-year ministry. By all accounts, as I learned in speaking with various parishioners and staff, as well as Callan himself, he seemed an extraordinarily "trustworthy" and admired Catholic priest. Here was an example of Vatican II's call to implement and promote the common priesthood all of believers. Sadly, this ministry was ended and Callan and Ramerman eventually became part of an independent Catholic Church in the Rochester area.

In June of 2004, APP initiated a letter campaign involving Pittsburgh area Catholics to promote the ordination of married men to the priesthood. They gathered 1139 letters with the intent of presenting them to the Catholic Conference of U.S. Bishops. In the letter they pointed out that with the dwindling number of celibate priests, ordinary Catholics would eventually be denied the celebration of the Mass and the receiving of the Eucharist on a regular basis. To publicize this campaign, APP held a press conference in downtown Pittsburgh near the chancery office of the diocese calling for optional celibacy and a married clergy. They pointed out that the Pittsburgh diocese had gone from 350 priests in 1999 to 299 priests in 2004. Again, the diocesan spokesman, Fr. Ron Lenguin, dismissed the effort of APP, suggesting the group had few active priests, didn't speak for the diocese, and that the number of signatures was not "that significant."[24]

In 2005, leading up to a special international bishop's synod in Rome in October, APP once again tried to raise publicly the issue of the ordination of married priests and the ordination of women, at least to the Diaconate, connecting it directly to the right of the Catholic faithful to have access to the Eucharist.

---

23. APP minutes, November, 1998.
24. Rodgers, "Group Backs Marriage," A-25.

As often is the case, APP began its process of raising a key church issue by first contacting the bishop and requesting a meeting in order to discuss concerns. John Oesterle, then APP's steering committee chair, sent the request to Bishop Wuerl. As always, Wuerl was very gentlemanly in his response, ever courteous and almost charming. However, his response made it clear that APP's decision of 1993 to alter its membership had the corresponding effect of changing Wuerl's interest in engaging with the group. Wuerl began his response by writing "As always I am pleased to meet with brother priests and would certainly be open to finding an occasion when we could discuss the Synod on the Eucharist." After this opening offer, the tone changed dramatically as he noted APP's interest in including other members of APP in the meeting. This represented a "dilemma" for Wuerl as it had for the official priests' council, described in its 2004 letter to APP, namely, the "ambiguity" that APP "is not made up entirely of Pittsburgh priests and does not represent nor speak for the priests of Pittsburgh." For Wuerl this only leads to "confusion and even a sense of misrepresentation that can cloud . . . issues." He ended, as he began, respectfully, "with every good wish, I am Faithfully in Christ, Donald Wuerl, Bishop of Pittsburgh."[25]

Oesterle's first response to the group concerning Wuerl's letter was "Most of us had believed Bishop Wuerl was the driving force behind the 'Priests Council effort.' That belief looks to be accurate." Oesterle then laid out possible options for responding to Wuerl, none of which included a "brother priests meeting by ourselves with the bishop," but left it up to the group to decide. However, he encouraged the group to reach consensus soon, as the next APP gathering was the annual picnic and "I hate to do business at picnics."

APP responded to Wuerl quickly with a note written by Oesterle and signed by the entire steering committee. It began by stating to the bishop: "We regret that you will not meet with the Association of Pittsburgh Priests." The letter went on to express their concern with the ongoing and deepening problem of priest shortage, raising the concern of the possible limited availability of the Eucharistic celebration in the future for the faithful who were used to frequent accessibility to this sacrament. In ten years, the letter continued, projections have the diocese down to "167 active priests. Is it time for the bishops to discuss optional celibacy . . . Is it time to discuss women as deacons?" Though they acknowledged that such issues were not part of the meeting's agenda, they asked Wuerl to carry these ideas to the synod meeting.

25. Letter from Bishop Wuerl, July, 2005.

Since no meeting between APP and Wuerl took place before the synod, APP implemented their next form of communication, to the public at large, by having a press conference downtown in front of the chancery office of the diocese in September of 2005. In it they highlighted that Bishop Wuerl would play a major role at the synod by being chosen as the representative by his brother bishops in the U.S. They emphasized that "over the past 20 years the number of Catholics in the U.S. has grown by almost 20 million while the number of priests has declined by over 15,000." APP spokesperson at the press conference, Fr. Garry Dorsey, asked: "What happens when the Eucharist is not available because of the shortage of priests . . . will bishops . . . listen to the Catholic community on this topic?" Dorsey mentioned that a letter to this effect was delivered to Bishop Wuerl earlier in the day along with the names of 28,500 Catholics (nationally, 1000 from Pittsburgh) who signed petitions gathered by a Cleveland group called Future Church, asking for such dialogue at the synod.[26]

Although APP decided not to accept Bishop Wuerl's offer to meet with "brother priests alone," it strikes me as somewhat notable that, despite the group's insistence on remaining independent and inclusive of non-clergy as full members, and the tension that this has created between the APP and five successive bishops, Wuerl's offer to meet with "brother priests" seemed a certain acknowledgment on his part of respect that he held toward the priests in the group. That is, not only did he never attempt to discipline them, but he seemed rather to desire a warm, collegial relationship with them. In a private interview, John Oesterle told me that Wuerl once commented to a non-APP priest that he had great admiration and respect for the APP members as loyal and faithful ecclesial servants, but couldn't ever understand their "other agenda," evidently referring to their frequent public dissent on both internal church issues and issues around social justice. Over the years APP performed an incredible dance between loyalty to and respect for each bishop, integrity in their quest for truth, as well as, independence and, at times, determined opposition and dissent.

Evidently the issue of priest shortage did get discussed at the October, 2005 synod—could APP's public pronouncements have influenced that? As a follow-up to the synod, a committee of bishops was formed with the title: "Post-Synod Exhortation Committee," and, as anticipated, Bishop Wuerl was appointed to that group and was assigned to help write Pope Benedict's final synod exhortation in the fall of 2006. In response to this, a coalition of any number of Catholic groups, organized by the same Future Church group in Cleveland, including APP, came together in March of 2006 to send

26. APP press release, September 28, 2005.

an open letter to Bishop Wuerl, to be published in the *National Catholic Reporter.*

According to this open letter, the bishops did discuss the shortage of clergy and the threat this posed to the availability of the Eucharist. Reportedly, four of twelve working groups at the synod recommended studying the feasibility of married priests, though the "final synod propositions" neglected to mention this issue. Disappointingly, "the ministry of Catholic women was essentially invisible at the synod." As the open letter praised Bishop Wuerl for some of his "interventions at the synod," they made a plea to "Please encourage Pope Benedict XVI to open ordination to married as well as celibate men, and reopen the long overdue discussion about women's full ministerial equality in the Church, beginning with ordaining women to the diaconate."[27]

Not long after this, a most significant event in the life of Roman Catholicism in the United States occurred on a boat, the Gateway Clipper, on the three rivers of Pittsburgh. On August first of 2006, eight women were ordained as Roman Catholic priests. This was the first such ordination in the United States. Roman Catholic *Womenpriests* organized the four-hour ceremony, presided over by three women bishops. Joan Houk, an APP member for many years, was among the ordained. At that point in time, *Womenpriests* counted five bishops and forty priests and deacons, along with one-hundred and twenty candidates, mostly from the U.S., in the clerical "pipeline." The first ordinations occurred in 2002 in Austria, when a "renegade" German (male) bishop ordained seven women; the Vatican immediately ex-communicated the women. Concerning the ordinations in Pittsburgh, the Pittsburgh Diocese's response was more nuanced. Diocesan spokesman, Fr. Ron Lenguin, released a statement that read: "This unfortunate ceremony will take place outside the Church and undermines the unity of the Church. Those attempting to confer Holy Orders have, by their own actions, removed themselves from the Church, as have those who present themselves for such an invalid ritual." Interestingly, though, the diocese said they would welcome back anyone who chose to leave the group. I have been told that no APP priests attended the ordination, but many other APP members did. Overall attendance was 425.[28]

27. No exact date found, but it was likely in April of 2006.

28. Information was gathered from several articles by APP member and married priest, William Podobinski, and sent as an e-mail to APP on August 3, 2006. Current APP members who were at the ordination are: Molly Rush, Joyce Rothermel, Jane and John Pillar, Evelyn Christi and David Aleva. There was actually a previous ordination of nine women, four priests and five deacons, on the St. Lawrence River, in international waters, in July of 2005. The boat had sailed from the Canadian side.

In anticipation of this event, APP decided to draft an op-ed for the local *Pittsburgh Post-Gazette*, supporting women's ordination. On July 30, the day before the riverboat ordination, the newspaper printed the piece under the name of a former Sister of Mercy and current member of APP, Marcia Snowden, in the name of APP. In this piece, Snowden pointed out that a papal commission of biblical scholars concluded in 1976 "that there was no scriptural reason to say that women cannot be ordained." The article also applauded all other Christian denominations, as well as Jewish congregations, who have ordained women or invited them into "public ritual leadership." The statement ended with the words: "This is a time . . . for all to share wisdom and recognize the call of women to the Roman Catholic Priesthood." The newspaper also printed an opposing view alongside APP's statement, entitled "Women Catholic Priests? It's a Non-Starter," written by the director of communications for the Catholic diocese, Robert Lockwood. In his rebuttal to the idea of women priests, Lockwood cites tradition and the fact that Jesus chose male apostles, arguing that this tradition cannot be undone.[29]

Shortly after the APP publication of its support for women's ordination and, by implication, the riverboat ordination itself, APP members Jack O'Malley and Neil McCaulley co-authored a letter to the editor strongly supporting the op-ed piece by Snowden and challenging the counter editorial. Pretty quickly the heat was turned up on O'Malley and McCaulley, and they were asked to meet with two diocesan officials about their support for this event, raising questions around canon law and the priests' public stance. There was enough concern about the meeting with diocesan officials, Frs. Frank Almade (an off and on APP supporter!) and Larry DiNardo, that APP brought a civil and canon lawyer, Paul Titus, a practicing Catholic layman and friend to the priests, with them to the meeting. The two APP priests refused to meet at the diocesan building, so the two diocesan clergy came to them. Sometime after the meeting, Titus helped O'Malley and McCaulley consider how to respond to the diocese, though no letter was sent.[30]

Finally, in late October, O'Malley and McCaulley submitted their formal response. Despite advice from the lawyer to the contrary, the two APP priests decided to write their own letter to the two diocesan officials as "fellow priests." In their response, they suggested "The spectacle of the river boat 'ordination' ceremony of last August created a media-frenzy. The underlying issue of the emerging role of women in the various ministries of the Church was lost in the overly sensational coverage of the event." They went on to

29 Snowden, "Now, More than Ever," and Lockwood, "It's a Non-starter," H-1.

30. APP minutes, August 28, 2006.

say that "statements in the media attributed to Church officials" as to the role of women in the Church "caused a great deal of anxiety among many women who are serving the Church well." APP felt it needed to respond to these concerns raised by many women, thus their initial letter to the editor. Interestingly, they wrote the letter to the newspaper not as parish priests, on church stationary, or even using their clergy titles i.e., they simply wrote as Jack O'Malley and Neil McCaulley. However, the paper "outed" them and printed their names with clerical designations. They ended their letter to the diocese by regretting "any misunderstandings or harms inflicted by inappropriate wording."[31] The matter faded, McCaulley and O'Malley got a hand slap, and APP members dodged yet another bullet with the diocese.

Four years later APP was at it again, this time in a direct communication to Pope Benedict. In a letter sent on June 2, 2010, APP asked the Pope to renew the priesthood by ordaining women and married priests, welcoming back resigned and married priests, and affirming gay women and men as worthy of priestly ordination. They concluded their plea for change by these words: "Dear Pope Benedict, we hope you will receive this call, which we make, and these thoughts and feelings, which we share in the same spirit in which they were forged: love for the priesthood, love for our Church and hope for the days ahead, Sincerely yours in Christ the Priest, Association of Pittsburgh Priests."[32]

Over the years since altering APP's membership to include other than ordained, celibate priests, one casualty of this decision has been APP's ability to use diocesan-related buildings. In 1996 APP invited Anthony Padavano, a married priest and president of Corpus, a national association advocating for married priesthood, to give a retreat at the Cardinal Wright Center. APP had met there many times over the years. That privilege was about to end. They received a letter from a diocesan official, Rev. Joseph Kleppner, that informed APP that the Wright Center would not be available for its use on this occasion, as such use "could be a source of scandal for the laity and priests of this local Church . . . [and as] contrary to the mind of the universal Church or this local Church and her bishop."[33]

Immediately APP wrote Bishop Wuerl to express its displeasure, reminding Wuerl that he had actually met with Padavano and Corpus while head of the Bishop's Committee on Priestly Life and Ministry some years back, demonstrating "openness and dialogue (reflecting) the spirit of Christ and the Church." This decision, they suggested, "closing the door for a

31. Letter to diocese dated October 24, 2006.
32. Letter dated June 2, 2010, "A Call to Pope benedict XVI."
33. Letter dated June 11, 1996.

retreat for resigned priests and wives, other Catholics, and priests who have served the diocese for many years does not reflect such spirit."[34] APP lost this round and held their retreat, instead, at St. Paul's Retreat House, run by the Passionate Fathers, a community of male religious very supportive of APP, and one of whose members, Fr. Tom Bonacci, was also a member of APP. Kearns Spirituality Center, a facility run by the Sisters of Divine Providence, a women's religious community also very sympathetic to APP concerns, had also become a gathering location for APP, especially for its Speaker Series, once diocesan buildings were no longer available.

APP lost another diocesan cite for meetings in 2006 at St Regis/St. Hyacinth parish in the city. APP member Don Fisher had been pastor there for a number of years, so it had become a regular meeting cite for the group. But Fisher retired in 2005. In November of 2006, new APP chair, Sr. Barbara Finch, CSJ, received a letter from the new administrator of the parish, Fr. James McDonough, denying permission for APP to continue meeting at the church. It seems that an APP member, William Podobinski, a former Holy Spirit priest, now married, participated in a Eucharistic liturgy at Christ Hope Ecumenical Catholic Church with a newly ordained woman priest (riverboat ceremony on August 1st of 2006), Joan Houk (also an APP member), and since the church was considered "schismatic" and Houk ordained "in an invalid and illicit ceremony," Podobinski, and by association APP, are "at odds with Church teaching" and the participants in that liturgy under "canonical sanction," thus "continued use of the parish facility is inappropriate." APP moved on and continued to meet where they were welcomed, not only at Kearns' Spirituality Center, but also in other parishes where they had sympathetic supporters.

In the early years of APP's new membership structure, moving beyond a merely clerical group while maintaining its original name, there was constant discernment and reevaluation as to the APP's structure and purpose. This comes out quite strongly in their annual mountaintop Retreats, in which they gathered for evaluation of the past year of activities and planned for the year to come. In 1996, three years out from its new membership structure, APP continued to see itself as a support group, though some felt that worked well for part of the group (clerics) and not so much for others. Meanwhile, the two-pronged focus on church renewal and social justice within the church and beyond continued.

By the mid-1990s APP counted about fifty dues-paying members, with a mailing list of non-active members and friends of 225. At the 1996 mountaintop gathering, they affirmed that its new identity was now pretty

---

34. APP letter to Bishop Wuerl, June 18, 1996.

comfortable for all, ordained and non-ordained women and men, and that they were still committed to the Vatican II agenda as priests and prophets, collegial and non-hierarchical, sometimes a voice on its own for justice, other times a collaborator with groups across the city and nationally.

On the negative side, they agreed their agenda was sometimes too broad, too unfocused, resulting in being spread too thinly, thus not always being effective. Regarding this latter acknowledgement, their list of social justice activities included affiliation with local and national groups: Haiti Solidarity Committee, the Cuba Coalition, Africa, especially South Africa (Don McIlvane had spent time in South Africa as it struggled with apartheid, and Don Fisher served five years with the Spiritan community among the Masai in Tanzania), Amnesty International, School of the Americas, as well as work on broad issues such as racism, eliminating the death penalty, welfare reform, and food and nutrition! A few years later they would affiliate with a new faith-based community organizing network, Pittsburgh Interfaith Impact Network (PIIN), later to become Pennsylvania Interfaith Impact Network.

On the church renewal front, they supported a diocesan revitalization program called "Salt and Light," a parish renewal program called Renew, women's ordination, priest retirement, church reorganization and other immediate issues that would spring up and need reaction and response. For a group of fifty active members, the agenda was ambitious.

Finally, there was growing concern that no new, younger clergy had joined, acknowledging that the younger clergy were much more conservative and traditional in their views, not exactly APP candidates, yet they remained determined to continue reaching out to invite new clergy to APP gatherings and actions.

Structurally they decided in 1996 to decrease their six member steering committee to four, always two ordained members and two non-ordained, and they remained committed to two standing committees, i.e., church renewal and social justice. They reaffirmed collaboration with national groups Catholics Organized for renewal (COR), Call to Action and National Federation of Priests Council (NFPC), and locally with the Thomas Merton Center for peace and justice and PIIN.

In the minutes of another mid-1990s Mountaintop experience, there was a reference to an organizational meeting of a "new clergy group" in Pittsburgh, which, like APP, decided to meet independent of the diocese. Evidently, it was a group not interested in alignment with APP but, nevertheless, unhappy with the current drift of the diocese. A few APP members attended this initial meeting of 113 Pittsburgh priests and APP felt "no conflict or competition" with this initiative. In fact, APP was glad for this development and felt there could be good collaboration. Also, since APP hadn't gained a new priest in its membership since 1979, at least here was a sizeable group of priests willing to have their own thoughts. However, it appears the group, despite a very good response and a healthy beginning, met only once. APP had been told by one of the key organizers that Bishop Wuerl took issue with this new initiative and singled out about twelve to fifteen of the participants, called them to a meeting and accused them of disloyalty to the diocese and him personally. Unlike APP which, over the years, has respectfully agreed to disagree at times with church hierarchy, yet maintained its existence, this group simply disbanded before it became further organized.[35]

In terms of national affiliations, in 1999, in what was undoubtedly a bittersweet moment for APP, especially for Neil McCaulley, APP decided to withdraw its membership from the National Federation of Priests' Council, a national group of Catholic priests that APP had helped initiate in 1968, and with whom McCaulley had served as President from 1980–82. This active, three decades-long affiliation, which APP devoted a good deal of energy and resources to, sending two delegates to the annual meetings and often initiating NFPC's social justice agenda, as well as freeing McCaulley to serve a two-year term as president, ended because of frustration on the part of APP with the NFPC's lack of ongoing prophetic witness, both within the church and in its social justice agenda. APP had reluctantly been discussing this move for a good many years, but by 1999 APP member Don McIlvane, after attending the annual meeting, reported that NFPC had become an organization with "no longer a justice agenda." It had become "toothless, passive and silent," according to McIlvane. Although McCaulley, always one of the most committed and active supporters of the NFPC, "would be sad if the APP would discontinue its membership," according to the May 17, 1999 minutes of the APP meeting, all but two members of APP voted to withdraw, the two abstaining. In its letter of withdrawal, APP applauded NFPC's long history of accomplishments on church renewal and social justice, stating: "In the past it was the NFPC that would lead us forward with its vision of Vatican II. Now it holds a convention every year for the guys to get together and talk about spirituality, but that spirituality doesn't address the changing needs of the American Church."[36] Though expressing deep sadness at this decision, APP renewed an ongoing commitment to other national Catholic groups, Catholic Organizations for Renewal (COR) and

35. Mountaintop meeting minutes and private interview with John Oesterle, November 19, 2018.

36. Letter from APP to NFPC, September 9, 1999.

the Western Pennsylvania chapter of Call to Action, both of whom the APP judged to be seriously committed to church renewal and social justice.

In priestly and wider Catholic circles the decision to withdraw from NFPC was a big deal and was picked up by the *National Catholic Reporter* (NCR) weekly newspaper. The NCR article pointed out that APP's membership change in 1993 made APP a unique presence among priests' groups in the NFPC. Explaining APP's decision to leave the national group, John Oesterle was quoted as saying: "They [NFPC] don't make waves. Yet Jesus made a lot of waves, and Peter and Paul got killed for making waves." When interviewed by NCR, the new President of NFPC, Fr. Robert Silva of Stockton, CA., said he "was having a hard time understanding" the withdrawal, although he did admit that the group (NFPC) "had made a deliberate shift in recent years from an adversarial style to one of being a partner to the local diocesan councils of priests . . . Our advocacy will hopefully be as strong as possible but it will not be like it was 15 years ago . . . we don't want to be adversarial (or) out to throw bombs, but rather productive and positive." They continued to be concerned about important issues of priest shortages, married priesthood and justice issues, "hard questions," but they would approach them differently, he went on, more studiously, seeking more input and consensus. Finally, Fr. Silva acknowledged, he would reach out to APP "in brotherhood," seeking to "heal any wounds and move forward in unity." But for APP, according to former NFPC President, Neil McCaulley, since the bishops took over all priests' councils due to a 1983 change in canon law, the NFPC's approach had been "muddled" and the group became too tied to the bishops. It was time for APP to move on, however reluctantly.[37]

Although two key APP leaders, especially on the social justice front, had reached different stages of their own ministerial journeys, Don McIlvane now retired (1994), though still somewhat active, and Jack O'Malley, since 2001 granted permission by Bishop Wuerl to work full time as chaplain of the AFL-CIO in Pennsylvania, thus no longer with a parish base, in O'Malley's own mind likely a relief for the diocese and Bishop Wuerl, as well as O'Malley himself, APP continued to speak and act out on social issues that mattered.

One such matter was the U.S. initiated war on Iraq in March of 2003. In chapter 3 I shared an encounter I, my wife and two friends, had with then Fr. Donald Wuerl, as we awaited an interview on a diocesan radio program in 1984 hosted by diocesan spokesperson, Fr. Ron Lenguin. Our topic was Central America and we engaged in a somewhat heated conversation with

37. APP meeting minutes and Lefevere,"Pittsburgh Priests Split from Federation," 10.

Fr. Wuerl as to the legacy of murdered bishop of El Salvador, Oscar Romero. Responding to our view that Romero was a hero, a prophet, and a saint, Wuerl countered he thought Romero was naïve and imprudent, and that he never should have put himself in a position to be assassinated. Given Romero's recent canonization, I think it fair to say Fr. Wuerl was on the wrong side of history, both church history and social history. In 2003, once again, Wuerl took a position on an international issue that seemed incredulous at the time, and seems even more so as history looks back.

Although the Vatican and the U.S. bishops condoned the invasion of Afghanistan after 9/11, as justified, the same judgment did not occur on the decision of the United States to declare war on and invade Iraq in 2003. In fact, Pope John Paul II and the U.S. Catholic bishops condemned the war as not justifiable according to the dictates of the traditional just war theory, a staple of Catholic social teaching dating back to Augustine. Two weeks after the start of the war, Wuerl, now Pittsburgh's bishop, led an interfaith prayer service for peace in downtown Pittsburgh, at which he acknowledged that a few weeks previously the impending war was being debated and the U.S. bishops declared that the war didn't appear to meet the "Church's standards for a just war." However, he went on, astonishingly to APP members:

> A great deal has been said about the just war theory, its conditions and its application. Several weeks ago it was fitting to debate this matter. Today the situation has changed. Our President, together with the leadership of allied nations, has concluded that the action they have ordered is justified. This is a gravely serious decision, but one I believe they have made conscientiously. Good people can arrive at differing conclusions using the same moral principles applied to a highly complex, concrete situation . . . We must pray for peace . . . May God Bless our President, our military personnel, our peacemakers, and all the human family . . . that still has so much to learn about Jesus' gospel, about Jesus' way and our following that path . . . Our role today as religious leaders is not to analyze the history or the geopolitical judgments that have led to this war. Our concern is to address the spiritual needs that come with this war in which we are now engaged.[38]

This statement by Bishop Wuerl represented to APP an astonishing lapse in moral and political judgment, and not only put him at odds with many in the peace community but also with the Pope and his brother bishops. Not only did he brush aside any moral concern with the traditional

38. Rodgers, "Wuerl Calls for Prayer."

just war theory, which also has components of moral theory that apply once war has begun, but he aligned himself with President Bush's own justification of what he called preventative or pre-emptive war, a concept not only in conflict with just war thinking but also international law. Many would say that the Iraq war has been among the very worst political and moral blunders of any presidency in modern history. For Bishop Wuerl to defer his own prophetic and moral voice to that of a wayward President was shocking for APP and, once again, the group decided to go public in opposition to Bishop Wuerl's stance.

APP acted swiftly by issuing a press release and participating in a larger anti-war march in downtown Pittsburgh. In its remarks, authored by APP member, Scott Fabean, married and father of four, APP pointed out the Pope's condemnation of the war and its solidarity with his pronouncements. APP challenged Bishop Wuerl's statements as contrary not only to the pope and other bishops but also Catholic moral teaching, incredulous that the bishop was suggesting "we ought not be debating its [the war's] justness," saying "the morality" of the war is such that "good people can differ." They accuse Wuerl of "ceding moral judgment to political and military authority," reminding the bishop that "morality does not suspend itself whenever you declare war." Finally, they conclude, "We are in solidarity with Our Holy Father and likewise believe this war to be 'immoral, illegal, and unjust.'"[39]

On another matter of deep social concern for APP, Scott Fabean was once again front and center. In the latter part of 2004, Fabean wrote a position paper he entitled, "Moral Values: Talk is Cheap," focusing on a consistent position of the APP for decades on what has become known as "the seamless garment of life," or "consistent ethic of life," a perspective originally articulated by the late Cardinal Joseph Bernardin. In the original reflection, Bernardin argued for a consistent "pro-life" perspective, in which he tied together multiple issues concerning life, not merely the central concern of the Catholic Church on abortion. Fabean wrote his reflection directly after the 2004 elections in late November, as a working paper for APP, suggesting that the "moral values" agenda that dominated the election was narrowly focused on the issues of abortion and gay marriage. In directing his comments on these two issues and their impact on the recent election results, Fabean argued that Catholic social teaching goes well beyond one or two issues. Furthermore, he suggested, being "pro-birth" doesn't mean one is "pro-life." He reminds us that Bernardin's "consistent ethic of life" involves not only protecting the unborn but also working "to end poverty, capital punishment, racism, mistreatment of workers and immigrants, sexism,

39. APP press release, March 25, 2003.

euthanasia, and nuclear proliferation, while also working to promote peace, justice, living wages, education, and care for the environment." Fabean's argument is that one can only claim to be "pro-life" if all of these life issues are addressed and included.

Focusing on abortion, he asks: "What kind of morality focuses on a baby being born without an equal devotion to that baby's health? food? education? housing? Can we really be so passionate about the mother not having an abortion and not be equally determined to see that she finds" other needs met after childbirth? Fabean attempts to open a dialogue as to just why a woman might choose an abortion, i.e., what are her circumstances? Often extreme poverty is a motivation, he suggests, citing various studies.

Ultimately, the document challenged Catholic bishops, Evangelicals and both Republican and Democratic leaders to work for a more just society and "fight to make abortions rare," focusing efforts on greater justice and equality, raising the standard of living, especially for the poorest, so that women are not put in the position of seeking to end the life of her unborn child because of a lack of resources to support this child and her other children. For Fabean and APP, Catholic social teaching in its broadest sense, if followed, would improve the lives of so many and be more effective in lowering the numbers of abortions, the ultimate goal. He concludes by describing himself as a "pro-life Democrat" and proud member of APP.[40]

A few months after Fabean's "seamless garment" working paper was circulated, Pittsburgh's St. Paul's Catholic Seminary—as well as the diocese and bishop, of course—became the focus of another APP public challenge, as church leadership, still under the guidance of Bishop Wuerl, once again looked like a wing of the Republican Party. Pro-Life, Catholic Republican Pennsylvania Senator Rick Santorum was invited to give a diocesan-sponsored lecture he entitled "Taking the Heat." The Social Action Committee of APP, most specifically Sr. Barbara Finch, Fr. Jack O'Malley and Scott Fabean, issued an open letter with the same title as Santorum's lecture, using his words "taking the heat" to refer to all of the people in the U.S. "taking the heat" because of poverty, job loss, food insecurity, etc. Despite his "pro-life" stance, retorts the APP open letter, Santorum supported the illegal war in Iraq, the death penalty, reduced taxes for the wealthy, while at the same time, opposing benefits for immigrants, raise in the minimum wage, and healthcare for all, etc. Their theme was as above, i.e., challenging the Catholic Senator to follow Cardinal Bernadin's "consistent ethic of life" perspective, which, again, opposes abortion as it advocates for ending poverty,

40. Fabean, "Moral Values."

racism, oppression of workers, the death penalty, war, etc. They end their letter asking for a dialogue about the "seamless garment" of life theology.[41]

In 2007, APP again meddled into the religion and partisan politics arena as Warren Metzler, in a letter to the editor in the *Pittsburgh Post-Gazette*, expressed deep "sadness and anger" that St. Vincent's College in Latrobe, PA, where a seminary is housed which many APP priests attended, invited Republican President George Bush, "the initiator of this dreadful war [in Iraq] . . . an international crime," to offer the commencement address. The letter suggests that the Benedictine Order, which runs the school, with its noble tradition of deep "learning and devotion to Christian principles of peace and justice," has scandalized us all. Furthermore, writes Metzler, "The invitation constitutes an endorsement of the invasion of Iraq and of inhuman social policies such as torture, illegal rendition of captured suspects . . . and illegal detention of hundreds of prisoners without trial at Guantanamo Bay. The moral disgrace that President Bush's visit will bring upon the Order, the College, the Catholic Church and the larger Christian community is well-nigh incalculable," Metzler concludes.[42]

One more time in the era of Pope Benedict XVI, APP, or at least one of its retired yet still active members, Neil McCaulley, waded directly into politics, this time of a very partisan nature, something the group generally avoided. I have no evidence that APP endorsed McCaulley's position paper, though I suspect they did as a decidedly collegial group, but in it he explains why he will be voting for the re-election of Barak Obama in 2012. Consistent with the APP's challenge to the Catholic bishop's pronouncements on pro-life issues, often focused singly on abortion, McCaulley expressed dismay that the Church's singly-focused moral stand seems to point to no other option than supporting an anti-abortion Republican candidate for President. In an ironic twist, McCaulley focused on a teaching that Cardinal Ratzinger—now Pope Benedict—articulated while head of the Congregation for the Doctrine of the Faith regarding the implications for a Catholic who would vote for a pro-choice candidate, in this case President Obama. Benedict would suggest that such a Catholic "would be guilty of formal cooperation in evil, and so unworthy to present himself for Holy Communion, if he were to deliberately vote for a candidate precisely because of the candidates' permissive stand on abortion." But there's an out here, as Ratzinger goes on to say, that one could still in good conscience vote for such a candidate if, at the same time he rejected the candidate's stance on abortion, he supported that candidate for a myriad of other reasons which would be

41. APP press release, "Redefining Taking the Heat," January 11, 2005.
42. Metzler, Letter to the Editor, April 20, 2007.

considered "remote cooperation, which can be permitted in the presence of proportionate reasons." McCaulley cleverly highlights this declaration from the Vatican to publicly announce to the Pittsburgh Catholic community that it is in keeping with Catholic teaching that one can, in good conscience, vote for a pro-choice candidate, i.e., President Obama. This was an important matter in the eyes of McCaulley and the APP because of consistent stories heard about pastors getting into the pulpit and reminding Catholics they can't vote for pro-choice candidates for any office, typically Democrat, and remain good Catholics. As McCaulley pointed out, that is erroneous, just ask Cardinal Ratzinger, or better, Pope Benedict! More subtly, I believe, it was McCaulley and the APP's way of once again exposing the Catholic hierarchy's (not so) "covert" support for the Republican Party.[43]

In the area of social justice, especially as it pertains to Church teaching, the issue around the institutional Church's undue emphasis and single-mindedness (in the eyes of APP) on the moral concern of abortion, has been one of APP's strongest critiques of the implementation by the hierarchy of the Church's social teachings. They have successfully and consistently, I believe, informed the Catholic community of this distorted or one-dimensional viewpoint, much to the detriment of the very expansive and profound teachings of the Church on other life issues such as war and peace, poverty and wealth and capital punishment, the latter which Pope Francis recently stated is no longer permissible under any circumstances. Not on the issue of abortion alone, but certainly quite profoundly on this issue, APP has been a prophetic voice for its willingness "to take the heat" from Church authorities in their insistence on proclaiming the breadth and depth of Catholic social teaching, much of which winds up on dusty shelves and rarely finds its way into the typical parish Sunday pulpit; unless, of course, one were to attend a parish pastored by an APP member or sympathizer.

However, one issue in which APP, in my judgment, has not taken a particularly clear or strong stand is that of the clergy sexual abuse crisis in the Catholic Church, despite its deep concern about this, as I can attest from many private interviews. One possible explanation for this relatively limited attention to the issue could be that, until the recent release of the Grand Jury report on clerical sexual abuse from the state of Pennsylvania in August of 2018, as far as the Pittsburgh Diocese was concerned, dealing with the issue of clergy sex abuse had been considered one area in which Bishop Wuerl, and his successor Bishop Zubik, had received positive press in their handling of various cases from the beginning of Wuerl's time in

43. McCaulley, "Pope Benedict, President Obama & Abortion," evidently an internally-distributed communication. I have no record that it was ever published.

Pittsburgh in 1988, until the present, under Zubik. As I have noted earlier, Wuerl has even been willing to buck the Vatican in his no tolerance policy in the Pittsburgh diocese during his lengthy tenure from 1988–2005. Under Bishop Wuerl's watch, in February of 2004, the diocese issued a press release on clergy sexual abuse entitled: "Pittsburgh report shows 1.9 percent of priests and deacons serving in diocese accused over five decades." This is low, as the national average seems to be about four percent. Of the fifty-one priests and deacons accused in Pittsburgh over these five decades, six were deemed falsely accused. Ninety percent of the accusations occurred between 1950 and 1989, before Wuerl's time, and six more during his time in the 1990s. No accusations occurred between 1997 and the issuing of the report in 2004. According to the press release, the diocese had implemented policies in 1993, constantly updating and revising them. The diocese reported what was found about Pittsburgh from a study done by The John Jay College of Criminal Justice, commissioned by the U.S. Conference of Catholic Bishops. "We requested this study to make certain that this terrible tragedy will not happen again," Bishop Wuerl stated at that time. Evidently, this was the first study of this kind in the country.[44]

Since the release of the Grand Jury report in 2018, there is need to re-evaluate this analysis. Although acknowledging that Wuerl and Zubik did indeed deal appropriately with a number of abuse cases, the report also suggests that they dropped the ball on a number of other situations, all, of course, under a veil of secrecy, lacking any transparency. Among other things, the report listed ninety-nine accused clerics, not the fifty-one reported by the John Jay study. Wuerl and Zubik disagree with those findings and have posed a vigorous defense of their actions, but indications are that there were errors made, despite the opinion of a few informed observers that the two bishops and the diocese handled clergy sexual abuse issues better than most. I will deal more fully with the Grand Jury report and the performance of the Pittsburgh diocese and the report's implications for APP—two of its deceased members have been accused in the report—in chapter 5.[45]

Although the clergy sexual abuse crisis has not been a front burner issue for APP, it has not totally neglected it and certainly has had open discussions about it during regular meeting times. In a May, 2002 APP meeting, after the revelations on clergy sexual abuse came out from Boston (*Boston Globe* Spotlight investigation), a married APP couple, Maynard and Carole Brennan, had prepared a draft statement on the pedophilia issue for the group's consideration. Nine APP members, a good, mixed group of clergy,

44. Report from the Pittsburgh Catholic Diocese, February 26, 2004.
45. Office of Attorney General, Commonwealth of Pennsylvania, "Report I."

laity and married, formed a committee to review the proposal, which raised themes that included: "justice, end of secrecy, repentance, healing, and outreach to victims." Furthermore, the Brennans had been interviewed by Fox TV on May 22, 2002. I presume the statement was eventually made public in the form of a press release from APP, but I can't find a record of it and no one has a good memory of it.[46]

The only other documentation available on this matter is a report from an annual mountaintop gathering in 2010, the minutes of which reported that "The re-energized focus on pedophilia throughout the world elicited much discussion. How much of this evil manifestation is really about power and the maintenance of an exercising of that power in the Church," they discussed. The group was clearly critical of the general "defensive attitude of the bishops [which] makes it apparent that they translate every investigation, article and question into an attack on the Church itself." APP concluded at its meeting that there needs to be "justice both for the accuser and the accused [and] it was noted that the publication 'Justice for Priests and Deacons' is an excellent perspective on the whole question."[47]

In several conversations I've had about this issue with APP priests, beyond their horror about the abuses themselves, as is clear from the mountaintop notes, another concern they have is their view that once the bishops finally started taking the issue seriously, and began removing priests from the ministry, the pendulum swung to the other extreme, from silently protecting and transferring priests accused to now throwing any accused under the bus, whether there was credible evidence or not, without due process. Hence, some of the priests felt incredibly vulnerable to false accusations. A Pittsburgh lawyer and Catholic, the aforementioned Paul Titus, a friend to APP who accompanied Jack O'Malley and Neil McCaulley when they were called to meet with diocesan officials over their comments on the "riverboat ordinations" of women, has consistently helped represent clergy who have insisted they were falsely accused.

As to why the APP did not seem to have had much to say about clergy sexual abuse and pedophilia issues, one APP member said to me that he guessed "they didn't think they had much to add to the discussion," and, what seemed true until the recent report, that the Pittsburgh Diocese under Bishop Wuerl was on top of this issue better than almost any diocese in the country. The John Jay study seemed to point in that direction. And Bishop

46. APP meeting minutes, May, 2002. I spoke with Carole Brennan on January 15, 2019 about this and she has a vague recollection of it. She is sure her husband, Maynard, now deceased, wrote it. She could not locate a copy of it, nor a record of where it might have been published.

47. Mountaintop minutes, April 19, 2010.

Wuerl's successor, Bishop David Zubik, who worked with Wuerl for many years in the chancery, seems to have continued Wuerl's track record with his no tolerance policy.

Along with their two-pronged focus on church renewal and social justice, one overall area in which APP has a stellar history is their constant and consistent determination to educate the Catholic community on both internal church and broader social justice issues. The group's annual speaker series hosts national religious speakers four to five times a year. Also, in an attempt to keep the wider public aware of their concerns around church and society, they constantly maintain access to the press, both the Catholic press—even though they've often complained the *Pittsburgh Catholic* regularly shuts them out—and the secular press. As an independent and often provocative voice in the diocese over the years, ready to critique politicians as well as their own Church leadership, they have generally not found it difficult to attract press coverage.

As for the speaker series, they have hosted such national religious figures as Fr. Charles Curran, former priest Anthony Padavano, Sr. Joan Chittister, OSB, pacifist Bishop Thomas Gumbleton, and most recently, silenced Irish priest and noted author, Fr. Tony Flannery of Galway, Ireland. John Oesterle gets a major share of the credit for keeping this program alive and relevant, doggedly pursuing some of the best public intellectuals, Catholic and otherwise, in the country to address often hundreds of Pittsburgh attendees.

There are many examples of the ongoing ability of APP to attract press attention, thus constantly having the opportunity to educate their own Catholic world, but also the wider Pittsburgh community, and, on occasion, a national audience through such publications as the *National Catholic Reporter*. Sometimes the press was brought in by one man, Fr. Don McIlvane. Several APP clergy told me the press would show up for anything McIlvane was selling. McIlvane, who died in 2014, was a colorful figure who would take on anyone, especially bishops, but also mayors, as we saw earlier in this study. More than a few APP members recalled to me that either former Mayor Richard Caligueri or City Council "Jeep" DiPasquale, or possibly both, had admitted McIlvane's influence by suggesting that elected officials were always wondering just what Fr. McIlvane's position might be on any number of pertinent issues of the day. McIlvane had power in the City and the Church. For some APP members McIlvane could be too much of a loner, not always a great team player. He was impatient and not always interested in dialogue and process. But could he stir the pot! The press seemed to love it. He got attention on lots of important struggles. He knew how to raise his voice and slam his fist on the podium with the best of them. And he was a great strategist, knowing where the pressure points were and when to push, and how hard. Mostly his APP counterparts loved it.

The *Pittsburgh Tribune-Review*, a newspaper based in Greensburg, PA, but with a wide circulation in Pittsburgh, especially since the closing of the *Pittsburgh Press*, published a piece about the history of APP in December of 1996, entitled: "Clerics' Group Tackles the Issues." McIlvane was quoted at the top of the article, even though retired at the time. His remarks were classic McIlvane. Reflecting back on APP's inception in 1966, McIlvane proudly declared, "But this association is not an official association meaning the bishop did not start it and the bishop did not sanction it. Now that doesn't mean we're bad Catholics or anything. We are, all of us, priests in good standing." The piece went on to list many of the APP's actions, both related to the church and the wider society, since 1966, most of which have been noted previously. Besides McIlvane, John Oesterle and Jack O'Malley also appeared in the article. Oesterle addressed the need for internal church reform, O'Malley the need for more involvement in social justice, suggesting the church is losing members because it doesn't address the issues and is seen as not relevant. And in a touching and personal moment in which he acknowledged the importance of APP for his life and ministry, O'Malley went on to say: "I think it's been a network of support and friendship. You don't feel isolated in your diocese . . . It makes you feel that you're connected . . . that you're not alone [and it] . . . encourages you to speak out, to reach out. The issues are much broader than just the parish." Another way to say this as one APP member did, "The APP always has your back."

And, as often has been the case with the press when reporting on APP, it immediately went to the diocese to get its response. As we've seen, for many decades, the voice of the diocese on such issues has almost always been Fr. Ron Lenguin, ironically both friend and classmate to a few APP members, but who regularly reminds the press that the APP has no official status in the diocese and, although he suggested APP "has not, strictly speaking, been at odds with the church establishment [not quite accurate] . . . Have they disagreed with the different bishops on issues? Yes, they have. I'm not sure that it's had any real effect on the Church as such." Lenguin went on to applaud APP for raising some important social justice issues, yet derided them for their occasional divisiveness. When McIlvane mentioned in the interview that surveys of priests suggest wide support for both "optional celibacy and women priests," Lenguin reminded the interviewer that "The Pope has said the issues—optional celibacy and women priests too—are closed and not ones that should be discussed publicly."[48]

48. Crumb, "Clerics' Group," B3.

In a *Pittsburgh Post-Gazette* article from 2000, "Decades Haven't Dimmed Activist Priests' Desire for Social Change," freelance writer Bette McDevitt acknowledged that "its members are a little less visible, a little less vocal, a lot less likely to get arrested. But they status quo push on several fronts, for justice and peace, for more open communication within the church, and yes, for married clergy."

After listing the many accomplishments of the group over the decades, McDevitt quoted Don Fisher, who after stating that he didn't hear any objections from the diocese about their existence and actions, speculated that: "I think, down deeply, the diocese had a sense of pride that we were involved in the issues, and what are they going to do anyway? Clearly, we were on the right side of history." McDevitt then quoted diocesan spokesman, Ron Lenguin, who said the name of the group confused people and the diocese "may wish" they would change it. He then, as he almost always does, diminished the impact of the group, citing their minutes as having maybe "15 active members."

Since Bishop Wuerl is pretty "conservative," offered APP member, John Oesterle, (in recent years) the group has chosen to be less confrontational and more dialogic in their interactions with him. He is not much into "peace and justice," Oesterle opined.

An issue not mentioned previously in this study, that of inviting to the "Eucharistic Table those in irregular marriages," was cited in the article as a new issue for APP (interestingly, Pope Francis has recently addressed that issue in a pastoral letter). McDevitt concluded her piece on APP by citing non-clergy members of the group. A former priest and his wife, Giles and Kathy Grabowski, APP members since 1993, appreciated "the spirituality and sense of community" that membership in APP offered them. Sr. Barbara Finch said about her joining APP: "I see it as a way to get in touch with my own sense of priesthood. I have the gifts of pastoral ministry, though I've never been ordained." Another lay member, Linda Werner, referred to APP as "a lifeline." Finally, McDevitt asked Fr. Don Fisher, "So why do you stay?" He responded that "he envisioned change on the way . . . I think the wave that brought Vatican II will be back, and with a greater force than before."[49]

In yet another article published in the *Post-Gazette*, inclusive of APP but with a larger focus on various Catholic groups seeking change, a senior editor, Clark Thomas, titled his piece: "Devout In Their Own Way: Talking to Catholics Who Feel Compelled to Challenge the Status Quo." Thomas referred to these groups as "the loyal opposition" to the institutional Church. Although he found the interviewees in various ways "angry, grief-stricken,

---

49. McDevitt, " "Decades Haven't Dimmed," D1–5.

even bitter," he opined, "they all still loved the Church, the nuns especially
... It never occurred to any of them to leave and join some Protestant de-
nomination." On a positive note, the interviewees focused on areas they
thought the Church was on the right path, e.g., certain justice issues. But
they also made clear their differences. Besides APP, Thomas interviewed
members from Call to Action, Pax Christi, Celibacy is the Issue (CITI),
and also, the LGBT[Q] Catholic group, Dignity. Call to Action focused lots
of interest on the question of women and priesthood, Pax Christi on non-
violence and demilitarization, CITI (whose website is rentapriest.com),
who according to co-founder, former priest, William Podobinski, "once a
priest, always a priest," encouraged married priests to go back into ministry.
Podobinski quoted one former, now married, priest as writing: "In one of
the best moves of my life I married a wonderful woman. I didn't steal money
from the parish funds, I didn't abuse children and I didn't have an affair
with the choir director, male or female. If I had done any of those things, I'd
be transferred or promoted, but not kicked out." The last Catholic group to
be cited in the article, Dignity, a support group for LGBT[Q] folks, felt the
most estranged from the church. Related to this estrangement, the Dignity
spokesperson said that the Church found its own group for the LGBT[Q]
community, "Courage," whose adherents committed to celibacy. They (the
Church) consider us to have a "disoriented nature," such a view creating
great "anguish," said the Dignity spokesperson. The group criticized the
Church for hypocrisy, suggesting that there are many "greying and gaying"
closet gay clergy. Despite a unanimous view that Pope John Paul II had set
the Church back in a deeply conservative direction, they weren't totally discouraged for, they suggested, "popes come and popes go," and change will
inevitably happen in a direction they—Dignity—were headed.[50]

As freelance journalist, Bette McDevitt, wrote—and I alluded to earlier—although APP is not quite as active as it might have been in the earliest
years when roughly forty-fifty full-time clerics were active members of the
group, inspired by the recent Vatican II Council, these more recent press
pieces still suggest great vibrancy in APP, both among the remaining clergy
and the new members drawn from the ranks of married priests, their wives,
nuns and laity. Furthermore, their mission, witness and activity seem still
quite worthy of ongoing press coverage, thus allowing APP to continue to
evangelize and educate on issues of Church reform and social justice, both
in the Church and in the wider society. The group's ongoing presence in the
diocese, despite what one might be tempted to call a kind of impasse with
the Church, as APP continues to press, not so successfully, for progressive

50. Thomas, "Devout," A-12.

reforms addressed over fifty years ago at Vatican II, remains a remarkable witness to truth and prophecy to all who choose to listen.

Before ending this chapter I wanted to highlight the contributions of one APP member who has died while I have been writing this history, i.e., Fr. Gene Lauer (died May 20, 2018). In this brief section, I want to especially highlight an article Lauer wrote in 2006 and point out its relevance to APP's ongoing efforts at advocating Church renewal. Although absent from Pittsburgh for many years as he labored at Notre Dame University and the Catholic Theological Union in Chicago, nevertheless, Lauer was not only a loyal dues-paying member of APP since joining in 1967, but he was also its theologian. Having earned his STD in 1966 from the Pontifical Gregorian University in Rome, he taught at many colleges and universities and wrote and edited several books as well as numerous theological articles. He had a hand in a few documents put out by APP, e.g., he co-authored the 1971 statement on priestly simplicity, and was often asked to serve as theme speaker for the APP speaker series or other occasions when the group wanted a sound, theological mind to address issues of ministry and Church. A quiet and humble priest, he had a very sharp mind, and in the years leading up to his death, he returned to Pittsburgh and continued to do ministry on the south side of the city, out preaching most Sundays and offering workshops and giving lectures. A close friend, Sr. Ellen Rufft, was quoted in his obituary as saying that Lauer was very progressive in his theology and an "avowed feminist." She went on to say about him: "He read books about feminism and he was very happy to announce to people that he was a feminist . . . [and] he thought women should definitely be priests."[51]

In a private interview I had with Lauer in the summer of 2017 he affirmed to me his interest in feminist theology, especially the works of Catholic scholar Elizabeth Johnson. But he was also a big fan of the nineteenth-century convert to Catholicism, John Cardinal Newman, who emphasized experience not philosophy as the key to good theology.

This emphasis on the importance of experience for theology came out in spades in a wonderful article Lauer wrote, published in 2006, "The Charism of the Priesthood Today," in which he went on to suggest it is time to seriously look at the role of the ordained priest in relation to the profound development of lay ministry, i.e., he asked, what are the specific roles priests play currently, and what are the roles specific to lay ministry, and how do these relate to one another? In the piece, Lauer does a quick historical look at the evolution of priesthood in Christianity and reminds us that the word priest was never used in referring to the apostles; rather, it only appears in

51. Crompton, "Obituary for Fr. Eugene Lauer."

the Letter to Hebrews and specifically refers to Jesus only. "The apostles and disciples were not a distinctively privileged class as were priests in the Jewish hierarchy." He goes on to write that there were five elements that were exercised by the "bishop/priest/minister/leader in the first two centuries of Christianity: . . . to evangelize . . . to take a leadership role in forming Christian community . . . to empower others to participate in ministering to the community . . . to preside at the Eucharistic table . . . and to model the teachings of Jesus to live out the Christian message."[52]

As the centuries went on, writes Lauer, slowly the priest became separated "from a necessary connection with a local community," as "ordination itself became an ultimate value," thus giving the priest "a privileged status in the community . . . [and] a definitive distinction between clergy and laity" developed, thus making the priest "a different kind of person . . . [in which] an ontological change took place at ordination." Furthermore, the priest was the only person who could preside at the Eucharist, giving the priest a certain "power" which allowed him to "control the act of worship." For Lauer such an evolution kept distancing the idea of ministry further and further from the original intuition of the early Church in which "the rite of initiation (baptism) has given to every one of the faithful a role in ministry," a more "practical" way to understand ministry, making use of the gifts of all the community, not just the priest.[53]

So what does this mean for the twenty-first century? At this point Lauer raises up the fact that as of 2005, according to a recent study, thirty-one thousand professional lay ministers were working in Catholic parishes and that this very positive development allows us to rethink ministry "to discern the authentic reality of lay ministry and the authentic reality of priesthood as interwoven ministries, functions, and realities, whereby the Church can reach its fullest expression." That is, we can only understand the ordained priesthood and the priesthood of all the baptized (common priesthood) "by viewing them together." And so in considering the relationship between ordained and lay ministry Lauer asks: "How do they fit together? Do they overlap? Does the ministry of one group intrude on the other? Are there some ministries that belong solely to one group that the other can never do?"

He concludes his article by stating that in the current situation and looking at the above five elements of church ministry, "full-time lay ecclesial ministers today often are doing four of the five functions of ministry . . . very successfully and faithfully, excluding only the presiding at the Eucharistic

52. Lauer, "The Charism," 197–98.
53. Lauer, "The Charism," 200–201.

table and administering certain sacraments." He goes on that it would seem very reasonable and possible that those currently "ministering very effectively out of their baptismal call . . . might be the ones who in the future will be called into the special circle of presiders at Eucharist and minister of sacraments . . . Practically speaking, they could be an ideal pool of candidates . . . [and] unlike seminarians, many and perhaps most have already passed the test of experience in their local communities and have been accepted as healthy, competent ministers of the gospel." Hence, maybe "there is no shortage of 'ministers' in the Church. Rather, there is a shortage of those who can preside . . . [and] in the light of the dramatic evolution of lay ministry . . . [which] will carry us into a new era, an era remarkably similar to the Church of the apostles."[54]

Lauer loved to use the word practical when referring to church polity, ever concerned that we think about what works and what is needed in church life and ministry. He does his theologizing out of his experience and the experience and pastoral needs of the contemporary Church. But he also has grounded himself and his theology in Church history and tradition. Specifically, he wonderfully raises up the recent evolution of lay ministry since Vatican II and the very positive experience of the development and professionalization of seasoned, tested and accepted ministers, already performing most of the necessary ministerial tasks. This piece by APP's resident theologian, a theologian recognized across the country as a major voice in the progressive and reform-minded Catholic camp nationally, is in keeping with APP's long history of promoting Vatican II's reclamation of the common priesthood, the priesthood of all baptized. In fact, Lauer, more than anyone, has helped shape APP's own theological viewpoints, on the Church and on ministry, especially priesthood. Given the institutional Catholic Church's seeming loss of this perspective on priesthood of all baptized in the post-Vatican era right up to the current period, it is really a quite radical and prophetic attempt to reclaim the notion of shared ministry and demonstrate how the Church can benefit from this going forward in the context of the needs of the Church in our current times. Lauer's proposal seems to me brilliant as a way forward for how the Church rethinks what has been termed the ministry shortage (priests), and rather focuses on the abundance of gifted and well prepared lay ministers. That was 2006. It's now 2019 and we seem no closer to this vision in how we reclaim and elaborate on the fullness of ministry in our day. Lauer's thoughtful and sound theology has truly given the Church and the APP a way forward in reimagining ministry. May he rest in peace.

54. Lauer, "The Charism," 203–7.

I'd like to comment briefly on one last and very interesting development regarding Catholic priests, both nationally and internationally, as this
study brings this formative era of Pope John Paul II (1978–2005) and Pope
Benedict XVI (2005–2013) to a close. I think it fair to say that John Paul II
and Pope Benedict XVI, formerly Cardinal Ratzinger, were on the same ecclesial and theological page, as together they moved the institution further
and further away from Vatican II's attempt to decentralize and empower
the local church, especially since Ratzinger's appointment by John Paul II as
head of the theological watchdog office, the Congregation for Doctrine and
the Faith, in 1983.

In 2011 there emerged in the Catholic Church two new associations
of priests with much the same spirit and agenda as APP's. One, the Association in the United States of Catholic Priests (AUSCP), has as its mission:
"To be an association of U.S. Catholic priests offering mutual support and
a collegial voice through dialogue, contemplation and prophetic action on
issues affecting church and society." Their vision is "to be a priests' voice
of hope and joy within our Pilgrim Church." Their interests are to "add a
priests' voice to the public conversation within the Church, among bishops
and lay persons, vowed religious, ordained deacons and others." They care
about "good liturgy, social justice, the role of women in our church, immigration policies that reflect Gospel values, the dignity of all human life, and
a Church that welcomes all the people of God."[55]

One APP member, Fr. Bernie Survil, not from Pittsburgh Diocese but
rather Greensburg, PA, is a founding member of this now eight-year-old
national priests' group with an independent voice for reform. Having withdrawn from the NFPC in 1999, APP is very happy for the development of
a more independent yet loyal and prophetic group of priests at the national
level. Several APP members have joined AUSCP.

The same year The Association of Catholic Priests (ACP) of Ireland
formed with a very ambitious agenda, which includes: "providing a voice
for Irish Catholic priests," especially around key "debates" in Irish society;
ongoing "implementation of the vision and teaching of the Second Vatican
Council, especially focused on "primacy of individual conscience, the status
and active participation of all the baptized," and "equal treatment" of all
Catholics. The group is also advocating for a "redesign of ministry" to be
more inclusive of all the baptized, and a "re-structuring of the governing
system of the Church," focused on "service" not "power," open dialogue and
participation of all in the choice of leadership in the Church. They advocate
a "re-evaluation of Catholic sexual teaching" and the "promotion of justice

55. Association of United States' Catholic Priests' website.

and peace" and care for "God's creation." Although unlike APP, in the case
of both AUSCP and ACP, full membership is limited to ordained priests.
However, associate membership is extended to all Catholics.

Each group meets annually and re-evaluates its agenda. I am told that
the AUSCP has up to twelve hundred members. In a personal interview with
a co-founder of Ireland's ACP, Fr. Tony Flannery, a Redemptorist priest, I
was told the ACP had between fifty and one-hundred members until it decided to work with lawyers to defend falsely accused priests of abuse claims.
At that point membership swelled to several hundred, as priests across the
country became concerned about false charges of sexual abuse. Sadly, Fr.
Flannery, though still a key ACP leader, has been "silenced" since 2012 by
Pope Benedict for his writings and preaching about married priesthood,
women priest and LGBTQ rights. As a leader of the ACP, and a year before
his silencing, he and several other priests sent a lengthy letter to Irish bishops asking that they postpone the implementation of the new overly "literal"
translation of the Catholic Missal for at least five years, objecting that the
texts are offensive and insensitive to many, with little input from priests and
lay people, and imposed on the international church with almost no consult. The group encouraged all Catholics in the international community to
give the Vatican feedback on this issue. Sadly, their efforts failed, and the
new translation issued, though it is currently under review at the Vatican.
Like the APP and AUSCP, the ACP issues frequent communications to the
press on issues of concern to the Irish Church. Flannery is the author of several books and recently traveled to the Pittsburgh to speak at APP's speaker
series in Pittsburgh in November, 2018. Flannery spoke on church reform
and future church. His lecture was attended by over two hundred.[56]

56. Association of Catholic Priests [Ireland] website. Also, private interview with fr.
Tony Flannery, in Galway, Ireland, September 15, 2017.

CHAPTER FIVE

The Francis Factor

A "Door Cracked Open" and the Vindication of APP

FROM ITS INCEPTION IN 1966, the Association of Pittsburgh Priests has consistently taken its inspiration and direction from the final documents of Vatican II, most especially "*Gaudium et Spes*: the Church and the Modern World." As recently as their March 14, 2016 annual mountaintop gathering they reiterated their mission and purpose with these words: "The Association of Pittsburgh Priests is a diocesan-wide organization of ordained and non-ordained women and men who act on our baptismal call to be priests and prophets. Our mission, rooted in the Gospel and the Spirit of Vatican II, is to carry out a ministry of justice and renewal in ourselves, the Church and the world."[1]

Despite their decades-old commitment, like many more liberal or progressive-minded in the Church, they have felt that the Council's best instincts and directives have never been fully realized. In the words of theologian Richard Gaillardetz, it's (Vatican II) an "unfinished project," or worse, a "failed promise." For Gaillardetz a fundamental problem was that "the task of post-conciliar reform was handed over to the Roman Curia for implementation," what he refers to as the "curialization of reform [which] basically meant asking a bureaucracy with a native inclination to preserve the status quo to take responsibility for reforming itself!"[2]

---

1. APP mountaintop minutes, March 14, 2016.
2. Gaillardetz, *An Unfinished Council*, x-xi.

Though a trusted ally of the Council's initiator, Pope John XXIII, Gaillardetz suggests that Pope Paul VI was "compromised" in his implementation of Vatican II by his "fear of schism"; thus he consistently tried to "placate conservatives" in an attempt to "keep the peace." And although Pope John Paul II made significant inroads regarding interfaith dialogue, openness to world religions and in the interaction of religion and science, he had little patience for "theological disagreement" and slowly re-established centralized authority in the papacy while, at the same time weakening the role of bishops, basically "emasculating collegiality," a key innovation of Vatican II. According to Gaillardetz, Pope Benedict XVI, John Paul II's key theologian for over two decades, pretty much followed the same line once elected pope.[3]

Perhaps one of the most pernicious aspects of John Paul II's papacy, particularly in light of the more recent revelations of the clergy sexual abuse crisis, is what Gaillardetz refers to as the gradual reassertion of a "sacral priesthood," i.e., the idea of the priest as part of "a clerical elite, separate from the rest of the people of God, superior in holiness and wisdom, and granted responsibility for all teaching and ministry in the church."[4] Along with this reassertion of a more elevated understanding of the priest under John Paul II, it's not a stretch to connect this to the often stated view of an ever more conservative or traditional candidate to priestly ministry filling up our seminaries. The current crop of seminarians is by and large not positively inclined towards a Vatican II perspective on priesthood, and ever more wants to distinguish themselves from the laity, symbolized by the inclination to wearing more traditional clerical garb, i.e., "the disturbing return of birettas, cassocks, and a sense of ecclesiastical entitlements," what Gaillardetz refers to as "neo-clericalism."[5] And likely not so coincidently, given the history and focus of APP and its vision of priesthood, no ordained priest has joined APP since 1979; as earlier asked, could this be a John Paul II effect? The early Church, Protestant Reformation, Vatican II and APP notion of a "common or baptismal priesthood" or "priesthood of all believers" seemed ever more distant during the time of John Paul II and Benedict XVI.

In my view what most sets apart the vision of Vatican II that has inspired APP from the post-Council perspective, most apparent in the papacies of John Paul II and Benedict XVI, is their divergent understanding of the modern world, demonstrated in their differing interpretations of the

---

3. Gaillardetz, *An Unfinished Council*, 14.

4. Gaillardetz, *An Unfinished Council*, 15–18.

5. Gaillardetz, *An Unfinished Council*, 69–70. This is also a constant theme of Pope Francis.

key Vatican II document, *Gaudium et Spes*. Simply put: is the world a challenging yet basically positive reality, ready to be engaged by a value-centered church (APP), or is the world a dark, scary reality, tainted by sin and corruption, thus a world to be encountered in a more cautious way (John Paul II and Benedict XVI)?

In a fascinating study entitled: *Vatican II: The Battle for Meaning*, Italian theologian Massimo Faggioli, argues that following Vatican II, key participants divided into basically two camps in their reception of the Council's documents, i.e., "neo-Augustinians" and "neo-Thomists." According to Faggioli, the "neo-Augustinian tendency" imagines the church's role to be at a certain distance from the "sinful world . . . an island of grace"; this camp is somewhat "skeptical or critical" of Vatican II, or at least cautious in its implementation. Faggioli suggests that two key theological influences on John Paul II, Jesuit Henri de Lubac, and even more, Joseph Ratzinger (later Pope Benedict XVI), more and more considered the Council as a "surrender to an excessive optimism about the modern world," thus representing a "crisis" for the church. Both theologians shared in "Augustine's pessimism about human freedom" and both were especially critical of what they viewed as the naïve optimism of the key document *Gaudium et Spes*.[6]

As early as 1975 Ratzinger spoke to this view of the Council and, in fact, the entire period of the 1960s, criticizing the notion that theology's job was primarily to "read the signs of the times" with these words: " Something of the Kennedy era pervaded the Council, something of the naïve optimism of the concept of the great society. It was precisely the break in historical consciousness, the self-tormenting rejection of the past, that produced the concept of a zero hour in which everything would begin again and all those things that had formerly been done badly would now be done well."[7]

Ratzinger went on to suggest that "the real meaning of Vatican II" and, in particular, the document of *Gaudium et Spes*—APP's alternate bible—has not been well understood. He calls certain interpretations of this document "astonishingly optimistic" in its take on modernity. He rejected what he called a "new modernism" and a "utopian interpretation" of Vatican II. Later, writes Faggioli, Ratzinger applied the same neo-Augustinian thinking to a critique of recent theological innovations such as European political theology and Latin American liberation theology.

The other camp of interpreters of Vatican II Faggioli refers to as the "neo-Thomists," those whom he depicts as the "progressives" in their take

6. Faggioli, *Vatican II*, 68–73.

7. Faggioli, *Vatican II*, 73. In a remarkable confirmation of Faggioli's take on Benedict's theology and reaction to Vatican II, see McElwee, "Benedict Blames Clergy Abuse," 1, 6.

on Vatican II. According to Faggioli, "a positive appreciation of history as a tool for theological work was at the center of the theology of the neo-Thomists." It was Dominican theologian Marie-Dominique Chenu who best articulated this viewpoint, which stands in sharp contrast to the vision of de Lubac and Ratzinger: "Given that the 'sacred doctrine' does not present itself as a system of abstract principles whose application depends from a mental or moral casuistry, but, according to St. Thomas, as the Word of God developing itself within human intelligence in the act of faith, the 'signs of the times' must enter, implicitly or explicitly, in the discernment of the impact of the Word in the historical community of the faithful."[8]

Reflecting his more positive view of humankind and creation, Chenu wrote of the "created autonomy and intelligibility of the world of nature, man [sic] and history . . . [and] the methodological autonomy of the sciences . . ." The social sciences are especially necessary for theology to read "the signs of the times," he concluded.[9]

Countering the more pessimistic view that Vatican II in its naiveté and optimism helped create a crisis in theology and the modern Church, neo-Thomist theologian Yves Congar, in Faggioli's view quite possibly "the most important theologian of Vatican II," reasoned that the crisis in society and the church preceded Vatican II by a decade or possibly two or three and, furthermore, "Vatican II has been followed by a socio-cultural mutation whose amplitude, radicality, rapidity, and global character have no equivalent in any other period in history. The Council felt this mutation, but it did not know every aspect nor its violence."[10]

Possibly the clearest neo-Thomist statement as to the positive values of the changes proposed at Vatican II, setting this viewpoint at odds with de Lubac, Ratzinger, and ultimately John Paul II, was made by Canadian Jesuit, Bernard Lonergan, when he stated: "They are changes, not in God's self-disclosure or our faith, but in our culture. They are changes such as occurred when the first Christians moved from Palestine into the Roman Empire . . . when Scholasticism yielded to Humanism, the Renaissance, the Reformation and the Counter-Reformation. Ours is a new age, and enormous tasks lie ahead. But we shall be all the more likely to surmount them, if we take the trouble to understand what is going forward and why."[11]

It's very difficult to say that any single historical event completely explains future occurrences, but one could reasonably speculate. I would

8. Faggioli, *Vatican II*, 77.

9. Faggioli, *Vatican II*, 77

10. Faggioli, *Vatican II*, 80.

11. Faggioli, *Vatican II*, 82–83.

argue that the key, or certainly a key, event in determining just how Vatican II would be implemented going forward under John Paul II and Benedict, was the 1985 international Synod of Bishops. The synod was called, according to Faggioli, to "celebrate" Vatican II and "to evaluate the 'application' of the council in the past twenty years." Although Faggioli acknowledges that the 1985 reception of the Council still leaned more towards "optimism" than skepticism, unlike the more negative perceptions held by many church leaders by the dawn of the twenty-first century, he states firmly that "The change in perspective about the Church and the world ["greater problems and anguish" as compared to 1965, according to the synod's final report] made the synod a turning point for the rise of the neo-Augustinian reception of Vatican II within the doctrinal orientation of the pontificate of John Paul II."[12] Faggioli suggests that John Paul II's impact on the synod was a mixed one, i.e., there was a clear development in the areas of "social teaching, interreligious dialogue and ecumenism," but a decidedly "more conservative" stance on internal church issues, e.g., "the notion of church as people of God" was diminished, "collegiality" was limited to "the relationship between the pope and the bishops," and "the role of the episcopal conferences . . . was decisively reduced to a mere tool and deprived of real ecclesiological meaning." Much of this had Cardinal Ratzinger's imprint all over it, writes Faggioli.[13]

Furthermore, argues Faggioli's, "the Catholic conservative narrative about Vatican II received a formidable boost by the election of Benedict XVI [2005]," although he also acknowledges that "the anti-Vatican II *revanche* mentality had already found important room for expansion" during the time of John Paul II with Ratzinger as doctrinal and theological watchdog. The end result of this post-Vatican II period is a serious polarization in the Church under Benedict between the anti, almost "Lefebvrian narrative" among "traditionalists," and the progressive position of "disappointment with Vatican II as a failed promise."[14]

Then something remarkable occurred: Pope Benedict XVI announced he was resigning the papacy. Looking old and tired, possibly worn out by an inability to deal with internal church corruption and a stubborn Vatican bureaucracy, he chose to step aside. In March of 2013 something equally remarkable occurred: the College of Cardinals elected Jorge Bergoglio, a Jesuit from Argentina whose parents had immigrated to South America from Italy. Bergoglio was the first pope from Latin America, as well as the first

12. Faggioli, *Vatican II*, 86.

13. Faggioli, *Vatican II*, 87.

14. Faggioli, *Vatican II*, 106–8.

post-Vatican II pope, having been ordained to the priesthood in 1966, one year after the conclusion of the Council. Bergoglio took the name Francis, not after Francis Xavier of Jesuit fame, but Francis of Assisi, the humble, nature-oriented medieval priest who founded the reform-minded Franciscan Friars.

Writing shortly after Bergoglio's election as pope, Jesuit theologian Paul Crowley suggests that "The Catholic Church is peering through a door cracked open by a new pope who has sparked the imagination of the world and rekindled a spirit of hope that many Catholics first encountered during the years of the second Vatican Council (1962–65)." Crowley points to early signs that under Francis this is truly a new moment in the Church. Like John XXIII, Francis would offer a pastoral rather than doctrinal approach to his teaching office by offering a "medicine of mercy rather than that of severity . . . love and inclusion . . . a humility in pastoral service and a church marked by poverty of the gospel . . . realizing the Church as an instrument of peace, justice and unity." And in a fairly startling moment when asked about the church's stance on homosexuality, Crowley reminds us of Francis' now famous reply, "Who am I to judge?" As to the proper understanding and interpretation of the documents of Vatican II, despite an acknowledgment that opinions differ on how to view and implement the Council, Francis clearly affirms that the gospel must be read "in light of contemporary culture [reading the sign of the times]," a pretty clear indication of Francis' preference for the more progressive perspective (neo-Thomist) perspective, following Faggioli's analysis.[15]

Though Francis is very careful to see himself as building on the legacies of his immediate predecessors, John Paul II and Benedict XVI, it seems clear that he considers the Council unfinished and is committed to completing the process. It's also clear that Paul VI is a kind of hero for Francis. Journalist Austin Ivereigh quotes Francis acknowledging that Paul is his "great light," often affirming that Paul VI's encyclical *Evangelii Nuntiandi* is not only Francis' "favorite church document," but "the greatest pastoral document ever written." Francis viewed its "great purpose . . . to reconcile eternal church teaching with the diversity of cultures."[16] I don't think it's a stretch to say that Francis is attempting to leapfrog over the legacies of the two previous popes and pick up where Paul VI left off, or maybe didn't quite have the courage to complete himself due to his aforementioned concern for unity.

15. Crowley, *From Vatican II*, xiii-xv.

16. Ivereigh, *The Great Reformer*, 122, 369.

In a wonderful study of Francis' roots in Latin America and their impact on his worldview, pastoral theologian Allan Figueroa Deck, himself a Latino, documents how the Latin American bishops (CELAM) took the documents of Vatican II much more seriously than any other regional conference of international church leaders. At the famous bishop's conference in 1968 at Medellin, Colombia, under the influence of the fledgling liberation theology movement, the bishops issued their now famous and central church teaching on "the preferential option for the poor," in their minds a clear biblical theme which they rediscovered and highlighted as central to the message of the Hebrew prophets and Jesus. A central theme of the conference was social injustice, what they called "systemic or structural injustice," referring to the situation as sinful, a great evil which serious Christians must confront and transform.[17]

Figueroa Deck counts Francis in the liberation theology camp, but clarifies that there are two strains, one more focused on social analysis with its influences of Marxism and dependency theory, the other specifically emerging out of Francis' home country of Argentina and referred to as a "theology of the people," equally focused on liberation and transformation of society, but more influenced by biblical foundations and the popular religious practices of the poor themselves. This latter perspective was what most influenced Francis and helps account for his deep sense of connection to the poor, the slum dwellers, and his call for clerics to mingle with the people, using the powerful image that priests should "smell of the sheep" as a sign of humility and a different way of being a priest. All of this fits with a constant theme of Francis, that is, railing against clericalism, a scourge that seemed to re-establish itself under John Paul II and Benedict, and considered a "poison" by Francis.[18]

Taking his "smell of the sheep" imagery one step further, Francis envisions the church as a "field hospital after battle," about the business of "healing wounds," always being near God's people. "The ministers of the Gospel must be people who can warm the hearts of the people, who walk through the dark night with them, who know how to dialogue and to descend themselves into their people's night, into the darkness, but without getting lost."[19]

But beyond this identification and solidarity with the people, which is part and parcel of Francis' Latin American ecclesial and theological roots, according to Figueroa Deck, "what is particularly distinctive about this

17. Figueroa Deck, *Francis*, 74–76.

18. Figueroa Deck, *Francis*, 32–59. Gaillardetz, *An Unfinished Council*, 69–70, 116.

19. Ivereigh, *The Great Reformer*, 168–69.

pope is his absolute insistence on political participation and commitment to social justice that flow from faith and love and not ideology," a particular mark of the liberation strain of "theology of the people" and Catholic Social Teaching dating all the way back to Pope Leo XIII. He has addressed the European Union and the United Nations as well as the U.S. Congress on the topic of socioeconomic inequality, and in his pursuit of linking faith and social justice Francis has shown a strong "prophetic orientation" in his teaching. In one famous sermon he makes it clear the role of political engagement: "It is not true that a good Catholic doesn't meddle in politics . . . A good Catholic meddles in politics, offering the best of himself, so that those who govern can govern. But what is the best that we can offer to those who govern?" According to Figueroa Deck, Francis' question refers to his admonition for the Church to be prophetic but not to "confuse the gospel message with partisan political ideologies of the left or the right."[20]

And Francis has often, both as bishop and pope, been fond of repeating words from Pius XI, who said: "politics is one of the highest forms of charity," which in a 2013 speech Francis elaborated on by saying: "Politics, according to the Social Doctrine of the Church, is one of the highest forms of charity, because it serves the common good."[21]

One of Francis' biographers, Austen Ivereigh, shares an amazing encounter that Francis had with fellow Argentinians while visiting Rio de Janeiro, Brazil, as he was reflecting upon what he would like to happen at the upcoming World Youth Day: "Sure, here inside [the cathedral] there's going to be havoc, and here in Rio, too, but I want havoc in the dioceses, I want us out there, I want the Church to go out into the street, I want us to avoid everything that speaks of worldliness, of comfort, of clericalism, of being closed in on ourselves. The parishes, the schools, the institutions—these are all places to go out from, and if we don't get out from them we become an NGO, and the Church cannot be an NGO."[22]

Whatever did the pope mean by the expression "create havoc"? Evidently some English translators decided the expression meant "create a mess," which thoroughly confused everyone. Instead, explains Ivereigh, the Spanish expression "*hacer lio* has a particular meaning in Argentina, where going out into the streets to bang saucepans and shout at the top of your voice indicates exuberant passion for a cause!"[23]

20. Figueroa Deck, *Francis*, 124–25.

21. Figueroa Deck, *Francis*, 11, 132.

22. Ivereigh, *The Great Reformer*, 45.

23. Ivereigh, *The Great Reformer*, 45.

And at various other times in his still young papacy, Francis has addressed issues of church and ministerial reform, such as renewed collegiality and re-empowerment of regionalized bishop's conferences, decentralization of authority, the common priesthood of all baptized, the possibility of married clergy and a greater role for women in the church, including ordaining women deacons. But in doing so, as theologian Richard Gaillardetz makes clear, it has put "Francis under fire" with members of the Curia, as any number have criticized him openly, afraid, writes Gaillardetz, that "Francis is the pope who might finally achieve the vision of the second Vatican Council." And some are cynically using his awkward, and at times, outright mishandling of the clerical sexual abuse crisis, to call for his resignation. Nevertheless, opines Gaillardetz, "The success of this pontificate likely represents the last, best chance for decades to come for the decisive realization of the vision of Vatican II. The stakes could scarcely be higher."[24]

In his book entitled: *An Unfinished Council: Vatican II, Pope Francis, and the Renewal of Catholicism*, Gaillardetz summarizes the current situation this way:

> Fifty years after the council, we are still waiting for a comprehensive program of church reform dedicated to the appropriate and necessary transformation of ecclesiastical structures. The focus of such a program would be to develop alternative ways to discipline ecclesial power in keeping with the Gospel. Such institutional reform is not a "liberal" project bent on accommodation to the values of the secular world, as is so often suggested; it is the necessary reform of a church that wishes to be more deeply rooted in the radical values of the Christian Gospel. It is a reform committed to unleashing the beautiful gifts of the Spirit lying dormant in our church.[25]

While interviewing Fr. Regis Ryan, current APP president, in a rectory he has been living in since arriving in the working class McKees Rocks section of Pittsburgh in 1975, I asked him what it meant for him personally and APP that Francis has been elected pope. "We feel vindicated," he replied, as Francis has spoken to so many of the issues APP has been advocating since 1966, e.g., collegiality and decentralization, increased role of women and ordination to the diaconite, openness to the possibility of married clergy, anti-clericalism, simplicity of lifestyle, social justice and

---

24. Gaillardetz, "Francis under Fire."
25. Gaillardetz, *An Unfinished Council*, 155–56.

political engagement, lay empowerment, common priesthood, respect for the LGBTQ community, etc.[26]

Shortly after the election of Pope Francis in March of 2013, APP took the occasion to make a public statement of congratulations, which they sent off to the Vatican. In the statement they expressed "best wishes to Pope Emeritus Benedict: May the Spirit accompany you always," but then added that this election represents an opportunity "to speak about a renewed vision for the whole Church for its days ahead." Speaking to the new pope specifically about their vision of the common priesthood, they declared:

> It is our conviction that ordination to the priesthood should be open to all baptized Catholics, just as they have always been taught and encouraged to claim as their legacy the sacraments of Baptism, Conformation, Eucharist, Reconciliation, Matrimony and Anointing of the Sick, so they should similarly be taught and encouraged to claim ordination as part of the same heritage. We feel this opening of ordination to all, without regard to gender, marital status or sexual orientation, will help to create the kind of equality truly worthy of a Church proclaiming good news. For this equality countless hearts are longing and when it is created, a waiting Church and world will rejoice.[27]

APP didn't miss a beat or a chance to engage the new pope as soon as he stepped into office. The so-called "Francis factor" became an immediate interest of APP and, in a real sense, gave the group new energy and hope. At a church renewal meeting not long after Francis' election the group declared "we were very excited about Pope Francis' statement that Vatican II has been only half implemented and that his goal is to implement 'the other half.'" From 2014 on, every annual mountaintop gathering of APP reflected upon the relationship between APP's agenda and mission and that of Francis. In 2014 they compared "common themes" with Francis: non-judgmental approach ("who am I to judge?"), inclusivity, life of simplicity and humility, rootedness in the joy of the Gospel, poverty and economic justice, openness to liberation theology, connection with youth, inclusion of women and laity in leadership.[28] At a follow-up to the annual mountaintop gathering, the group pretty much agreed that they were doing a good job of integrating the "Francis factor" into their initiatives and their programming. It had been many decades since the APP felt in sync with much of what was coming out of the Vatican, to say the least.

26. Private interview, June 15, 2017.

27. Letter to Pope Francis sent on March 28, 2013.

28. Minutes of mountaintop meeting, April 14, 2014.

In 2015, on the fiftieth anniversary of the end of Vatican II, Fr. Neil McCaulley, APP's most passionate member in its indefatigable struggle for Church reform, wrote an inspiring summary of APP's accomplishments since 1966. Despite determination, doggedness, and undying joy for reform in the Church he so loved, McCaulley cautioned that much work still needs to be done. He warned about the need to be on guard "against revisionism, an attempt to roll back Vatican II effects" and to stay focused on the "unfinished business of the documents," acknowledging that "as soon as the Council was ended some in the Church began to oppose . . . it, especially among the *Curia.*" But, McCaulley reminded, "The 16 documents of the Council stand; become familiar with them again. Be inspired again! . . . We may have the loneliness of the long distance runner but Jesus says it's worth it."[29]

The following year, in October of 2016, APP celebrated its own fiftieth year since that first clandestine gathering of nineteen priests, a lively affair attended by about seventy-five members and supporters—at the time APP had approximately 40–50 active members and an overall membership of 160. In typical APP fashion, the anniversary committee was made up of canonical priests, married priests and their spouses, and lay folks, all under the lay leadership of Marcia Snowden, a long time APP member and former sister of Mercy for over thirty-five years. I had the privilege of delivering the keynote address, offering an overview of APP history which also served as a launching pad for this current writing project. Although, sadly, some key APP member priests had died in recent years—Don McIlvane, Neil Mc-Caulley, Warren Metzler—many other original members were present. A highlight of the event was the acknowledgement of the participation of several APP members who had participated in the historic freedom marches in Selma and, later, Jackson, Mississippi (Don Fisher, Mark Glasgow, posthumously, Don McIlvane.) A lively period of discussion, reflections and stories followed as the group pledged commitment to carrying on with its historic mission and to seeing this writing project through to its completion.

Long before APP altered its membership to include married priests and their spouses, religious sisters and women and men laity, in 1993, APP members had a long history of working very closely with laity and, more especially, religious sisters. Plowshares activist and Thomas Merton Center co-founder, and great friend to APP as a Catholic lay leader, Molly Rush often has spoken of the deep impact of APP leaders on many lay Catholics, as has been mentioned earlier in this study. Also, from its inception in 1966, APP formed close bonds with various communities of sisters, e.g., Sisters of

---

29. Neil McCaulley, "The Church of Vatican II," undated letter, likely late in 2015.

Mercy, Sisters of St. Joseph, Divine Providence, Sisters of Charity, Benedictines, et al. To this day most all of the APP's ongoing speaker series meets at the motherhouse of the Sisters of Divine Providence, north of Pittsburgh. One might say the sisters of Pittsburgh have always had APP's back and APP has always advocated for a much greater recognition of the work of vowed sisters, but also for expanded roles of leadership for the sisters.

In a time in which many of the younger clergy seemed to have reverted to a pre-Vatican II perspective on priesthood and priestly life, whether in their theology or, symbolically, in their daily garb, as previously cited by a number of authors, they have also shown remarkably little interest in working with women religious.[30] In contrast, APP clerics have almost all maintained very deep and close friendships and working relationships with religious women. It is my belief and observation that these relationships have been essential in the healthy and prophetic ministries of APP clerics, and has solidified their deep convictions about shared ministry that has kept APP viable and effective for over fifty years as a model for priestly witness. Given that women in general, and women religious in particular, are the lifeblood and backbone of the Catholic Church, it is vital that male clerics have healthy personal relationships with women as well as good working relationships and regard for women as they carry out their priestly ministry. Furthermore, writes Fr. Donald Cozzens, a former seminary director, in his probing, insightful and engaging study of the priesthood, priests need to deal openly and honestly with questions of intimacy and, despite celibacy, are in need of intimate friendships. The health and vitality of the Church itself is at stake, he argues.[31] Over the years I have observed any number of such relationships between APP clerical members and women, religious and lay. Such relationships, in my view, have served only to strengthen their prophetic witness to a truly inclusive and shared sense of priestly ministry.

Not only has APP a long history of working with women religious congregations, but individual APP clerics have often formed special working relationships with individual sisters, not only related to certain parish situations, but also in the wider work of church reform and social justice. Although many women religious have worked side by side with APP clergy, too many to mention in this study, in particular three women religious have played major leadership roles with APP right up to the present moment. Two of these women, Joyce Rothermel and Marcia Snowden, after many years as vowed religious, moved on from their respective religious communities but continued to work in the fields of social service and social justice, and have

---

30. Author's private interviews with any number of sisters over these last years.

31. Cozzens, *The Changing Face*, 25–43.

also been key activists in the ongoing work of APP. Snowden is point person for the writing of this APP history project. The third, Sr. Barbara Finch, still a member of the Sisters of St. Joseph in Baden, PA., and a recently retired nurse working in the county jail system, works tirelessly in a leadership role with APP, currently serving as a member of the APP's steering committee.

In the cases of Rothermel and Snowden, there is also a long-term relationship with the Thomas Merton Peace and Justice Center, a group initially funded by APP donations and now a partner with APP and other activist groups in the struggle for social justice in the greater Pittsburgh region. Snowden and Rothermel have served the Merton Center as both board and staff members at various times and have helped ensure that APP and the Merton Center work collaboratively on key issues.

Snowden remembers well living in a Sister of Mercy convent in the Manchester neighborhood of Pittsburgh as Jack O'Malley served as curate, then later pastor of St. Joseph's Parish. With the support of pastor Ed Joyce, St Joseph's was one of the training grounds for seminarians who were attracted to both Joyce and more especially activist O'Malley, who, as a newly ordained priest, attended the first APP meeting. When Cesar Chavez, the great organizer of the California farmworkers, contacted O'Malley to implement grape and lettuce boycotts in Pittsburgh, Snowden remembers hosting the farmworkers in the convent.

Later many priests and sisters together attended urban ministry programs at the University of Notre Dame (CCUM) under the leadership of co-founder of the Association of Chicago Priests, Monsignor Jack Egan. Among other things the priests and sisters learned about faith-based community organizing, initiated by Saul Alinsky in Chicago in the late 1930s, and carried on by disciples like Egan. Some APP members and sisters like Snowden became founding members of a local community organizing group that lasted for several years.

Rothermel, currently chair of the Church reform committee of APP and a close collaborator with Fr. John Oesterle on APP's speaker series group, joined APP as soon as membership changed to include more than just priests in 1993.

Sr. Barbara Finch, besides serving on APP's steering committee, also serves as the group's resident liturgist. Barbara can put together a prayer service in short order whenever called upon. She met Don Fisher and Jack O'Malley in the late sixties and became active at St. Joseph's somewhat later. Finch has inexhaustible energy, never misses a rally for justice, no matter what the issue, and admits that she once wondered about priesthood for herself, as so many of her mentors have been ordained priests. Although Finch, like others I've interviewed, thinks APP might one day close up shop and its members, the majority now lay, might consider becoming part of a Catholic reform group, Call to Action, she still finds great meaning in her participation in APP. "Every age needs a prophetic group, always ahead of its time," declares Finch. The APP has been a "phenomenal witness" over the years and has truly served as a vision of the "future church."[32]

Given APP's long and vital connection to women religious, it is no surprise that the group stepped up in support of women religious members of the Leadership Council of Women Religious (LCWR) when, in 2012, under Pope Benedict, the Vatican's Congregation on Doctrine and Faith initiated an investigation into LCWR, purportedly for its overemphasis on issues such as economic inequality and war and peace, and lack of deeper concern for traditional church issues around personal and sexual morality, most especially abortion. Not only did APP pass and circulate a "statement of support for the LCWR," lauding their many accomplishments, but demanded an "immediate end to the outrageous, hurtful and scandalous mandate of the Congregation for the Doctrine of Faith (CDF)." They encouraged all APP members to write protest letters to three members of the U.S. hierarchy in charge of the investigation. APP sent off its own letter of protest to Cardinal Muller, new head of the CDF as of August of 2012, asking him to "make this [investigation] go away." They characterize it as "deeply offensive" and a "cause of division in the Church," as it has "attacked the reputation of our Sisters." Furthermore, APP organized vigils at St. Paul's Cathedral in Pittsburgh in support of LCWR and demanding an end to the investigation.[33]

Shortly after Pope Francis' election, in April of 2013, at a monthly gathering, APP members expressed concern that Francis had yet to distance himself from this investigation, thus giving the impression of tacit support, despite widespread outrage on the part of many in the Church that this group of male hierarchy members would have the gall to challenge the great work and witness of women religious.[34] Although I could not locate a copy, APP drafted, adopted and sent off a letter to Pope Francis in June of 2014 expressing grave concerns about the LCWR investigation and recommending a quick resolution with a statement about the excellent work of LCWR since its inception in 1956 in the era of Pope Pius XII.[35] Thankfully, by mid-2015, after a fifty minute meeting between LCWR leadership and Pope Francis, a report was written and the investigation came to a resolution;

32. Multiple interviews with Rothermel, Snowden and Finch from 2016–2018.

33. APP brochure in support of LCWR; Letter to Cardinal Muller, August 9, 2012; APP minutes, June 4, 2012.

34. APP minutes, April 14, 2013.

35. APP minutes, May and June, 2014.

the end of another tragic chapter in the recent history of the relationship between the hierarchy and its faithful.

Although APP has always been an association, initially of clergy from the diocese of Pittsburgh, then eventually married priests, their spouses, religious sisters, women and men in the laity, pretty much all from the Pittsburgh diocese, for many years a priest from the neighboring diocese of Greensburg, PA., Fr. Bernie Survil, has been a faithful friend and member of the group. Survil, a very committed social gospel priest for many decades, has always found great support and solidarity with the Pittsburgh group. For many he is a true prophet, often in the forefront of both Church renewal efforts, as well as social justice activism. Regarding the latter, Survil has been so identified with radical politics that at a 2017 APP general meeting the minutes recorded him as "Fr. Bernie Sanders," a beautiful slip by the recorder of the meeting, associating Survil with the outspoken socialist Senator from Vermont, not a stretch at all.

Among other ministries in his five decades of priesthood, Survil has had an almost twenty-five year stint as a Maryknoll priest volunteer, spending a few decades in various countries in Central America. He also spent time on the U.S.–Mexico border in the early days of the church sanctuary movement, as refugees were pouring over the border in the early 1980s, fleeing from civil war and in search of safe passage. A few actually made it to Pittsburgh and stayed in a Mennonite church for over one year before moving on to Canada. For the past many years Survil has been back in the Western Pennsylvania area, active both in Greensburg and Pittsburgh, faithfully participating with APP, and joining in and, in some cases initiating, internal Church reform efforts as well as social justice outreach. With the support of APP, he has helped initiate a new, independent national clergy group calling itself the Association of U.S. Catholic Priests, who have, among other things, been advocating for the ordination of women deacons. Several APP priest members have joined the AUSCP. However, unlike APP, AUSCP has not invited into full membership all baptized Catholics who agree with their agenda. When Survil first approached APP in 2011 about the idea of starting up a national clergy group, APP supported the idea but expressed disappointment that it would be an all clergy group, although, as of 2016, they do welcome associate members or "friends" from the laity.

As an outspoken and activist priest, Survil has always had a somewhat tense relationship with the leadership of his own diocese, although he may not share that viewpoint completely. Deceased APP priest, Don Fisher, once shared with me an encounter he had with Survil. Seems that Survil was acknowledging to Fisher that he was having some difficulty with his then bishop, Anthony Bosco, a Pittsburgh native, when Fisher, who knew

Bosco pretty well, offered to intervene and speak with the bishop on Survil's behalf. Survil responded that he wouldn't want that, as it might strain his relationship with the bishop! Fisher thought that hilarious, though he wasn't sure that Survil had a similar reaction. More recently, in the Fall 2013, APP minutes related that Survil had received a "formal canonical warning" from the Vicar General of the Greensburg diocese for what was described as his "parking lot ministry." It seems that he had been leafletting automobiles in church parking lots in the Greensburg and Pittsburgh dioceses during Sunday Mass. A legislator whose district covered one of the parking lots in question and who was named in the leaflet as defying the U.S. Bishop's position on immigration reform, contacted the Greensburg diocese to complain; thus, Survil received a "canonical warning and fraternal correction" to immediately stop this "ministry," or face the consequences. Survil respectfully replied by citing the pope's own words on immigrant rights and, while defending his actions, acknowledged he needed to consult his own canon lawyer as to the meaning of formal canonical warning. Fr. Bernie "Sanders" strikes again.

On a somewhat more serious note, though, Survil's rather harsh letter from the diocese, with its threat of a "formal canonical warning," raised for APP, yet again, the question of due process for priests, as another APP priest had previously received such a "warning." What rights do priests have when questioned by their diocesan officials? To its credit, over the years, whenever issues did arise for one of its priests, and one was called down to the chancery for interrogation, APP never let anyone appear alone. APP was always there to support its members.

Also in 2013, Survil became APP's point person on another issue central to its church renewal advocacy, i.e., lay and clergy participation in the selection of bishops. Survil had raised the issue at an APP meeting as his own bishop in the Greensburg diocese was retiring in 2014 and he thought, with its history and research on this issue, APP might want to get involved in the process. He was commissioned to draft a statement for the group. While drafting the statement for APP, Survil cited the words of the Archbishop Emeritus of San Francisco, John Quinn, who stated in a March 2013 address at Stanford University: "A very large number of bishops are of the opinion that there is not any real or meaningful collegiality in the Church today . . . [and that] . . . local bishops have no perceptible influence in the appointment of bishops. Instead, appointments are made in Rome, often by men who do not adequately know local diocesan needs."[36]

36. APP policy statement, August, 2013.

At the same time a group of lay people from the Greensburg diocese, friends of Survil, formed what they called the "Ambrosians of Greensburg," with a mission statement that read: "In light of Pope Francis' emphasis on transparency and collegiality, the Ambrosians of Greensburg were formed to act as a conduit for messages and concerns of local Catholics particularly as they pertain to assigning a new bishop for the diocese of Greensburg." They chose their name in honor of St. Ambrose who, in 374 CE was elected bishop of Milan by the local clergy and laity. They also cited Pope Celestine (422–432 CE) who required lay and clergy input into the selection of bishops. The group then organized a petition drive to Pope Francis highlighting the qualities they felt the next bishop of Greensburg ought to possess. The group had the full support of the APP, and APP member Neil McCaulley sent a letter to Greensburg laity and clergy offering to serve as a resource, as he was thoroughly familiar with a manual developed by the NFPC on procedures as to how best to select bishops with full local input.[37]

Edward Malesic, a priest from York Haven, PA, was chosen as Greensburg's bishop in April of 2015. At the time one of the leaders of the Ambrosians who helped organize the petition drive to Pope Francis, Angela Rudick, said that she felt the process worked well and "was encouraged" by what she had heard of the new bishop. "I'm hoping he will be a bishop who can put the image of Christ in our minds, that he cares for the poor, that he is not a king, but simply a holy man, someone more in line with our Pope," said Rudick.[38] APP followed up with a letter of congratulations to the new bishop, introducing themselves and their mission and activities, with an offer to meet up and collaborate "to build up the kingdom of God in southwestern Pennsylvania."[39]

As I've suggested before, one of the admirable qualities of APP leadership over the decades has been its willingness to constantly discern and reimagine its ongoing mission, its goals and purposes, and to analyze just how effective its work is. Particularly in these last years, most especially with the death or disablement of some key APP clerics, there has been a critical sense that one of its main contribution to the life of the church and the greater Pittsburgh region is its educational outreach, i.e., specifically its speaker series, which brings in five to six nationally recognized figures who have their pulse on key religious and moral issues of the day. Some, though not all, of the Catholic speakers have found themselves on the margins of the Church,

37. Letter from McCaulley to Ambrosians, October 11, 2015.
38. Internal communication among Ambrosians with quote from Rudick, citing an article in the *Tribune Review*, in Greenburg, PA, April 25, 2015.
39. APP letter, June 16, 2015.

such as "Nuns on the Bus" Sister Simone Campbell, married priest Anthony Padavano, Kathleen Kennedy Townsend, Fr. Charles Curran, Bishop Tom Gumbleton, expelled Maryknoll priest, Ray Bourgeois, and, more recently, "silenced" Redemptorist priest from Ireland, Tony Flannery, who drew two hundred people to his presentation on the future church and new language and thinking.

Over the years two religious sisters drew the largest crowds. Local sister Janet Mock, who had recently finished up a leadership role with LCWR, spoke on the "Sense of the Faithful," in September of 2013. Then, in March of 2016, evolutionary theologian, Sr. Ilia Delio, addressed a standing room only audience with a talk entitled: "Co-creating an Unfinished Universe." Besides keeping the Catholic community, as well as the wider religious and secular community, apprised of key social and religious issues, the speaker series allows APP, a group considered marginal by many in the Pittsburgh Catholic community, to maintain contact with people who have little interest in participating in APP directly, but nevertheless appreciate this high quality speaker series and wish to help promote its success by attending lectures and spreading the word. One seemingly progressive diocesan priest whom I interviewed, who is not a member of APP and was clear he had little interest in becoming a member, despite his respect for the individuals involved and the justice projects the group has undertaken, nevertheless actively promotes the speaker series and expressed great appreciation to APP for the depth and relevance of its programming.[40]

Fr. John Oesterle serves as the key facilitator of the speaker series and deserves much of the credit for making this series so successful. He considers it one of his main contributions to the group as a member of the church renewal committee. He seeks out recommendations for speakers from the wider community, gathers information on the candidates, and circulates that information for group consumption. The group then votes on whom to actually reach out to. Oesterle does the bulk of the follow up to engage speakers and to arrange details. Over and over in APP minutes in these last few years, I have read similar statements to the effect that "all agree that our speaker series is our very best product at this time. It should be continued and expanded."[41]

Regarding their ongoing mission, APP members can be hard on themselves. For example, by late 2017 at a general meeting while reflecting on "APP's response to peace and justice issues," one participant asked: "What

---

40. Two telephone interviews with Fr. Michael Stumpf, November 20, 2017 and June 15, 2018.

41. APP minutes, April 13, 2015.

do we do beyond making statements?" One member suggested that now "the Merton Center is our voice." Another chimed in: "we partner with others on issues."[42] The truth is, though, despite the depletion of full-time clergy in APP, some of whom took the lead in areas of social activism—Don McIlvane and Don Fisher deceased, Jack O'Malley disabled—in the Francis years APP still has remained relatively active on social justice issues even as they partner up with other activist groups such as the Thomas Merton Center and Pennsylvania Interfaith Impact Network, as well as a newer configuration of mostly Catholics lay people called "Social Justice Seekers."

One very tangible local justice issue APP engaged in as early as 2012 is the ongoing attempt by adjunct faculty to unionize at Duquesne University, a local Catholic school.[43] Some of APP's best work over the years has been to call to account the very Catholic institutions it is so deeply imbedded in. At a January, 2013 APP general meeting, two of these faculty members were invited to address the group because "The good Catholic University has denied them the right to see that the NLRB [National Labor Relations Board] intervene in this struggle." APP offered "to support them [the two professors] in any way which they might consider helpful."[44] In April of 2014 Fr. Neil McCaulley, APP letter writer extraordinaire even in his retirement and only two months before his death, sent off a letter to a faculty dean that was vintage McCaulley, citing Church sources while delivering a slightly sardonic request:

Dear Dr. Dougherty,

This coming Divine Mercy Sunday the Church Universal will canonize two great popes—John XXIII and John Paul II. It would seem an opportune time to honor them by recognizing the adjunct professors' union efforts and enter into collective bargaining with them.

John Paul II and John XXIII were such strong teachers of Catholic social teaching, especially the basic human right to form a union to enter into collective bargaining.

Doesn't that seem like an appropriate gesture for a Catholic University?

Peace in the Resurrected Christ,
Fr. Neil McCaulley[45]

42. APP minutes, October 9, 2017.

43. "APP Support Statement of the Adjunct Faculty at Duquesne University," September, 2012.

44. APP minutes, January 14, 2013.

45. Letter sent April of 2014.

In the early part of 2016 as the teachers' the struggle continued, APP declared "no progress to report": the University was still looking for a "religious exemption" from the NLRB, and the unionizers were "threatening to go all the way to the Supreme Court." It was noted at this February 8 meeting of APP that union organizing for adjunct faculty was happening all over the country, including many Catholic schools, some of whom settled, others not. For APP it was reminiscent of the fight with the diocese over teacher unionizing attempts in primary and secondary Catholic schools in the diocese in the 1970s. According to a recent issue of *The Duquesne Duke*, the university's campus newspaper, "The NLRB ruled in a unanimous decision ordering Duquesne University to bargain with an adjunct faculty union group." Nevertheless, the struggle goes on as the University will appeal the NLRB decision in court.[46]

In October of 2013, APP members Neil McCaulley, Jack O'Malley and John Oesterle took on another diocesan organization, The Catholic Cemetery Association, supporting an attempt by the Cemetery Workers' Union to negotiate a new contract. At a public gathering of Pittsburgh priests at Oglebay, WV, Neil McCaulley spoke up and addressed Bishop Zubik in support of the cemetery workers. It seemed Zubik knew nothing. After the meeting, Oesterle spoke privately with Zubik. Two days later Oesterle received a phone call to join a conference call with the bishop and other diocesan officials. He shared with them the issues the workers raised at a recent APP meeting they attended. Sometime later, reports Oesterle, "The union leaders came back to a future APP meeting, saying that they settled for a far better contract than they ever expected; All this because Neil [McCaulley] opened his mouth in the right place at the right time."[47]

APP also had deep concerns about institutional Catholic opposition to aspects of the Affordable Care Act, specifically looking for a religious exemption related to the issue of artificial contraception. They shared their differences with the bishop at a meeting in 2012. Sometime later that year Bishop Zubik and the bishop of Erie filed law suits on this issue, and in response APP and "various Catholic groups" filed "amicus briefs in opposition to the suits filed then by the bishops." Catholic lawyer and friend of APP, Paul Titus, helped file these briefs.[48]

In 2016 leading up to the elections in November, APP participated in a major effort to circulate a document entitled, "A Revolution of Tenderness:

---

46. Arke, "NLRB Rules."

47. E-mail communication from Fr. John Oesterle, November 9, 2018.

48. Minutes of meeting with Bishop Zubik, March 20, 2012; McElwee, "Pittsburgh Priests to Bishop."

A 2016 Pope Francis Voter Guide." It was written and circulated by a co-alition of national Catholic organizations, including various women's and men's religious communities, Pax Christi USA and a number of Catholic advocacy groups. The content of the document discussed the importance of political engagement, reminding Catholics that Pope Francis considers "politics one of the highest forms of love, because it is in the service of the common good." The document also raised concerns about the economy, global peacemaking, immigration and refugees, the environment, racial justice and freedom of religion and conscience. The document was complete with discussion questions and encouraged all dioceses to distribute the material. APP went all out on this task.

One issue of social justice and equality that the APP has given relatively little attention to until recently is that of LGBTQ rights; although there is one significant exception. Though several APP members have a very clear recollection of the event, I could not document exactly when it took place. To the best of anyone's recollection, sometime in the late 1980s, early 1990s, the Pittsburgh City Council was considering a resolution to protect the rights of LGBTQ folks to be classroom teachers. The Catholic diocese, with auxiliary Bishop McDowell as point person, opposed the resolution and McDowell testified at City Council. APP decided to support the resolution in direct opposition to the diocese. APP sent out a press release to that effect and Neil McCaulley volunteered to speak at City Council. The night before the hearing McCaulley received a call from Bishop Wuerl, asking him not to testify. They argued for a bit, McCaulley insisting that the issue was one of civil rights and the dignity of persons, not faith and morals, which might have demanded that McCaulley follow his bishop. During McCaulley's testimony in front of an overflow crowd in City Council chambers, according to a clerically-garbed John Oesterle who was in attendance, an agitated listener shouted: "I can't believe that a Catholic priest is saying this. He's probably a fag himself." Oesterle went on to recollect: "I could feel myself tighten up and anxious, wondering if people would think I was gay, and immediately I knew why I was there and why Neil was testifying." Gary Dorsey also received a call from Bishop Wuerl expressing disappointment that APP took a public stand against the diocese. "I thought we were friends," the bishop said to Dorsey. "We are," responded Dorsey, "we just see things differently on this issue." One year later the diocese reversed itself and dropped its opposition to the resolution.[49]

49. E-mail communication with John Oesterle, November 9, 2018. Private interview with Gary Dorsey, May 5, 2018.

APP pastors have always had a very positive history of supporting Dignity, a gay Catholic group, by celebrating Eucharist with them, generally at Protestant churches, as they were prohibited from such celebrations in their own churches. Nevertheless, until 2013, with the one exception of the City Council resolution issue in the late 1980s, as reported above, there is not much indication that gay rights' issues were on the APP radar. Then, in the minutes of the April 14, 2013 general meeting it is written that a Catholic bishop had made a public statement saying those in "same sex marriages should refrain from going to communion." In response to this, activist and progressive Bishop Thomas Gumbleton, who had been part of the APP's speaker series in 2012, made a public statement welcoming those in same-sex marriages to the "communion table." John Oesterle was commissioned to send Gumbleton a letter of "support and thanks."[50]

Later in 2013 "the group agreed that gay and lesbian issues should be supported in future donation decisions." But it wasn't until 2014 when a bill emerged in the State of Pennsylvania legislature (HB and senate Bill 300) dubbed "Equality PA," adding "sexual orientation, gender identity and expression" to the current Pennsylvania laws regarding protection of human rights, that APP began taking a more activist role on LGBTQ rights. The prime mover in this effort was Don Fisher. After agreeing to invite a speaker representing the LGBTQ community to address this piece of legislation at two different meetings in April and June of 2014, the group decided to participate in the annual Pride march. In announcing the decision to participate for the first time in the Pittsburgh Pride Parade, Fisher handwrote an incredibly compelling statement of explanation and solidarity with the LGBTQ community. In it, he apologized to the gay community that the priests had "come late to this journey—this historic struggle for equality." He talked about it as "a transformation of our society" and aligned it with the civil rights struggles of the 1950s and 1960s, which he participated in at Selma, Alabama and Jackson, Mississippi, by declaring "the old ways of 'separate but equal' no longer hold." He ended by decrying the role of the Church in this history of discrimination by writing: "Years of prejudice have infected our parishes, our places of learning, even our seminaries and have made them sick in this regard and called us into silence. Our hearts break when we think of this. It is high time for the silence to be broken on this issue." Participating in the march represented for Fisher a breaking of this silence, as he looked for "greater days ahead."[51]

---

50. APP minutes, April 14, 2013.
51. Undated press release from APP, signed by Don Fisher.

In July of that year, it was recorded that after the parade "We received a positive response from parade watchers. Next year we may want to have a table at the pride festival." At the same meeting it was discussed that APP weigh in publicly on the issue of gay marriage, as the state had recently approved legalization of marriage for same-sex partners. It was also noted that when questioned about gay issues and the Church, the pope had recently been quoted as saying: "Who am I to Judge?" Fisher was asked and agreed to draft a letter to the editor of the *Pittsburgh Post-Gazette* in support of gay marriage as well as the aforementioned legislation proposed in the state legislature.[52] The letter appeared in the September 19th edition of the *Pittsburgh Post-Gazette*. It is clear that the published letter was drafted by Fisher, as many of the same points addressed in his handwritten statement appear again in the published piece, even though his name doesn't appear in the newspaper, only the names of the current APP steering committee, "sent in the name of the Association of Pittsburgh Priests." The major addition to the printed piece is a call for advocacy for the legislative bill being debated at the time in the state legislature. Interestingly, the heading of the letter became a challenge to the institutional Church as it read: "Our Church Must End its LGBT [now LGBTQ] Prejudice."[53]

Participating in the Pittsburgh Pride Parade and issuing a public statement of support for same-sex marriage, LGBTQ equality, and advocating for the legislative bill on equality, but most especially condemning its own church for prejudice and silence, were yet more examples of courageous actions taken on the part of APP, in these cases in direct opposition to church leadership. APP was calling out the leadership of the local and national church to change its teaching and public witness on this issue. However, there was not total unanimity in the group on moving forward with participation in the Pittsburgh Pride Parade the following year. In a meeting immediately preceding the annual parade, the minutes read: "After a vibrant discussion, we voted to march in the Gay Pride Parade. Registration of $200 was approved. There were two abstentions." Both were clerics. Although nothing is said in the minutes as to the controversy regarding participation, one APP member remembers there being discomfort about an invited singer.[54] Nevertheless, shortly after the parade John Oesterle received a call

52. APP minutes, July 7, 2014.

53. Letter to editor, *Pittsburgh Post-Gazette*, September 19, 2014.

54. APP minutes, June 8, 2015. John Oesterle recalls that "the organizing group for the parade had invited a popular singer who was pro-gay but also racist. The younger leaders in the LGBTQ community asked the 'old guys network' to disinvite the singer. They refused. So they organized their own parade at a different time. I thought the negative votes came because of this."

from Don Fisher, who in exclaiming great joy about the APP's participation, declared to Oesterle, "We're all gay today," implying solidarity and oneness with the gay community.

One other related involvement of APP in very recent social justice education and organizing has to do with an initiative started by Social Justice Seekers, a group of lay Catholic activists with some links to APP. The prime mover behind this initiative is an APP supporter, Kevin Hayes. Hayes has attended APP meetings in the past, both to share his ideas but also to seek input and support from APP. The idea of Social Justice Seekers is to organize around regions of Greater Pittsburgh defined as north, south, east and west. It is a kind of cluster concept that The Thomas Merton Center developed back in the early 1980s. Indications are it is an excellent initiative to engage Catholics (and others) in important issues of the day. The group also has serious interest in a model one might call "contemplation and action," centered on the importance of grounding social activism in prayer and reflection. To that end, Social Justice Seekers and others sponsored two days of "reflection with the theme of reconciliation" in November of 2018. Many APP activists participated.

On a totally different front, though only involving APP minimally, the Pittsburgh diocese under the leadership of Donald Wuerl as bishop from 1988 until 2006 had a pretty good track record of dealing with the clergy sexual abuse issue. That perception continued under the leadership of his successor, David Zubik, who had been an auxiliary bishop under Wuerl before assuming leadership when Wuerl moved on to Washington, DC, eventually becoming a Cardinal of that diocese and a close confidant of Pope Francis. This perception dramatically changed with the publication of the Grand Jury of Pennsylvania report on clergy sexual abuse that covered six dioceses: Pittsburgh, Greensburg, Erie, Harrisburg, Allentown and Scranton. The dioceses of Altoona-Johnstown and Philadelphia were not part of this investigation as they had already been under scrutiny from 2003 to 2011. The report was issued on August 14, 2018. It had been held up for two months as the State Supreme Court heard challenges from approximately two dozen current and former clergy who claimed that allegations against them were false. In the final report several names were redacted until their challenges could be heard in full.[55] The State Supreme Court recently determined that the names should not be listed.

According to the report, over three hundred priests were accused of abusing more than one thousand children or teens in these six dioceses, and suggested there were likely many more. Most of the abused were boys,

55. Ward et al., "They Hid It All," A-1, A-6.

though there were also girls. Although there were instances as recent as 2010, "most occurred before the early 2000s, and many of the reported abuses go back decades to the 1960s, 70s and 80s . . . [T]he cover-up was sophisticated," according to Attorney General Josh Shapiro. "For decades, monsignors, auxiliary bishops, bishops, archbishops, cardinals have mostly been protected; many, including some named in this report, have been promoted. Until that changes, we think it is too early to close the book on the Catholic Church sex scandal," the report goes on. Ninety-nine priests from Pittsburgh were named: forty-three are deceased, twenty-six alive and thirty "unknown . . . redacted or omitted."[56]

Regarding former Pittsburgh Bishop Donald Wuerl's reputation for "helping victims" of sexual abuse and even standing up to the Vatican and prevailing in one particular case, the Grand Jury Report accused him of badly mishandling several cases of clerical abuse. Furthermore, it suggested he was responsible for coining an expression regarding these cases as the importance of a "circle of secrecy," an expression both he and his former assistant, now current Pittsburgh Bishop, David Zubik, vehemently deny. Knowing that the report was on its way and also knowing that he would be criticized in it, Cardinal Wuerl of Washington, DC, sent a pre-emptive letter to fellow clergy to the effect that, despite criticism, the report "also confirms I acted with diligence, with concern for survivors and to prevent future acts of abuse." He concluded by suggesting that a "just assessment of my actions . . . and my continued commitment to the protection of children will dispel any notions otherwise made by this report." Current Bishop Zubik has also attempted to defend both former Bishop Wuerl's actions and his own during these past 30 years, although the report stated that, as late as 2012, after offering a victim money for his children's college tuition as well as counseling help, Bishop Zubik asked him to sign a statement that he would not talk publicly about the abuse. The man reportedly declined to sign the confidentiality agreement. When asked about this, the bishop declared the church no longer asks victims to sign such agreements, stating, "We learn from the past. It's an evolving understanding." If true, it certainly took many years to come to such "understanding," a painstakingly slow evolution.[57]

---

56. Ward et al., "They Hid It All," A-1, A-6. To be fair, there have been only two known instances of child sexual abuse reported in the last ten years. John Oesterle made me aware of this as he cited the Jesuit columnist Thomas Reese. Also, despite the horrific nature of the clerical sexual abuse scandal, most especially the cover-up, according to psychologist Thomas Plante, since the bishops implemented new policies at a meeting in Dallas in 2002, there have been "'barely a trickle' of new clerical child sexual abuse cases." See Morris-Young, "Psychologist," 5.

57. Smeltz, et al., "Zubik Apologizes," A-1, A-9.

According to a piece in *The Washington Post*, the Grand Jury's report on the handling of clergy sexual abuse cases by then Bishop Wuerl can be best characterized as "mixed, at times stopping abusive priests from continuing in their ministries in the diocese and at other times guiding them right back into parishes." He was probably most applauded for his unwillingness to reinstate a priest, Anthony Cipolla, whom the Vatican directed him to restore to ministry. Wuerl prevailed in that case. But he also returned some to ministry, "often based on the advice of psychiatrists at the sometimes secretive church-run treatment centers where the diocese sent accused priests." Yet Wuerl did not seem guilty of many of the worst behavior, in which bishops named in the report hid cases from the authorities and lied to families. Maybe he relied on "faulty science" in his dependence on certain psychiatrists, but in the view of *National Catholic Reporter* journalist, Michael Winter and Canon Lawyer, Nicholas Cafardi, Wuerl was ahead of most bishops on this issue and "overall exercised his oversight properly." Furthermore, writes longtime religion reporter at the *New York Times*, Peter Steinfels, in a stinging rebuke of the grand jury report and its key author, Attorney general, Josh Shapiro, "The Pennsylvania grand jury report on sex abuse by Catholic priests is inaccurate, unfair, and fundamentally misleading. Its shortcomings should not be masked by its vehement style, its befuddling structure, or its sheer bulk."[58]

Nevertheless, Fr. Thomas Doyle, a Dominican priest and trained canon lawyer who worked for many years at the Conference of Catholic Bishops in Washington, DC, said in an interview in 2002 that by 1985 there was a massive report written on clergy sexual abuse that he helped produce, outlining the problem and suggesting precise strategies to deal with it. The bishops chose to disregard it. I don't think Fr. Doyle would buy the "faulty science" argument after 1985.[59]

Maybe the fairest or kindest statement concerning Wuerl's record on handling of this crisis was made by Monsignor John Engle, President and CEO of Catholic Charities, who said, in a somewhat tortured manner, "He [Wuerl] has integrity and care and commitment to honesty. I don't think he'd say he's done all the right things, but he did his best. It may seem like he made some wrong decisions, and maybe he did, but he didn't mean to."[60]

Both Cardinal Wuerl and Bishop Zubik have been pressured to resign by local groups as well as national networks. Beginning in late August, a

58. Zaumer & Thebault, "Cardinal Wuerl's Actions"; Steinfels, "Vehemently Misleading," 13–26.

59. Panaritis, "Priests Report Went Unheeded," A-1.

60. Boorstein, "Abuse Report."

number of protest vigils outside St. Matthew's Cathedral took place calling for Wuerl's resignation.[61] Although APP took no official position on the calls for resignation, I do know at least one APP member who wrote Bishop Zubik and called for him to resign (the request was not made in the name of APP but solely by the individual). Also, the national group Survivors Network of those Abused by Priests (SNAP) called for Zubik's resignation.[62]

And a group of approximately 7,000 theologians, educators, parishioners and lay leaders signed a statement calling on "The Catholic Bishops of the United States to prayerfully and genuinely consider submitting to Pope Francis their collective resignation as a public act of repentance and lamentation before God and God's People."[63]

After spending nearly two months defending his actions, on October 12, Wuerl asked the Pope to accept his resignation. The Pope did, but with seeming reluctance, offering praise for Wuerl's willingness to "put the good of the Church above his personal interests." The Pope characterized Wuerl's decision as "noble." And, curiously, the Pope asked him to stay on as apostolic administrator until a replacement is found.[64] Bishop Zubik remains in place as of now, resisting calls for his resignation. And he is currently attending listening sessions organized by many local Catholics, including APP.

Wuerl seems a tragic figure, highly respected among colleagues, yet guilty of, at minimal, poor judgment in some abuse cases. Furthermore, in some ways he looks much worse on the ongoing scandal of the sexually abusive behavior of former Cardinal, now defrocked priest, Theodore McCarrick. Wuerl had been told of McCarrick's behavior by one of his victims in 2004. After initially denying any knowledge of McCarrick's transgressions, Wuerl recently acknowledged that he had forgotten about the meeting with the victim, what he refers to as a "lapse in memory," and offered his apologies for "any additional grief my failure might have also brought the survivor."[65]

Zubik comes off as someone still in denial as to the gravity of the crisis, with a deaf ear towards the pain of his own people, and more than a little defensive. When quizzed at a press conference the day the report was publicized, Bishop Zubik was asked whether or not he considered resigning. Instead of acknowledging the general failure of the Church and its leadership

61. Bourbon, "Protesters Outside Churches."
62. Goldstein, "Abuse Survivors Group," A-4.
63. Dailytheology.org website, August 17, 2018.
64. Allen, "Abuse scandal."
65. Boorstein, "D.C. Prelate."

to protect children and teens, and that it has given him grave pause as a key leader as part of an institution responsible for such failure, thus humbly and honestly acknowledging deep regret, he chose to defend himself by stating, "I think that when you take a look at what I'm named for—I'm not named for any activity that would be a break of the trust that the pope places in me, and we are certainly doing a number of good things in the diocese that I would want to see continue."[66]

Seems to me a more appropriate and, ultimately, a more honest and healing response, would have been something like that of Bishop Eamon Martin of Armagh, Ireland, who said at the October internal bishop's synod "that there are still areas of life in the Church where this has not yet come to the fore, come to light." He went on to say there is still some "denial" going on in the international Catholic Church. When asked at the synod whether or not the Church could ever get beyond this scandal, he replied: "No, and nor should we, because people who have been traumatized by abuse never put it behind them. They carry it with them throughout their lives, and therefore so should we."[67]

Meanwhile, as fallout from the still recent grand jury report continues to play out, the Pittsburgh diocese moved forward with a significant new consolidation of parishes and clergy reassignments, thus further disrupting and wounding the faithful. Though advised by some to at least temporarily delay such a re-organization given the abuse crisis, the bishop moved ahead with the consolidation, given the green light at a gathering of diocesan priests following the grand jury report. One wonders where the voice of the people was in this decision-making.[68]

As for APP, the grand jury report was a devastating blow, especially for the clergy members. As faithful and prophetic servants of the Gospel and Church for over fifty years, they are part of a clerical system that is now under intense scrutiny. After the report came out I called a few APP priests on the phone and one expressed gratitude for the contact, admitting the day following the report was a deeply depressing and onerous day in his ministerial life. He deeply appreciated the support. However, concerning the grand jury report and the clergy sexual abuse crisis itself, there is little or, at least, no credible APP connection in terms of accused clergy. Of the

66. Goldstein, "Abuse Survivors," A-4.

67. Harris, "Irish Prelate."

68. One APP priest told me he thought the consolidation ought to be put on hold, particularly in light of the recent Grand Jury Report. He focused on the impact the latter is having on lay people. Another shared that, at a meeting of diocesan priests, most encouraged Bishop Zubik to proceed with the consolidation. Nevertheless, where was input from lay people?

ninety-nine Pittsburgh priests on the list of priests accused, two have some APP connections, one peripheral, Ed Joyce, the other direct, Don McIlvane. Joyce was pastor at St. Joseph's on the Northside when APP was founded. He was not at the first meeting, nor was he in a leadership role. But he was a supporter and a kind of mentor to the younger clergy, especially his curate, Jack O'Malley, who was ordained in 1965 and assigned to St. Joseph's at Joyce's request. Joyce was an intellectual, a great preacher and teacher, and a very progressive clergy voice regarding the reforms of Vatican II. He died in 1969. Though some knew Joyce had an alcohol problem, there was no indication he was involved in sexual abuse. A number of APP priests questioned were completely surprised when his name appeared on the list of those accused. Furthermore, sexual abuse was not on the radar in the 1960s. Few even imagined the problem or had any understanding of it. Interestingly, all I spoke to, including O'Malley, were unaware that Fr. Pat Jones, now deceased, actually turned Joyce into the diocese in 1968, having "caught [Joyce and a young person] in a compromising position." Joyce was yanked out of St. Joesph's (no one but Jones seemed to know the real reason) and served as chaplain for the Sisters of St. Francis for four months. He died the next year at the age of fifty-four.[69]

The other APP priest on the list, Don McIlvane, who died in 2014, was, for a good while, a key APP activist. McIlvane was at the initial gathering, took a leadership role, and until his somewhat early retirement in 1996, at the age of 68, was very active with the APP and in city politics. We've discussed McIlvane's profound impact in an earlier chapter. After retirement he was less active with APP, especially after the group changed its constitution and invited non-canonical priests into full membership. In later years he began to have some cognitive difficulties and spent his final years in a retirement home. Even in his APP active days he was often a loner, according to many APP clerics. McIlvane could be impatient and less interested in process. He would often call press conferences on his own. He was strident and uncompromising, although mostly about the right issues. He was particularly strong on racial justice and labor rights and he was a mentor to many.

McIlvane was accused of abuse by one man in 2006. The incidents (many, according to the accuser) occurred from 1973–75. He vehemently denied the accusations and several APP clerics accompanied him to the diocese to support him during the investigation. It was concluded that the accuser was not credible and the case was dropped. Several APP clergy

69. Office of Attorney General, Commonwealth of Pennsylvania, "Report I,," 670. Joyce's accuser filed his allegation in December of 2002, describing sexual abuse from 1966–1968.

remembered that the diocese did give some amount of money to the accuser, who evidently had personal issues and limited income. The Grand Jury Report confirmed this. The payment was not an admission on the part of the diocese that the accusations had any merit. There was an attempt by a lawyer to remove McIlvane's name from the Grand Jury Report, since there was never credible evidence, and he was deceased, but the attempt failed.[70]

Feeling the need to respond both to the Grand Jury Report and the listing of McIlvane, John Oesterle sent the following letter to the *Pittsburgh Post-Gazette*:

> I applaud the grand jury for its two-year investigation of sexual abuse by priests and cover-up by bishops over the past 70 years. Your paper has shared the devastating news. Hopefully it leads to continuing changes by dioceses worldwide in facing this issue. Hopefully legislators will respond to all four recommendations so that the Catholic Church and all institutions and organizations will protect children and teens.
>
> The August 18 PG listed Pittsburgh priests and their grand jury information. One is Rev. Don McIlvane, who was a champion of civil rights and racial equality and an outspoken critic of corruption in city, state, federal and Vatican affairs. He was opposed to the war in Vietnam and the militarization of our country.
>
> For those who did not have the time to read his entire report, one man accused him of abuse. An investigation was conducted and the Diocesan Review Board "voted unanimously that there was no semblance of truth to the allegations."
>
> Rev. John Oesterle, Uptown [71]

McIlvane's case raises another side of the horrific clergy abuse scandal, i.e., due process. Once the clergy abuse issue hit the news back in 2002 with the award-winning report of the *Boston Globe*'s "Spotlight" team, exposing widespread sexual abuse on the part of Boston clergy, some clergy, APP members among them, have felt that now some bishops will immediately

---

70. Office of Attorney General, Commonwealth of Pennsylvania, "Report I,," 702–3. The accuser described "at least 40" incidents from 1973–1977. In 2008, the diocese gave the accuser "$5000 to help him through some additional financial difficulties. The money was not intended to be considered as any type of reimbursement or 'settlement' related to his claim." Later the diocesan review board "reviewed the allegations ... [and] determined that the allegations could not be substantiated because the information was inconclusive and unable to be verified." McIlvane was "restored to priestly ministry" as the board "voted unanimously that there was no semblance of truth to the allegations."

71. Letter to the editor, *Pittsburgh Post-Gazette*, August 2018.

remove clergy when accused without due process. They feel vulnerable. There is a sense that some bishops are more interested in, as one APP priest expressed, "covering their own asses" and appearing to be strong on protecting victims. Though totally disgusted by brother priests who have sexually violated children and youth, they have also felt that false accusations do happen, and the falsely accused need some protection. And they've had personal experiences with at least one APP member who was withdrawn from ministry, not for sexual abuse, but for other perceived indiscretions, without due process and a fair hearing. That priest, by the way, was ultimately vindicated and allowed to resume ministry, but not without experiencing much pain.

Neill McCaulley first raised this issue of due process at the annual Pittsburgh clergy gathering at Oglebay, WV, in October of 2013. McCaulley followed this request to the diocese with a letter to all the priests and deacons in the diocese alerting them to their rights and sharing with them that a number of clergy had been called to the diocese about accusations. They were immediately put on "administrative leave" and lost pay, residence and ability to continue in ministry until an investigation was conducted. Citing a publication from a group called "Justice for Priests and Deacons," McCaulley offered to advise the Pittsburgh clergy, and in his letter he shared detailed recommendations as to what to do once summoned to the diocese because of an accusation.[72]

The issue continued to be discussed at several APP meetings through the summer and fall of 2014, as the diocese had still not acted on the previous year's request to clarify policy. Gary Dorsey was commissioned to draft a letter to the bishop asking when there would be such a policy. Finally, an answer came from the Vicar General of the diocese that recommendations were forthcoming.[73]

So what would be APP's next steps after the release of the Grand Jury Report? What else but to organize a listening session, thus giving members and supporters an opportunity to speak and be heard as the first stage of bringing about some kind of solace and healing in the midst of a crisis. The APP session, jointly sponsored with the Sisters of Divine Providence and the aforementioned Social Justice Seekers (other listening sessions took place in individual parishes), took place on September 20, 2018. One hundred sixty people attended. Stories of abuse were shared, anger, disgust

72. Letter dated February 4, 2014.

73. Letter received from Larry DiNardo, Vicar General of the Pittsburgh Diocese, October 12, 2014.

and pain expressed. Some spoke of leaving the Church, others expressed the willingness to work for change.

As an outcome of the session, the group decided to summarize what was said in a document sent to local Pittsburgh bishop, David Zubik; the President of the U.S. Catholic Conference of Bishops, Daniel DiNardo; a national bishop's leader, Cardinal Kevin Farrel; the Papal Nuncio in Washington, DC, Christopher Pierre; and, finally, Pope Francis. After expressing deep "anger" and "broken hearts," and sharing some of the more compelling stories, leading to "broken trust" yet still "hope," the document expressed the interest in both "dialogue and need for structural reforms." They then went on to analyze how they see the ongoing problems in the current life of the institutional Church. In this part they identified serious problem areas in the Church, e.g., the "sin of clericalism, " the grave error of trying "to avoid bringing scandal to the church" leading to "a far greater and more complicated tragedy," declaring "mandatory celibacy" as leading to many negative consequences, and condemning "patriarchy" and the "excluding of women to positions of high influence."

In a very powerful conclusion the document very pointedly suggested that those in leadership roles do "not dismiss the depth of this crisis with phrases like, 'improvements have been made' [or] 'we acted with the best intention' or 'we cannot judge past actions by today's standards.'" Whether true or not, they write, such expressions "are unhelpful—they ignore the deep, systemic reforms necessary and generate increasing resentment." They ask those who cannot accept this to have the "courage and the humility to step aside." Among others this seems directed specifically at their own leader, Bishop Zubik, who has made precisely such comments. Finally, the document challenges the laity to step up and gain its voice, accepting the call to fully implement the directives of Vatican II and helping remake the future church. The communication to the members of the institutional hierarchy ends with these words: "We pray that you not ignore our concerns and we look forward to hearing your response, approved by and respectfully submitted for the Board of Directors of the Association of Pittsburgh Priests." APP received a cordial response to their letter from a representative of the Papal Nuncio in Washington in early November.[74]

I am not sure that an Alinsky-trained community organizer would have ended this powerful and heartfelt sharing of an angry, violated and pained community, in such a meek fashion, without demanding response, dialogue and action on serious reform. Nevertheless, it certainly stands as

74. Document sent on October 4, 2018. Letter from the Papal Nuncio, signed by Msgr. Walter Erbi, was sent on November 5, 2018.

an important first step by the group in moving forward with their mission and commitment to continually work for transformation of this ancient institution. Time will tell if their efforts bear fruit.

Meanwhile, ongoing meetings and listening sessions are taking place in all four Pittsburgh regions and a new group calling itself Catholics for Change in Our Church (CCOC) has emerged. Four focus groups have been developed out of these gatherings: "(1) Supporting Victims/Survivors and Families; (2) Financial Transparency; (3) Reducing Clericalism; and (4) Lay Oversight of Diocesan Functions." Bishop Zubik himself has organized some listening sessions. APP member Jim McCarville reported on two such sessions. He described them as "raw and direct," with "frequent calls for the bishop to resign because he 'just doesn't seem to get it.'"[75] The next meeting with Bishop Zubik took place in February of 2019, furthering the dialogue and continuing to press for change.

It seems to me that a key issue, or possibly the key issue, in this horrific history is the hierarchy's lack of transparency and secrecy in the way it has dealt with the problem of sexual abuse by clergy. Who was overseeing the bishops? Where was the laity? Recently, during the special synod in Rome on clergy sexual abuse, the Irish prelate Eamon Martin spoke directly to this when commenting on the issue of "the need for greater transparency," stating that "secrecy must go out the window . . . Secrecy has been one of the root causes of the problem we are in today . . . my files have to be open . . . [and] anything that I have that may have been sent here to the Holy See . . . it's open to my national board, it's open under proper rules of disclosure in legal cases to the police and civil authority."[76]

Previous to the devastating Grand Jury Report of August, 2018, after which APP's relationship and dialogue with the diocese has gone through huge changes, as all attention has been focused on the abuse crisis, in an otherwise very interesting and surprising development, APP had invited Fr. Joe Mele, a friend though not member of APP, and Vicar for Leadership Development and Evangelization in the Pittsburgh Diocese, to address APP during the summer of 2016 with the purported aim of assessing "how can the APP help build leadership in the Church of Pittsburgh in the spirit of Pope Francis?" Could this represent the possibility of actual "cooperation between the diocese and APP," wondered the group?[77] After so many decades of APP attempts at cooperation and dialogue, through

75. Correspondence from Jim McCarville, APP steering committee, received by author in December of 2018.

76. White, "Irish Archbishop."

77. APP minutes, August 8, 2016.

misunderstanding, mistrust, and frequent tension, there was reason to be skeptical and cautious about this initiative and a number of veteran APP members were certainly that. One APP cleric shared with me, humorously of course, that "Don McIlvane is turning over in his grave" at the very thought of such cooperation with the diocese.

Nevertheless, some members thought one contribution APP might be able to offer the diocese, specifically lay people in the pews, was a speaker's bureau around issues of social justice, thus aiding the diocese in its outreach around key issues of concern. APP had special interest in educating folks about *Laudato Si*, the papal encyclical on the environment. At a summer 2017 meeting of APP, the current Vice President, Jim McCarville, reported on a meeting he had arranged with Dr. Michael Therrien, a lay employee of the diocese, as part of the Secretariat for Leadership Development and Evangelization, the same office where Fr. Joe Mele works. In fact, it was Mele who helped set up the meeting with Therrien. McCarville reported that the meeting with Dr. Therrien was hopeful as Therrien admitted the diocese had no current program "to teach the social gospel and was very interested in our efforts." He expressed openness to providing opportunities to spread the word on *Laudato Si*. Why not invite him to an APP meeting, the group thought? Beyond this, Sr. Barbara Finch reported that she was attempting to access a mailing list of parish contacts that the APP might use to offer programs. "It appears that his [Dr. Therrien] goal and ours were closely aligned." The next step would be to put together a list of resource people to do presentations and then meet with Dr. Therrien in the Fall of 2017. APP was also in touch with a theology professor at Duquesne University, Dr. Daniel Scheid, who might also be a collaborator.[78]

Next, President Fr. Regis Ryan and Vice-President Jim McCarville met with the Vicar-General of the diocese, Fr. Larry DiNardo, in order to further the conversation about cooperation between APP and the diocese. DiNardo was encouraging and offered to publicize APP events and speakers; he even agreed to send information to parishes, and offered to come to an APP meeting. Regis Ryan, an APP member from its inception, was in partial shock about the meeting, never imagining such a development. By February of 2018, DiNardo had invited APP "to assist in the development of a social teachings formation program for parishes." APP began to develop a list of resource people to help carry this effort forward.[79]

By late spring of 2018, APP had a conference call with Dr. Therrien and talked of ongoing communication, as well as of more talk of collaboration.

78. APP minutes, June 25, 2017.
79. APP minutes, February 5, 2018.

As the communication continued through letter and e-mail, a potential glitch surfaced. Dr. Therrien raised a caution as to the role of "advocacy" in the collaborative work. He described the work of advocacy as "a tightrope," explaining that the diocese's role is to teach the social gospel and encourage "our parish leaders to do that advocacy work at the parish level . . . when it comes to diocesan officials, however, advocacy work has to proceed with great prudence for any number of reasons—mostly legal—but also because of what their actual role needs to be . . . the primary role of a parish is not to advocate. Rather, it is to form our people so that, as citizens of the commonwealth, they will do that work as members of the parish." At the same time, Dr. Therrien acknowledged that the experience of the diocese with this model, of imagining parishioners actually doing the advocacy, and thus implementing the teachings, was often disappointing or non-existent: "a problem we have to fix," though he offered no strategy for the "fix."[80]

In a carefully worded reply APP said, "Regarding advocacy, we do not think we are so far apart . . . advocacy, we understand, must be more than legislative fixes. It is also, as you know, [about] transformation of people, parishes, and institutions."[81]

Sadly, with the sexual abuse crisis taking center stage and calls for serious structural change in the Church, this dialogue is on the back burner. Truth be told, a number of current APP members have had serious doubts about this proposed partnership. And I must say that I'm guessing Don McIlvane is indeed now "turning over in his grave," as are Don Fisher and Neil McCaulley, at the thought of such collaboration; they would not have been surprised by the diocese's caution around advocacy. Another, Fr. Jack O'Malley, no longer as active (due to health issues), also has his doubts. Their earliest vision for APP involved serious advocacy on a myriad of teachings of the Catholic Church. They were on the front lines at every turn, often leading their parishioners, or certainly walking with them. Though they loved it when the faithful stood in solidarity with them, they weren't about to wait for the teachings to sink in, despite their agreement, I'm sure, that educating folks on the social teachings through preaching and classes remains essential. But they would respond, I'm sure, not with "prudence" but with reasoned and strategic direct action, in their minds the best form of education. They would have little concern with the "legal" consequences of their actions.

In fact, at the next APP meeting of the church renewal committee (May 13, 2018), when the idea of collaboration with the diocese emerged,

---

80. E-mail to APP from Dr. Therrien, May 2, 2018.

81. APP reply to Therrien, May 2, 2018.

"concern and doubts [were] expressed." Nevertheless, the group imagined going forward with contacting parishes for Advent and Lenten programs around social teachings. Also, APP and Social Justice Seekers had already, on their own, contacted a number of Pittsburgh pastors about their ideas. And, at the July 30, 2018 APP church renewal meeting, John Oesterle reminded the group that the 2018 mountaintop retreat "made a priority of connecting with the diocese." And APP had already received a request from a parish in Beaver County to assist them in setting up a "Social Justice and Peace Committee," which Barbara Finch and Joyce Rothermel had already agreed to pursue. Could this have been APP's new mission as they continue their remarkable, ongoing legacy of now fifty-three years advocacy around social justice and church renewal? Furthermore, will new members continue to infuse new energy into this legacy? Will younger clergy finally catch APP's vision in this new era of Pope Francis, with his passion for justice and reform? Will there be any canonical clergy left in the group going forward or will lay folks Like Jim McCarville, the Pillars, Kevin Hayes, David Aleva and other lay women and men, priests of the laity, be the primary carriers of the APP legacy? Will APP finally decide to become a chapter of Call to Action, as some members continue to advocate? Or will the new developing group of Catholics for Change in our Church (CCOC), currently focused on a serious dialogue with Bishop Zubik on institutional change and reform, in light of the clergy abuse crisis, become the main driving force in finally implementing the vision of Vatican II?

Whatever the future holds for APP, the current group continues to consistently carry through its ongoing mission of support and solidarity, church renewal and the implementation of the Church's social teachings. And, as already referred to, APP is front and center in the deep call for serious structural change in the Church, especially in light of its current crisis around clergy sexual abuse.

Back in its March 2016 mountaintop gathering it renewed and slightly revised (in italics) its mission statement to read: "The Association of Pittsburgh Priests is a diocesan-wide organization of ordained and non-ordained women and men who act on our baptismal call to be priests and prophets. *Our mission, rooted in the Gospel and the Spirit of Vatican II, is to carry out a ministry of justice and renewal in ourselves, the Church and the world.*

At that same gathering the group considered "things we have done well" and "hopes, dreams and visions for APP" going forward. As to accomplishments they listed the following:

> Been supportive; been current; been persistent; witnessed to injustice [many times going to jail in acts of civil disobedience];

assisted in the foundation of the Thomas Merton Center, PIIN, and the Association of US Catholic Priests; always been a support group to progressive Catholics. The opening of APP to married priests and their spouses was one of the best things we did. Stayed open to new directions, e.g., Gay Pride; supported women in ministry, both religious and lay; been faithful to the idea and practice of renewal; been a voice for justice and peace, eg., Letters to the Editor, Op Ed pieces; attempted to influence diocesan policies and activities in the light of the teachings of Vatican II; collaborated with other organizations for justice; offered speaker series to Catholics of western, PA.; survived as friends for many years; we lasted [while] taking on hot topics.[82]

At the conclusion of the 2016 mountaintop gathering, the participants also dreamed of APP's ongoing life imagining "perseverance" with more and more takeover by lay people, always remaining faithful to the "spirit of Vatican II," while continuing to address "social inequities." They committed themselves to being an ongoing "force in the Church of Pittsburgh," as they work to incorporate new members into their vision. They even completely updated their 1966 constitution in 2017, yet another sign of their ongoing commitment to that vision.

Considering the future direction of APP brings me back to its beginnings, laid out in chapter 1 of this history, and, more especially, the individuals who came together with a vision of what Church should be and what kind of priesthood they thought it appropriate to live out. Many of the original crew, of course, moved on and married and found other vocations; some of those are still members of APP, in some cases with their wives. But those who stayed in the priesthood considered APP an essential part of their ministry and vocation, as well as their lives, finding in APP not only an avenue for their actions, but a support group, a solidarity group, a brotherhood which served as a real community of shared vision and values. For these, APP was and is a joy.

One of my most memorable interviews with APP came about because of a suggestion by APP member Marcia Snowden, a former Sister of Mercy, who after leaving religious life also found APP a spiritual community, a support group that has helped her live out her most cherished values. Snowden suggested that I consider doing some interviews for this history project in groups, imagining that especially when discussing the early years, several together would help one another remember past events, or help get some of those events straight, especially when there isn't always documentation.

---

82. Mountaintop minutes, March 14, 2016.

Although I only did group interviews on occasion, one I relish involved three APP priest members who were at the initial gatherings in 1966 and 1967: Jack O'Malley, Gary Dorsey and Don Fisher. Aside from its evoking great stories and valuable information, I was particularly struck by the sheer pleasure in the group, especially in Don Fisher, as they recalled so many memorable moments of APP activities. Fisher loved talking about the actions, the fellowship, the solidarity, the human joy of trying to live out one's principles with fellow travelers. During the over two-hour session, he beamed with excitement, with memories. Away from APP from 1975–80, as a priest associate with the Holy Spirit Congregation in Africa, he said he couldn't wait to get back to be part of APP. When the joint interview was over, he was sad and expressed the wish that we could do it again. "I love talking about APP," he said.

Unfortunately, there was not an opportunity to do another group interview, at least with that particular threesome, as Fisher died in February of 2017, a good while before I even started writing this story. He is one of several key APP members who have died in these last few years: Warren Metzler, Don McIlvane, Neil McCaulley, Don Fisher, and, most recently, in May of 2018, APP's key theologian, Gene Lauer. Among these five, Fisher and McCaulley were most active and faithful to the APP community, though all were good, faithful priests, and remained part of the fellowship. In the case of Fisher and McCaulley, they attended meetings, wrote letters, showed up at rallies well into their retirement and right up until their last days.

One other key APP activist, Fr. Jack O'Malley, one of the participants in the group interview, although very much still alive, has been slowed by a number of significant health issues, hence has not been able to participate in regular APP activities for a while now. Nevertheless, O'Malley's long, incomparable career as a priest and most assuredly a leader in the social justice arena of APP work, though he was never much for meetings and long strategy sessions, he was always ready to be on the front lines when it was time to demonstrate, do civil disobedience, speak up at rallies or gatherings with bishops, other clerics or targeted politicians. O'Malley always spoke truth to power. As Lauer shared with me in a personal interview, previously reported, "O'Malley was always so quick to name the issue, so clear on message." And O'Malley had the courage to challenge fellow activists as well as the opposition. As Lauer related in the same interview, he remembered that at dinner sponsored by the NAACP, in which O'Malley was recognized as a true champion of civil rights and a true brother in solidarity with African Americans in the struggle for equality, he challenged the "black brothers and sisters" to support their "brown sister and brother farmworkers," who were also in a struggle for just wages and working conditions, as they called for grape and lettuce boycotts.

As mentioned previously, O'Malley had been freed up by then Bishop Wuerl to work directly with the AFL-CIO as chaplain (O'Malley always quips that he thinks the bishop was delighted to get him out of a parish where he might drag others into his activism!) and was feted as AFL-CIO "Citizen of the Year" in 2015. And, in May of 2018, though pretty hobbled by a chronic back condition and Parkinson's disease, O'Malley showed up at the City-County building in downtown Pittsburgh to accept a key to the city from current Mayor Bill Paduto, for his long years of activism on a myriad of issues.[83]

McCaulley focused much of his energy on church renewal in his APP work. His funeral homilist, fellow APP member, John Oesterle, said "he loved the church" and served on clergy councils, both at home and nationally. He advocated tirelessly for lay people and priests to help select bishops, thought married men and women should be priests, and he tried to get good books of theology and spirituality into the hands of lay people. On his deathbed Oesterle asked him "how many books he had bought" over the years? "13, 400," he replied. Reluctant to say how much he had spent, he finally acknowledged "$75,000." "What's he doing now," asked Oesterle, "He's talking to the theologians who wrote all those books he read. He's with the bishops who were at Vatican II. He's with all the people whose funerals he celebrated. He's part of the communion of saints."[84]

Don Fisher's death rated a special obituary in the *Pittsburgh Post-Gazette* and was entitled "Priest at Forefront of the Civil Rights Fight." Fisher was more representative of the social justice wing of APP and spent many days in jail because of his activism, a few with the current author of this history. Even before APP began, in 1965, then a young cleric, after watching Martin Luther King Jr. protesting in Alabama, Fisher went to his pastor and said: "Excuse me, Monsignor, I have to go to Selma." To which his pastor responded, make sure you "wear a helmet." As his sister was quoted as saying at his funeral, "Every parish Don went to, he was committed to the work of the church, but he was not committed to staying in that rectory. His feet were on the street with the people." His many APP activities and even some beyond APP involved nuclear disarmament, civil rights, local community organizing, immigration work with the sanctuary movement, tax resistance, etc. Fisher, also an accomplished potter, was also very spiritually grounded,

---

83. May 30, 2018.

84. Funeral sermon for Neil McCaulley, delivered by John Oesterle, July 3, 2014.

and, appropriately, the obituary writer observed, his life was marked by "protest, pottery and prayer."[85]

In retirement he remained a very active APP member and, at an APP meeting in 2012, maybe sensing his body was losing steam along with other APP colleagues, he opened the meeting, usually set aside for a time of reflection, by reading Mary Oliver's famous poem, "When Death Comes." It's a wonderful piece on the meaning of life and death. For APP activists it might seem Oliver had Fisher in mind when she wrote this.[86]

I chose to end this history about two deceased priests and one significantly disabled, not because I want to give the impression that death is also nearing for APP, but rather to highlight key APP activists who represent, in my view, the very best of what it has meant to be a priest to so many of us who are children and inheritors of the transformative vision of the Second Vatican Council. It seems to me an important thing to make note of such priests, as the current pope and so many others, most especially women, decry the new forms of clericalism they have seen appear in these last years. In the view of one Korean nun, Sister Mina Kwon, who was a participant in a recent gathering of bishops in Rome (October, 2018), clericalism is a key underlying reason that most leadership roles don't include women. "Clericalism is linked to the authority of clergy over their duty of divine service. The main key words about clericalism would be: hierarchy, authoritarianism, a sense of entitlement, superiority and demand for excessive respect," said Kwon. "Clericalism . . . goes against the way of Jesus' teaching and it needs to be overcome before it is too late," she warned.[87]

And in an address to fellow Jesuits in Lithuania the month before this synod, Pope Francis declared, "I believe the Lord wants a change in the Church," and echoing the words of Sister Kwon, he went on to say: "I have said many times that a perversion of the Church today is clericalism." In his talk he also asked his brother Jesuits for their support in fully implementing Vatican II, since we are only "halfway there," given that "historians tell us that it takes 100 years for a Council to be applied. So if you want to help me, do whatever it takes to move the Council forward in the Church."[88]

APP members couldn't have said it better, as so many have lived out their clerical lives offering to God's people a model of priest very much in the vein of the simple, humble and generally progressive priest, who likes to be known as the bishop of Rome, Pope Francis. Although still early in his

85. Smith, "Donald Fisher."

86. Mary Oliver poem read by Fisher at APP meeting, January 16, 2012.

87. Harris, "Clericalism a Key."

88. White, "Pope Tells Jesuits."

papacy, maybe yet there will be a truly Francis effect on the priesthood—"A Door Cracked Open"—and we will look upon the APP as pioneers in such a vision of what it is to be priest, a calling, as we've written, to be shared by all baptized Christians. Few have ever accused the APP of clericalism. To the contrary, As APP member and married priest Joe DiCarlo said in an interview with me in 2016, "The APP is my idea of priesthood," humble servants, seekers of justice, builders of community. Many I have spoken with in the course of this research share DiCarlo's sentiments, as do I.

Although APP has lost some key priests in these last years, along with many lay members, canonical priests Regis Ryan, John Oesterle, Gary Dorsey, Bernie Survil, Greg Swiderski and Vince Stegman continue to play a major role in APP's ongoing "mission, rooted in the Gospel and the Spirit of Vatican II . . . to carry out a ministry of justice and renewal in ourselves, the Church and the world." And, with Pope Francis they are well aware that, indeed, such a mission may be only "halfway there."

In a recent telephone interview with longtime APP member, Scott Fabian, a former seminarian, now married, he wondered what impact APP has actually had over these fifty-three years. Whose lives has it influenced? What institutional changes have occurred because of its witness? What victories for social justice can it claim? APP priest Gary Dorsey shared a similar question with me. In somewhat answering his own query, Dorsey said to me, "APP has been a constant voice that the diocese always had to be aware of." This assessment is too modest. I'm hoping that I have unearthed innumerable examples of APP's positive impact over the years, whether in the lives of individuals, in the Pittsburgh Catholic Church, in the wider Pittsburgh community or in the United States. As APP member and former Christian Brother Jim Ruck shared with me in an e-mail, in the midst of the deep systemic troubles the Catholic Church is currently facing, "APP is the counter story." Whatever direction APP takes going forward, I suspect the legacy will be lasting, and its dreams ultimately realized by those who are following in their footsteps. May it be so!

CONCLUSION

APP's Legacy

Victory, Success or Prophetic Hope?

IN OCTOBER OF 2014, I had the privilege of co-leading a weekend retreat for Pittsburgh's Thomas Merton Center with IHM sister, Nancy Sylvester. After many years as a social activist, working both on church renewal and reform, as well as social justice in the wider community, Sylvester and a group of other women religious created a new endeavor they called Institute for Communal Contemplation and Dialogue. As Sylvester explains in the introduction to a publication of the institute entitled *Crucible for Change: Engaging Impasse through Communal Contemplation and Dialogue*, she and many other women came to the conclusion that "Our assumptions about how the world works, who we are as humans on this planet, how we live with each other in our diversity, and why we are here are called into question, no longer providing the meaning and direction they had in an earlier time." Such "changes" and "shifts" led these women to characterize the current situation as one of "impasse," arguing that "seemingly intractable issues involving the Roman Catholic Church and our society" are the order of the day, which "evokes frustration, fear, desolation, [and] depression." Despite the inclination "to walk away from," such a situation, thus "not engage," suggests Sylvester, she and her colleagues decided the better response was rather to engage "impasse and seeing that as a crucible for change; a process that holds the potential for something new to emerge."[1]

The inspiration behind the insight of an impasse, both in church and society, are the writings of a Carmelite contemplative nun, Constance Fitzgerald. In two very dense articles, one first published in 1984, the other in 2009, Fitzgerald argues that in a time of impasse it becomes most important that the community deepen its contemplative practice. Employing insights

---

1. Sylvester and Klick, *Crucible for Change*, 1–2.

174

from the medieval mystic, John of the Cross, in the 1984 piece Fitzgerald compares the current impasse as a "dark night of the soul," a spiritually arid period which, ironically, becomes an opening to deepening insights about the spiritual life. Rather than seek to escape from such a situation of impasse, Fitzgerald says: "our experience of God and our spirituality must emerge from our concrete, historical situation," which is the only way we can "feed" and "enliven" the spiritual journey. Secondly, she writes, we are currently experiencing a "dark night of the world." In this context, she asks, "What if, by chance, our time in evolution is a dark-night time—a time of crisis and transition that must be understood if it is to be part of learning a new vision and harmony for the human species and the planet?"[2]

Instead of impasse leading to paralysis and bringing "acting and living . . . to a standstill," Fitzgerald goes on to state that such a situation "provides a challenge and a concrete focus for contemplation . . . [which helps search for] intuitive, symbolic, unconventional answers, so that action can be renewed eventually with greater purpose." Thus, through a deepening of the contemplative life, "paradoxically, a situation of no potential is loaded with potential, and impasse becomes the place for the reconstitution of the intuitive self."[3]

Twenty-five years later, in 2009, in an updated view of her initial insight about impasse, in an address to the annual meeting of the Catholic Theological Society of America, Fitzgerald deepened her call for serious "theological reflection," despite the fact that we are living: "at a time when polarization, suspicion, denouncement, investigation, silencing, alienation, anger, cynicism and sadness divide our Church, and when our country is rocked with economic meltdown precipitated by years of wrong-doing and greed, our earth menaced with global warming and ecological distress that threaten all planetary life with eventual extinction, the religions of the world plagued with extremism and age-old distrust that fuel war and terrorism, the people of the world abused with violence, slavery, and deprivation too great to measure."[4]

In this address, Fitzgerald takes her analysis to the next level as she focuses great attention on the theological notion of "prophetic hope" with its emphasis on the future, both the historical future, and the fullness of the kingdom of God which is approaching us from the *eschatological*—end time

2. Fitzgerald, "Impasse and Dark Night," 93.

3. Fitzgerald, "Impasse and Dark Night," 94; Fitzgerald shares insights from a theologian named Belden Lane, who wrote a piece in *America* magazine entitled: "Spirituality and Political Commitment: Notes on a Liberation Theology of Nonviolence," March 14, 1981.

4. Fitzgerald, "From Impasse to Prophetic Hope," 22.

or God's time—future. Hope allows us to envision a different future beyond the current impasse, and prophetic action helps show us the way forward. Quoting philosopher Leon Blum, Fitzgerald affirms "we work in the present, not for the present," that is, we act for a "world that is coming."[5]

A theological colleague of Fitzgerald's, Dominican sister Mary Catherine Hilkert, whom Fitzgerald credits with helping her work through some of her insights about "prophetic hope," in a book on preaching entitled *Naming Grace*, writes that Christians, especially preachers, are "people of the future" and are called to be prophets of hope. And, according to biblical scholar Walter Brueggemann, the role of the prophet is "to nurture, nourish, and evoke a consciousness and perception alternative to the consciousness and perception of the dominant culture around us." Hilkert goes on to write that "the prophetic imagination remains focused on the promise of the future reign of God," at the same time that it critiques and "laments" the current situation of, if you will, impasse. And this "promise" offers "hope and energy for discipleship."[6]

I'm not sure any APP member would necessarily use the word impasse to describe his or her relationship with the hierarchy of the Catholic Church whether in Pittsburgh, at the national level, or the Vatican. Certainly no one in the group has used this expression in my conversations with them. Nevertheless, given the lack of progress in the Church on so many of the issues dear to the heart of APP, it seems to me an apt description. Despite APP's tireless efforts at Vatican II-inspired reforms over a fifty-three year period, we seem no closer to a married clergy, ordained women, or even female deacons, significant lay leadership in church management and decision-making, decentralization and more collegiality between local dioceses and the Vatican, transparency and open dialogue among hierarchy, priests and laity, etc. Pope Francis offers hope for some movement back to the reforms advocated by Vatican II, but we are still waiting.

Although always committed to maintaining a positive, respectful and open relationship with their local bishop, including the current Bishop David Zubik, many APP members express growing disinterest in continuing serious dialogue with him. There is a general feeling that such meetings are a waste; the bishop listens, thanks them for the visit, and goes about his business as if all is well with the Church. Part of this is fatigue. After many years of dialogue, little change has occurred. The recent Grand Jury Report on clergy sexual abuse, which has provided a new opportunity for honest and open dialogue, has forced the bishop to meet with APP members and

5. Fitzgerald, "From Impasse to Prophetic Hope," 31–36.
6. Hilkert, *Naming Grace*, 81–84.

a new lay-led Catholic organization, Catholics for Change in Our Church. APP is an integral part of these efforts and is working very closely with CCOC, which represents hundreds of Pittsburghers from all across the city and suburbs and clearly shows great promise. There is renewed hope that such efforts will bear fruit, though no one I've spoken with in Pittsburgh is convinced that the bishop sees the need for any major, systemic reform of the Catholic Church that APP, CCOC and any number of national and international Catholic organizations are calling for.

At the end of chapter 5 I recorded that during private interviews that both APP priest Gary Dorsey and APP lay member Scott Fabian raised very similar questions: in the end, what real impact has APP had, whether in the church or society? Neither was sure of the answer, though both wanted to believe the group had made a significant difference for good. In a similar vein, pondering the question of what difference his life and work as a law professor has actually made, but more especially what impact his actions as a litigator around issues of social justice issues have had, APP supporter and professor of international law at the University of Pittsburgh, Jules Lobel, tried to answer the question by writing a book entitled: *Success without Victory: Lost Legal Battles and the Long Road to Justice in America.*[7]

According to his book, published in 2003, it would appear Lobel has enjoyed no real "victories" and little "success," based on his reporting on any number of cases he and colleagues have lost. Admittedly, much like APP, Lobel has tackled big issues, such as "challenging United States Interventions Central America," litigating against U.S. foreign travel policy on Cuba, taking on U.S. foreign policy decisions, and fighting corporate America and its closing of steel plants in towns such as Youngstown, Ohio. He and others took on big institutions, knowing "victory" was unlikely.

Whether it be the Vatican, The U.S. Catholic Bishops, the Pittsburgh Diocese or, like Lobel, the U.S. war machine or U.S. foreign policy, APP has also taken on big institutions, not expecting victories, at least not in the short run. Pondering a life dedicated to legal activism, hence, Lobel asked the question: what does "success" mean? What is "failure?" Knowing victory was unlikely, part of Lobel's motivation was to use litigation as both a means of "political action" and organizing, as well as an attempt "to educate the public." But he also saw his work and engagement in such endeavors as a personal "calling," citing the witness of American Transcendentalists, Ralph Waldo Emerson and Henry David Thoreau, who wrote of the importance of "cultivating [one's] moral sensibilities" as a self-expression of who one wants to be. Lobel has also been inspired by former Supreme Court Justice

7. Lobel, *Success without Victory.*

William Brennan, who explained his many dissents as "expressions of his own conscience," and an attempt "to define himself and not to change society." Ultimately, writes Lobel, "Success inheres in the creation of a tradition, of a commitment to struggle, of a narrative of resistance that can inspire others similarly to resist."[8]

But most compelling to me and, I believe, most related to the life and legacy of APP, beyond seeking to redefine what constitutes "success" and victory, Lobel links his own "calling" to his deep roots in Jewish culture and religion and the vision of justice voiced by the great prophets of Israel, found in the Hebrew Bible. Many years ago, as I developed a personal friendship with Lobel, we used to jog in one of Pittsburgh's urban jewels, Schenley Park. The ever inquisitive Lobel, whose grandfather was a Rabbi, would quiz me and APP priests Don Fisher and Mark Glasgow, who often joined us on these urban jogs. Lobel often wanted to discuss deep theological dilemmas. We often talked about the prophets of old from the Jewish tradition, as well as modern Jewish prophets like Rabbi Abraham Heschel and philosopher Martin Buber. I'd like to think that Lobel's musings on this great tradition, that managed to wind their way into his brilliant book, was even slightly influenced by those long, hard, sweaty jogs. Remarkably, and I'd say appropriately, given his cultural roots, Lobel ends his fascinating and probing analysis of just what constitutes "success" and "victory" and his own legal career, by making a profoundly theological assertion about "the Jewish prophetic tradition": it "emphasizes redemption." That is, beyond its call for "reform" and "justice" and its "duty to speak to the people," this tradition has "an optimistic [I'd prefer to say hopeful], redemptive view of the future."[9]

By ending his book on this profoundly prophetic, theological insight about "redemption" and the "future," it seems to me Lobel has transcended the more mundane discussion about "success" and "victory" in one's life's work, and engaged in a deeper exploration of the ultimate meaning of one's life's and work. And it is consistent with the view of another great Jewish prophet and philosopher, Martin Buber, who once said: "success is not a name of God."[10] In a similar vein, in considering whether or not APP has had "success" or attained many "victories," or made any real difference, ultimately, what matters more is that APP has consistently offered, by its proclamations and actions, the "prophetic hope" that the future is God's future and the belief that the reign of God will ultimately prevail.

8. Lobel, *Success without Victory*, 1–7.

9. Lobel, *Success without Victory*, 268.

10. Soelle, *Dorothee Soelle*, 71–76.

Nevertheless, despite this view that APP's major contribution to renewal of Catholicism and the struggle for justice in the world lies in its
enduring hope-filled and prophetic vision focused on the coming kingdom
of God, there are still numerous examples of significant impact—success?—
APP's actions have actually had over there many years of priestly witness.
This book has documented any number of these examples: The letter of appreciation for local organizing from the United Farm Workers' co-founder,
Cesar Chavez, who used the word "victory" in describing a positive 1972
ruling by the National Labor Relations Board regarding UFW's campaigns;
victory in forcing the regional bishops to open up their annual meetings to
other than a small cadre of the church hierarchy; letter of gratitude from the
head of the Pittsburgh Catholic teacher's union for support on the picket
lines; acknowledgement of crucial support for the successful battle for better wages of the Catholic cemetery workers; appreciation from the nuns in
West Virginia in their struggle with church hierarchy over the question of
pro-choice; letter of gratitude from the major seminary head in the diocese
of Seattle over APP's public statements to oppose the role of Pittsburgh's
Bishop Donald Wuerl in his perceived undermining of Archbishop Hunthausan; successful lobbying in support of Pittsburgh's City Council's legislation to protect LGBTQ rights in direct opposition to the Pittsburgh Diocese;
consistent education of Pittsburgh Catholics and the wider population
through numerous published documents, letters to the editor and public interviews, some of which received national attention; and significant
participation and encouragement in the development of the newly formed
national group of priests, Association of United States' Catholic Priests, as
well as the very recent formation of the mostly lay-led Pittsburgh group,
Catholics for Change in Our Church (CCOC).

An early invitee to APP's wonderfully successful speaker series is
Catholic moral theologian, Fr. Charles Curran. Banned from teaching in
any Catholic theology department back in 1986, due to his perceived het-
erodox theological writings and lectures, at times in opposition to Vatican
teaching, Charlie, as he prefers to be called, published a memoir in 2006
which he entitled: *Loyal Dissent: Memoir of a Catholic Theologian.*[11] In it,
Curran shares that some of his colleagues in the world of Catholic moral
theology "object" to his use of the word "dissent" as too "negative" a word,
too "associated with opposition and confrontation." He goes on: "The term,
in their view, risks obscuring all that is positive about what is involved in the
position—its respect for tradition, concern for truth, love of the church, and
recognition for shared responsibility within the church." Several thought

11. Curran, *Loyal Dissent.*

that embracing the word represents what I would call a strategic mistake, that is, taking attention away from the important issues involved, and focusing attention on "rebellion and disloyalty." Though deeply respectful of these colleagues, who for the most part agree with Curran's theological viewpoint, he argues that in the political realm, dissent "has often been expressed as the highest form of patriotism . . . [and] . . . in the context of the church, for me [Curran], dissent means speaking the truth in love."[12]

Although acknowledging that over the years he has received much encouragement and appreciation from fellow priests for his "courageous" acts of public dissent, an appreciation shared by many APP members, Curran ends his memoir by humbly suggesting that local pastors have a much more challenging ministry in the church than he, as theologian, as they face their everyday pastoral responsibilities in the parish:

> Many priests have told me how they admire the way I have worked for change in the church and dealt with tension and adversity. But I remind them that as pastors they play a much more difficult role than I. Within any local church community today, there are Democrats and Republicans, liberals and conservatives, rich and poor, male and female, introverts and extroverts, young and old, gays and straights. Parish priests have to deal every day with the tensions and problems that arise from all this diversity, and they must try to both challenge and unify the people of God. If I give more than five percent of my true time to addressing these tensions, that is a lot.[13]

APP has never been reluctant to accept the charge that it has, at times, been in dissent from official church teaching. This fact has caused them to be subject to much criticism from ordinary Catholics as well as many priestly colleagues. It has caused many priests, even some sympathetic to their positions, to stay clear of public identity with APP. Yet, much like Charlie Curran, they have always thought of themselves as *loyal* dissenters, ever faithful to the church, and motivated by love for the church and its people. And Curran's acknowledgment that the role of the local pastor, even more so APP types, I would suggest, is ever more challenging than the Catholic theologian, as he exercises pastoral care for the entire parish community, even with those who are angered by his dissenting positions and his politics and social activism.

Although it seems to me appropriate to "accuse" APP of being, at times, loyal dissenters in the Catholic Church, I would argue that a much

12. Curran, *Loyal Dissent*, 67–68.
13. Curran, *Loyal Dissent*, 259.

more appropriate and profound way to describe the group's decades-long ministry is as an example of what Latin American theologian Jon Sobrino calls an exercise in "political holiness." The group's consistent and enduring witness to biblical values, and its unflinching commitment to the implementation of the calls for reform of the Second Vatican Council have been a truly holy endeavor as it continues to witness to the social implications of the bible and church social teachings.[14]

Acknowledging that some may find the expression "political holiness" a bit "odd," uniting "two realities normally presumed to be separate," Sobrino goes on to define precisely what he means by the expression: "In general, by holiness I mean the outstanding practice of faith, hope, and especially charity and the virtues generated by the following of Jesus. By politics I mean action directed toward structurally transforming society in the direction of the reign of God, by doing justice to the poor and oppressed majorities, so that they obtain a life and historical salvation."[15]

Sobrino cites slain Salvadoran Archbishop Oscar Romero as one who proclaimed the necessity of "political involvement" by religious people due to "a crying need for social justice." Such involvement is an act of love for Sobrino, a response to the "will of God," Who calls us to love those who are especially oppressed by social conditions of poverty and marginalization. But there are serious consequences to such witness: for Romero, the four church women and so many others, assassination. For pastoral agents such as APP clerics, they are subject to alienation, marginalization and often condemnation, both by the hierarchy as well as ordinary Catholics. Yet, cautions Sobrino, one must be aware that politics can be messy, what he calls a "creaturely area," by which he means "it has its own special temptations ... [and] sins because ... it is about the use of power." Therefore, one needs to "engage in politics in the right spirit, so that political love may be and remain *love* ... [and] remain open to the kingdom of God."[16]

Finally, writes Sobrino, if the poor are "to receive the good news and for history to move toward the coming of God's kingdom," it is "necessary" for there to be people who practice what Sobrino has referred to as "political holiness." The church, too, he calls to "political holiness" for the sake of the poor, if it is to "recover the truth of the gospel and make this the foundation of its mission." For Sobrino, such a witness is the only way for the church to "retain its credibility."[17]

14. Sobrino, *Spirituality of Liberation*.

15. Sobrino, *Spirituality of Liberation*, 80.

16. Sobrino, *Spirituality of Liberation*, 81–84.

17. Sobrino, *Spirituality of Liberation*, 86.

As loyal dissenters and ministers of the church, It is apt to proclaim that APP members have consistently exercised a ministry of "political holiness," as they have stood in picket lines with teachers, cemetery workers, and anti-war activists, and advocated for women's role in the church and the rights of members of the LGBTQ community. Ultimately, it is an expression of love and pastoral care. By such a witness, they have paid a certain price of marginalization yet, because of their strong sense of community and faithfulness to how they view their priestly calling, they have remained both strong and joyful in their exercise of ministry.

So, after fifty-three years of existence, what does the future hold for APP? Furthermore, especially given the recent revelations of clergy sexual abuse reported on by the Pennsylvania Grand Jury, as well as other reports from across the nation and the wider Catholic world, what is the future of the Catholic Church? In 2016, as part of its speaker series, APP invited evolutionary theologian and scientist, Franciscan Sister Ilia Delio, OSF, to address an audience of several hundred people in Pittsburgh. She not only mesmerized the attendees, of which I was one, with her ability to merge theology and science, helping the group to imagine something amazing is happening as the creative process in the universe continues, but she also imagined a different future for the Church. She applauded APP for its ongoing witness to a church yet to be adequately renewed, and encouraged the group to continue on in its quest to create a new church. More recently, in an article entitled: "Death in the Church: Is New Life Ahead," published by an organization she founded, The Omega Center, she argues, "the Church has deep structural problems" and if it does not radically alter those structures, there may well be a "schism." She goes on to lay most of the blame on the "male-dominated" and "closed caste system of clerical elitism" and "corporate ladder-climbing" of some of these clerics. She further argues that it is crucial for theology to incorporate science, especially in the theological education of these clerics. While calling for a "systemic re-organization," she also insists on the full inclusion of women in all areas of church ministry and leadership, including "Holy Orders." The Church must look "forward" not "upwards . . . towards heaven above," she states, suggesting "that Christianity is less an historical religion than a religion of the future." Much like the theologians of hope and liberation, Delio imagines God as coming towards us from the future. She ends her piece with a clarion call to all to be "cooperative co-creators" with God in forging the future church as she declares that despite the deep brokenness of the current church in light of "the abuse crisis . . . our faith must remain unshaken. Christ is risen from the dead . . . [and] . . .we cannot stand still nor can we turn back. Our hands are now put to the plow and we must forge a new path ahead. The Church will be born anew, for God is doing new things."[18]

As was referenced in this book, Pope Francis has said that it will take one hundred years for the full implementation of the teachings of Vatican II; we are only halfway there! Though no APP member expects to be there when the full implementation of Vatican II takes place, the group lives and acts as if it fully expects the ultimate flourishing of God's promised kingdom. That is the group's faith and hope. Continuing to bring in such speakers as the brilliant evolutionary theologian, Ilia Delio, helps keep APP's "hands" on "the plow" in the meantime.

Concluding this historical journey of chronicling the fifty-three year history of the Association of Pittsburgh Priests, I, like many in the Catholic community in Pittsburgh, can't help but wonder what the group's future is. But having worked closely with APP for many of the years of their existence, thus being privy to an insider's perspective, I also still wonder, somewhat amazed, as to just how this group has survived, despite tension with and scrutiny from five different bishops as well as the official clergy council of Pittsburgh.

As to the future, APP's original ordained clergy association made a bold move in 1992 and 1993 when it decided to open membership to resigned priests, many of whom were married, as well as religious sisters and lay women and men. Motivated by the ancient notion, revisited during the Reformation, most especially by Luther, and raised up once again at Vatican II, of the priesthood of all believers, APP instilled new life into their organization with this decision. And, most prophetically, the group decided to maintain its initial name, Association of Pittsburgh Priests, despite the fact that it was no longer merely an association of ordained priests. With this bold move, it was looking both backward and forward, reclaiming an ancient tradition no longer in play, at least in the Catholic world, but also looking to the future, envisioning the day when all baptized, men and women, will be acclaimed as minsters of the Gospel. Despite some calls by active lay members of APP to either change the group's name or join up with another progressive Catholic reform-minded group, such as Pittsburgh's new, reform-minded and lay led organization, Catholics for Change in Our Church (CCOC), to this day it is still Association of Pittsburgh Priests, an independent, voluntary and prophetic group of ordained and non-ordained priests, ever a voice for renewal and Vatican II-inspired reform in the Catholic Church.

18. Delio, "Death in the Church," 5.

But, as earlier mentioned, an even more intriguing question for me than APP's future, as important as that may be, is, given the group's history of challenging, at times, both church doctrine and the pastoral implementation of the church's social teachings by five different Pittsburgh bishops, how has it been able to avoid ecclesial sanctioning? Although the book has documented a number of instances in which certain APP members had to explain and defend themselves and their actions to church officials, usually representatives of the bishop, each time they managed to escape anything close to suspension. As far as I can document, the only punishment key members of APP have endured has been a pastoral transfer, generally into a rural parish, far removed from center city and the chancery. Although, as I reported in chapter 4, a former member of the official clergy council claimed he saved APP from Bishop Wuerl's desire to force APP to alter its organizational name, my research leads me to conclude that all five bishops recognized that APP clerics were good priests and faithful to their ministerial calling. They have been good, honest pastors, beloved by their parishioners or other recipients of their pastoral care, and, despite their often critical views and disagreements with their hierarchical superiors, they have been loyal and generally respectful of church authority. The group has also been very astute and strategic; they knew what buttons to push, when to push them, and when to ease off and engage in open and honest dialogue. And they stayed together. As many have stated to me, "APP always has your back." Even when the group reached what might be called an "impasse" with their local bishop, most especially with Bishop Bevilacqua, but also with the current bishop, David Zubik, leading some to see ongoing dialogue as fruitless, they have remained loyal dissenters.

There is another possible explanation for the group's survival, shared with me on numerous occasions by an APP leader, Fr. Jack O'Malley. Now retired and physically limited, but for many decades one of the key proponents of APP's social justice activities and, undoubtedly, the APP member serving the most jail time for acts of civil disobedience, O'Malley has often said to me that APP clerics avoided sanctioning because of the presence in the group of Frs. Gary Dorsey and Regis Ryan. O'Malley, an astute observer of persons, firmly believes that the stature, respect and credibility that Dorsey and Ryan have had with diocesan leadership over the years, enormously helped APP avoid sanctioning despite many skirmishes. No one in APP whom I've questioned about O'Malley's intuitions on this have dismissed the notion that Dorsey and Ryan's presence and prominence in the group has given them credibility and, possibly, saved them from sanctioning. This seems also true of priests in the diocese who are critical of APP. One sharp critic of APP, himself a priest of the diocese, told me recently that Regis

Ryan is one of his heroes and mentors. Another, despite his view that APP operates outside of the diocesan "tent," still admires many of its members and much of its ecclesial and social vision.

Beyond all of this, it's clear to this author that APP's endurance has most of all to do with community and solidarity. That is, this unique group of Catholic priests formed a bond around personal relationships and collegial support, deep commitment to their calling as priests in the ministry begun by Jesus, and deep love for God's people and the Church that they have served so faithfully. And as the group welcomed into full membership non-clerics in the early 1990s, this same sense of community and solidarity remained central to their vision, recognizing that all baptized Christians share in in the one priesthood of Christ and that they represented the future of the Church.

How did the group deal with impasse over its long history? It consistently went to the "mountaintop" in order to step back, re-evaluate, contemplate and recommit to the calls for fidelity and renewal put forth by the reform-minded leaders of the Second Vatican Council. These consistent times of withdrawal and replenishment led the group to continue to affirm its role as loyal dissenters and practitioners of what Sobrino calls, "political holiness."

In the end, what are we to say about priesthood according to the vision of the Association of Pittsburgh Priests? I'll give the final word to Don Fisher, now deceased, but one of APP's earliest and most committed members until his death in 2017. No one I know or have interviewed from APP has expressed such joy and love for the organization as Fisher. After a two-hour collective interview with three APP members in 2016, Fisher being one of the three, along with Jack O'Malley and Gary Dorsey, he expressed disappointment that the interview had to end. "I just love talking about APP," mused Fisher. What follows are excerpts from a personal sharing Fisher offered at the celebration of his twenty-fifth anniversary of ordination in 1986. Although deeply personal, I consider his words a collective expression of what priesthood is in the eyes of APP members. These words also serve to be a prophetic call to all who exercise priesthood going forward. I was privileged to be present as he delivered these words:

> O God, you have given each of us a yearning for the truth. It undergirds all our desires to be honest with each other, to be in on what is happening, to know how it is. As the forsythia and the dogwood blossoms of spring are another name for beauty, so the truth, O God, is another name for You.

... I think of these gifts of Your truth and Your call to love as I reflect on the priesthood ... They are powerful gifts; they send us forth ... to search ... to be with.

... I was taught well, O God, through all my seminary training, to see You in Jesus of Nazareth, of Galilee: I'm learning in the years since to see You as a Salvadoran, a Nicaraguan, a South African, A Tanzanian ... all neighbors on this small planet. Help us to see You in the many, many people who do not even call out Your Name, but whose goodness and suffering are sure signs of Your presence.

Through all the piles of books and notes, and the years of lectures, prayer and meditation I sought for You, O God, and gained some valuable insights, but it was some later experiences that made me wonder what it was that I really knew. For a while I was glad about being, as they say, "elevated to the priesthood." I "kind of" enjoyed this pedestal arrangement. Now it makes me nervous, and more ashamed than glad to be "pedestalized" while so many others are put down, and kept down. For now it is no longer time for special uniforms to mark us off from the world, or special status to make sure we're taken care of. Rather, it's time for especially strong commitments to our broken world, and time to serve, not be served.

... When first ordained I was grateful, O God, for Your power in me to forgive sins, to invoke Your blessings, to celebrate at Your Eucharistic table. I'm somewhat clearer now that forgiveness is really the power to forgive myself, and to help others to see that they can forgive themselves, and forgive others. I'm beginning to see that I celebrate the Eucharist with the whole community of believers, and I want to help make that community more and more representative of all Your people, O God. And the power to bless? Not a power, but a privilege, a gift to see that life itself is the blessing ... and that we bless each other along the way by not standing apart from each other, but by standing with ... and standing for.

Let us feel Your life within us, O Spirit of God ... You have always been with Your people. Manifest Yourself with great power in our time, like a mighty wind blowing. We need You. May our search for the truth, and our experience of Your love lead us to direct our lives toward the things that really matter, to rejoice today and every day in Your mysterious companionship with us. Amen. Alleluia.[19]

19. Words from a sharing Don Fisher gave on the twenty-fifth anniversary of his ordination, May 18, 1986.

Bibliography

Abbott, Walter M, ed. *The Documents of Vatican II*. New York: The America Press, 1966.

Allen, John. "Abuse Scandal Isn't the Only Chapter in Donald Wuerl's Story." *Crux*, October 12, 2018.

Arke, Raymond. "NLRB Rules Against Duquesne, Orders University to Bargain with Adjunct Union." *The Duquesne Duke*, November, 2018.

Association of Pittsburgh Priests. "Chastity, Yes; Obedience, Of Course; but also, Simplicity." *National Catholic Reporter*, February 5, 1971.

———. "The Priest and Politics." Unpublished document. June 1983.

———. "Priests Retain Right to Debate, Promote Women's Ordination." *National Catholic Reporter*, November 11, 1994.

Atzinger, Jack. "Protest: Priests Hold Back Portion of Income Tax." *Beaver County Times* (PA), April 16, 1984.

Baumann, Paul, et al. "An Unhealed Wound." *Commonweal* (June 15, 2018) 9–24.

Beach, George K, ed. *James Luther Adams: An Examined Faith*. Boston: Beacon, 1991.

Bergholz, Eleanor. "Priests Ask Wuerl to Leave Seattle." *Pittsburgh Post-Gazette*, December 3, 1986.

Bernardin, Joseph, et al. *Consistent Ethic of Life*. Edited by Thomas G. Feuchtmann. Kansas City, MO: Sheed & Ward, 1988.

Boorstein, Michelle. "Abuse Reports Puts Unwelcome Spotlight on Cardinal Wuerl." *Washington Post*, August 20, 2018.

———. "D.C. Prelate Says He Forgot Abuse Charges." *Boston Globe*, January 17, 2019.

Bourbon, Julie. "Protesters Outside Churches Call for Wuerl's Resignation, Church Reform." *National Catholic Reporter*, August 26, 2018.

Bradley-Steck, Tara. "Catholic Clergy in Nuke Protest." *Beaver County (Pa.) Times*, April 15, 1983.

Brown, Francis F. "The Association of Pittsburgh Priests: A Brief History." Unpublished pamphlet. January, 1987.

———. *Priests in Council: Initiatives toward a Democratic Church*. New York: Andrews and McMeel, 1979.

Bunnik, Ruud J. *Priests for Tomorrow: A Radical Examination of Christian Ministry*. New York: Holt, Rinehart and Winston, 1969.

Burghardt, Walter. "What Is a Priest?" *The Way* 23 (Autumn 1974) 55–67.

Clifford, Catherine E. *Decoding Vatican II: Interpretation and Ongoing Reception*. New York: Paulist, 2014.

Collins, Paul. "Pope Hamlet: Paul VI's Indecisive, Wavering Papacy." *National Catholic Reporter* 55/1 (October 19–November 1, 2018) 16–17.

Comblin, Jose. *People of God*. Edited and translated by Phillip Berryman. New York: Orbis, 2004.

Cozzens, Donald B. *The Changing Face of the Priesthood*. Collegeville, MN: Liturgical, 2000.

Crompton, Janice. "Obituary for Fr. Eugene Lauer." *Pittsburgh Post-Gazette*, May 22, 2018.

Crowley, Paul, ed. *From Vatican II to Pope Francis: Charting a Catholic Future*. New York: Orbis, 2014.

Crumb, Joseph. "Clerics' Group Tackles the Issues." *Pittsburgh Tribune-Review*, December 30, 1996, B-3.

Curran, Charles E. *Loyal Dissent: Memoir of a Catholic Theologian*. Washington, DC: Georgetown University Press, 2006.

Dahm, Charles. *Power and Authority in the Catholic Church: Cardinal Cody in Chicago*. South Bend: University of Notre Dame Press, 1981.

Delio, Ilia. "Death in the Church: Is New Life Ahead?" The Omega Center, August 28, 2018.

Eagan, Margery. "The Church's Dismaying Anti-abortion Rhetoric." *The Boston Globe*, May 17, 2019, A8.

Fabean, Scott. "Moral Values: Talk Is Cheap." Unpublished document. November 29, 2004.

Faggioli, Massimo. *Vatican II: The Battle for Meaning*. New York: Paulist, 2012.

Faggioli, Massimo, and Andrea Vicini. *The Legacy of Vatican II*. New York: Paulist, 2015.

Farrell, John A. *Tip O'Neill and the Democratic Century*. Boston: Little, Brown, 2001.

Figueroa Deck, Allan. *Francis, Bishop of Rome: The Gospel for the Third Millennium*. New York: Paulist, 2016.

———. "Commentary on *Populorum Progressio*." In *Modern Catholic Social Teaching: Commentaries and Interpretations*, edited by Kenneth R. Himes et al., 292–314. Washington, DC: Georgetown University Press, 2004.

Fitzgerald, Constance. "From Impasse to Prophetic Hope: Crisis of Memory." *CTSA Proceedings* 64 (2009) 21–42.

———. "Impasse and Dark Night" In *Living with Apocalypse, Spiritual Resources for Social Compassion*, edited by Tilden Edwards, 93–116. San Francisco: Harper & Row, 1984.

Frisbie, Margery. *An Alley in Chicago: The Life and Legacy of Monsignor John Egan*. Chicago: Sheed & Ward, 2002.

Gaillardetz, Richard R. "The Ecclesiological Foundations of Modern Catholic Social Teaching." In *Modern Catholic Social Teaching: Commentaries and Interpretations*, edited by Kenneth R. Himes, 72–98. Washington, DC: Georgetown University Press, 2005.

———. "Francis under Fire." *The Tablet*, September 19, 2018.

———. *An Unfinished Council: Vatican II, Pope Francis, and the Renewal of Catholicism*. Collegeville, MN: Liturgical, 2015.

Gigler, Rich. "Priest Group backs W. VA. Nuns' Stand against Vatican." *Pittsburgh Press*, September 10, 1986.

Goldstein, Andrew. "Abuse Survivors Group Seeks Zubik's Resignation: Bishop Denies Any Part in Cover-up." *Pittsburgh Post-Gazette*, August 16, 2018, A-4.

Groutt, John. "The Second Vatican Council: A Memoir." *Journal of Ecumenical Studies* (Winter 2014) 1–8.

Gudorf, Christine E. *Catholic Social Teaching on Liberation Themes.* Lanham, MD: University Press of America, 1980.

———. "Commentary on *Octogesima Adveniens.*" In *Modern Catholic Social Teaching: Commentaries and Interpretations,* edited by Kenneth R. Himes et al., 315–32. Washington, DC: Georgetown University Press, 2004.

Harris, Elise. "Clericalism a Key of Women's Exclusion, Korean Nun Says." *Crux,* October 26, 2018.

———. "Irish Prelate Says Some Nations Don't Grasp 'Severity' of Abuse Crisis." *Crux,* October 26, 2018.

Hilkert, Mary Catherine. *Naming Grace: Preaching and the Sacramental Imagination.* New York: Continuum, 1997.

Ivereigh, Austen. *The Great Reformer: Francis and the Making of a Radical Pope.* New York: Picador, 2015.

Kelly, Timothy. *The Transformation of American Catholicism: The Pittsburgh Laity and the Second Vatican Council, 1950–1972.* South Bend: University of Notre Dame Press, 2010.

Lauer, Eugene. "The Charism of the Priesthood Today." In *Priests for the 21st Century,* edited by Donald Dietrich and Kenneth Himes, 195–207. New York: Crossroad, 2006.

Lefevere, Patricia. "Pittsburgh Priests Split from Federation." *National Catholic Reporter,* September 24, 1999, 10.

Lobel, Jules. *Success without Victory: Lost Legal Battles and the Long Road to Justice in America.* New York: New York University Press, 2003.

Lockwood, Robert P. "It's a Non-Starter." *Pittsburgh Post-Gazette,* July 30, 2006, H-1.

McCann, Patricia. "Call for Pluralism." *Thomas Merton Center Newsletter,* January, 1985.

McCray, Pat. "Priests Protest Bishop Conference." *Chester Local Daily News,* April 25, 1975, 21.

McDevitt, Bette. "Decades Haven't Dimmed Priests' Desire for Change." *Pittsburgh Post-Gazette,* May 23, 2000, D1–3.

McDonald, Arthur J. "The Practice and Theory of Liberation Theology in Peru." PhD diss., University of Pittsburgh, 1993.

———. "A Prophet in the Monastery: Why Thomas Merton's Radical Social Vision Still Inspires Forty Years Later." Unpublished keynote address celebrating the 40th anniversary of the Thomas Merton Center for Peace and Justice. Pittsburgh: January 31, 2012.

———. "The U.S. Catholic Church and Foreign Policy: An Historical Perspective." Unpublished address given at the annual meeting of The National Federation of Priests' Council. Pittsburgh: October, 1983.

McElwee, Joshua J. "Benedict Blames Clergy Abuse on Sexual Revolution, Vatican II Theology." *National Catholic Reporter,* May 3–16, 2019, 1 & 6.

———. "Pittsburgh Priests to Bishop: Listen to Laity on Contraception." *National Catholic Reporter,* April 5, 2012.

McIlvane, Donald W. "Non-violence in America: An Extended Review." *The Priest* (November, 1967) 923–28.

Morris-Young, Dan. "Psychologist: Communication Failures Obscure US Bishops' Progress on Abuse." *National Catholic Reporter,* November 30–December 13, 2018, 5.

O'Brien, David J., and Thomas A. Shannon, eds. *Catholic Social Thought: Encyclicals and Documents from Pope Leo XIII to Pope Francis.* 3rd ed. New York: Orbis, 2016.

Office of Attorney General, Commonwealth of Pennsylvania. "Report I of the 40th Statewide Investigating Grand Jury." August 14, 2018.

Panaritis, Maria. "Priest's Report Went Unheeded." *Philadelphia Inquirer,* May 11, 2002, A1 & A6.

Paul VI. "Decree on the Ministry and Life of Priests." In *The Documents of Vatican II,* edited by Walter M. Abbott, 532–79. New York: America Press, 1966.

———. "*Gaudium et Spes*: Pastoral Constitution on the Church in the Modern World." In *The Documents of Vatican II,* edited by Walter M. Abbott. New York: America Press, 1966.

Rodgers, Ann. "Group Backs Marriage for Priests." *Pittsburgh Post-Gazette,* June 10, 2004, A25.

———. "In 15 Years Wuerl Has Dealt with Red Ink, Downsizing, Sex Abuse." *Pittsburgh Post-Gazette,* March 22, 2003.

———. "Wuerl Calls for Prayer, Warns Against Bigotry." *Pittsburgh Post-Gazette,* March 21, 2003.

Schillebeeckx, Edward. *The Church with a Human Face: A New and Expanded Theology of Ministry.* New York: Crossroad, 1985.

Seate, Mike. "Rogue Priests Challenge John Paul's Statements." *Pittsburgh Tribune-Review,* October 26, 1994.

Sherwood, Topper. "The Right to Disagree: Pro-choice Nuns Take Issue with Vatican." *Observer-Reporter,* September 25, 1986, C1.

Smeltz, Adam, et al. "Zubik Apologizes, Says Pittsburgh Diocese Has 'Learned From the Past.'" *Pittsburgh Post-Gazette,* August 15, 2018, A–1 & A–9.

Smith, Peter. "Retired Priest Was at Forefront of Civil Rights." *Pittsburgh Post-Gazette,* March 2, 2017, Obituary.

Snowden, Marcia. "Now, More than Ever." *Pittsburgh Post-Gazette,* June 30, 2006, H1 & H4.

Sobrino, Jon. *Spirituality of Liberation: Toward Political Holiness.* Translated by Robert R. Barr. New York: Orbis, 1988.

Soelle, Dorothee. *Dorothee Soelle: Essential Writings.* Edited by Diane Oliver. Essential Readings in Modern Spiritual Masters. Maryknoll, NY: Orbis, 2006.

Steinfels, Peter. "Vehemently Misleading: The Pennsylvania Grand Jury Report Is Not What It Seems." *Commonweal* (January 25, 2019) 13–26.

Sylvester, Nancy, and Mary Jo Klick, eds. *Crucible for Change: Engaging Impasse through Communal Contemplation and Dialogue.* San Antonio: Sor Juana, 2004.

Thomas, Clarke. "Devout In Their Own Way." *Pittsburgh Post-Gazette,* April 10, 2002, A-12.

Tobias, Eileen. "A Maryknoll Film Weighed for Oscar." *The New York Times,* April 10, 1983. https://nyti.ms/29yh1Ac.

Trainor, Ken. *Unfinished Pentecost: Vatican II and the Altered Lives of Those Who Witnessed It.* Oak Park, IL: Chauncey Park, 2013.

Wallace, Andrew. "Priests Call Secret Talks by Bishops 'Embarrassing.'" *Philadelphia Inquirer,* April 25, 1974.

Ward, Paula Reed, et al. "They Hid It All: Report Accuses 300 Priests of Abusing More Than 1,000 Children." *Pittsburgh Post-Gazette*, August 15, 2018, A-1 & A-6.

White, Christopher. "Irish Archbishop Says Abuse Summit 'Much Closer' to Worldwide Policy." *Crux*, February 23, 2019.

————. "Pope Tells Jesuits Clericalism a 'Perversion' in the Church." *Crux*, October 17, 2018.

Wills, Gary. *Why Priests? A Failed Tradition*. New York: Penguin, 2013.

Zauzmer, Julie, and Reis Thebault. "Cardinal Wuerl's Actions in Pittsburgh Scrutinized by Catholic Sexual Abuse Investigation." *Washington Post*, August 14, 2018.

CPSIA information can be obtained
at www.ICGtesting.com
Printed in the USA
LVHW030731111119
636962LV00011B/4920